Unsung Heroes

Unsung Heroes

Janet Carroll Richardson *with* Brad Bailey

WRS
PUBLISHING
A DIVISION OF WRS GROUP, INC.
WACO, TEXAS

Text © 1996 by Janet Carroll Richardson

First published in the United States of America in 1996 by WRS Publishing, a division of WRS Group, Inc., 701 N. New Road, Waco, Texas 76710

Book design by Georgia Brady
Jacket design by Joe James

10 9 8 7 6 5 4 3 2 1

Library of Congress Cataloging-in-Publication Data

Richardson, Janet Carroll.
    Unsung heroes / Janet Carroll Richardson with Brad Bailey.
        p.   cm.
    ISBN 1-56796-117-7
    1. United States--Biography. 2. Biography--20th century. 3. Heroes--United States--Biography. I. Bailey, Brad, 1953-   . II. Title.
    CT220.R53   1995
    920'.009'04--dc20

                                                    95-22486
                                                        CIP

DEDICATION

THIS BOOK IS DEDICATED to the three people who have taught me most about what's important in this life of mine: my parents, Mary and George Richardson, who started my incredible journey with their own legacy for "making a difference," and to my precious daughter, Bethany Laura Richardson Carroll, who picked up where they left off, and who has taught me more about pure love than any other human being. Bethany, my heart actually grew two sizes larger December 14, 1985, the lucky day I met you!

CONTENTS

PART I
SAVING THE CHILDREN

PART II
THE WORST IS
OVER—STORIES OF
OVERCOMING

PART III
THE HEALERS

FOREWORD

UNSUNG HEROES IS BEST DESCRIBED with this tribute by Dr. Joseph R. Sizoo: "Let it never be forgotten that glamour is not greatness; applause is not fame; prominence is not eminence. The man of the hour is not apt to be the man of the ages. A stone may sparkle, but that does not make it a diamond; a man may have money, but that does not make him a success. It is what the unimportant do that really counts and determines the course of history. The greatest forces in the universe are never spectacular. Summer showers are more effective than hurricanes, but they get no publicity. The world would soon die but for the fidelity, loyalty and consecration of those whose names are unhonored and unsung."

The book, *Unsung Heroes*, by Janet Carroll Richardson, is certainly a classic example of what Dr. Sizoo was saying. Here's a book that offers hope and encouragement through story after story of ordinary people doing extraordinary things. These people come from every walk of life and fill every imaginable role in society. They are everyday people who saw problems and got involved in solving these problems. They became unsung heroes because they forgot self and got involved in making a difference in the lives of others.

Unsung Heroes is a book parents should read to their children. Read the book one story at a time and discuss it at the dinner table or on long walks. It's filled with lessons about life and the importance of abandoning the hooray-for-me, to-heck-with-you, I'm-going-to-do-it-my-way, and I'll-win-even-if-I-have-to-do-it-through-intimidation-and-looking-out-for-number-one attitude. Without saying so, this book clearly demonstrates that those who get the most out of life are those who give the most to life. In story after story it becomes clear that when you do things for others, you are the recipient of even greater benefits. Maybe that's the reason most unsung heroes are astonished that anyone would consider them a hero.

Unsung Heroes is a classic example of the fact that other people can give you pleasure, but you'll never experience genuine happiness until you do things for other people. In that sense, this is a "happiness" book, because these unsung heroes are living complete, fulfilled lives. Few of them make the headlines, but they do affect the heartlines of the people they benefit through their unselfish service.

I encourage you to read one unsung hero story at a time. Do not pick it up and go from cover to cover, though you will be sorely tempted to do so. After each story, stop and ask yourself a question: What did this individual have that enabled him or her to get involved in and enrich other people's lives? You will find yourself looking around and wondering if you could and should get involved in doing more for others.

Underneath the messages each story contains you will discover that the cover of the book is right on target. It does give hope, encouragement, and inspiration, and, in a world which too often focuses on poverty, crime, drug abuse, adultery, divorce, violence, and a host of other negatives, this one shines brightly as an example of what an unselfish individual is capable of doing for others. I like it, and you will, too.

—ZIG ZIGLAR
Author of *Over the Top*

ACKNOWLEDGMENTS

I HAVE SO MANY PEOPLE to thank for helping me with my quest—too many to list here, and so many that I would surely leave someone out if I were to try to list them all. But a few special thank-yous are definitely in order: Thank you, Brad Bailey for working your miracles with my simple words; to Dr. Wayman Spence, my publisher, Georgia Brady, my editor, Tom Spence, and all the great people at WRS Publishing for your continued support and for making some sense out of these jumbled words; and a special thanks to April Looney for seeing that we got the correct words and punctuation on paper. Buff Parham, for giving me my start with the television show at WFAA-TV, Channel 8. You always had great insight; and to Dave Lane and all my friends at Channel 8 for believing in me and my idea; to Jerry Cadigan for being the real talent behind the original television programs; to Steve Price for your editing magic; to Brian Hawkins for teaching me how to produce good TV; to Art Young for all your help in launching the show; to Nancy Cunningham for always encouraging me; to Jeanne Prejean for helping to get "Unsung Heroes" the recognition it so needed; to Herb Kelleher and our great friends at Southwest Airlines for sponsoring "Unsung Heroes," without whose support there would not have been an "Unsung Heroes"; to Sharon Freeman, a great friend and my right hand for so many years; to all the great people who've worked on our staff and crews including: Jay Payne, Betty Shaw, Shelly Roll, Darrell Cartright, Kate Shaw, Cathy Cumming, Robert Johnson, Rawson Stovall, Duane Conder, Jon Cermin, Jody Dean, Alyce Caron, Mr. Zig Ziglar; to my friends at AMS Productions for taking my television show to higher heights; to Paul Frank, my agent at The William Morris Agency, for believing in me and my wonderful stories; to my mom and dad, Mary and George Richardson, for being my real inspiration, to my sisters Kathy and Betty Lyn, to Randy, Nicole, Miranda, Ken, Zac, Jake, and my entire family for always believing in dreams; to my wonderful grandparents for your love and wisdom—especially Myrtis and Meme; to the Reverend Joe Murphy, one of the first saints I ever met; to Mike Carroll for being a good dad and friend; to my precious daughter, Bethany, who reminds me every day to blow bubbles, roller skate in the park, feed the ducks, and to never let go of the child within me; thanks to the wonderful unsung heroes I have had the honor of meeting along the way. You are teaching me the real purpose of life; thanks to my first hero and special friend, Bobby Dotson. After meeting you, I knew I'd found a true unsung hero, and after telling your story, I knew there was no going back. And thank you, God, for giving me a purpose, and for making all things possible. I love you all!

PREFACE

ALL OF THE PEOPLE you are about to meet in the following pages are worth full-length books in their own right. And all of these profiles are the result of an obsession—albeit a magnificent one. "Unsung Heroes" is not just the name of the television program that I created and produced. It is also my baby, born of that obsession.

The stickiest obsessions are those that revolve around an unanswered question. The question may begin half formed, at the not-quite-conscious level—just a vague feeling of unease, the nagging feeling that while nothing's really wrong, things aren't entirely right, either—the feeling that something indefinable is missing from life. It's like craving a food, but not being able to quite figure what it is.

I began to have these feelings as a young woman shortly after I left home, this nagging itch I couldn't quite scratch. In retrospect, I'd enjoyed a childhood that was straight out of *It's a Wonderful Life.* My dad, George "Skeet" Richardson, was a sort of Texas version of George Bailey. He was, by trade, a homebuilder, but that was not the love of his life; instead of presiding over the Bailey Building & Loan, his great love was politics. He was a die-hard public servant and would have gone far had he not been too honest for the political trade. So my father was my first hero: the man who did the right thing and was willing to pay the price.

I had just assumed that my life was like that of any other small-town girl, but it was not, due to my father, in large part. Dad is a populist who believes not only in the vote of the "little man," but in his inherent greatness, goodness, and wisdom, as well.

On any given Saturday afternoon, our house would be filled with family and friends. Ringmaster of this circus, there was my mother, Mary Richardson, a schoolteacher who saw the imparting of wisdom—and concern—to her students not as just a job, but an almost holy vocation. She has a perennial brightness of outlook and a desire to help others that is remarkable, given her background. She was a dirt poor farm girl. Her father was a smart man, but an alcoholic. She has an eternally sunny optimism that I did not, as I was growing up, realize was out of the ordinary.

There was an openness between my parents that I also took for granted. They loved each other in front of us daughters, and they fought in front of us, too.

My friends didn't know what to make of what they thought were the Sunday-morning discussion groups, where my parents hashed out the great issues of the day over breakfast. It was like living on the set of "Meet the Press."

Kids who spent the night with me would wonder on those Sunday mornings why they were fighting all the time about stuff that was going on in the world and what that had to do with anything.

What my friends didn't know was that *every* breakfast was that way, seven days a week, and that my parents included us in those current-events free-for-alls. Every single morning we started out with, "Well, here's what's going on in the world today—what do you think about it?" Every morning was a community-affairs program, because they wanted to make us think, to help us to realize that we were part of the world and partly responsible for changing it.

My parents would get very mad about things like hunger and deprivation—but they were not mad at each other; the argument was usually over what should be done, because they both believed, more than any two people I've ever met, that Something Should Be Done, and the question was usually, What can *we* do?

In short, my mother and father were (and are) the kind of people who did (and do) great and good things according to their means, and who have lived in a world of liberalism and ideas. And they attract that kind of people, too.

I was raised around so many big people, strong people, good people: people of plan and purpose who demanded equitable treatment for others.

Somewhere in the middle of all this light and heat, I grew up. I guess I expected that life would hold more of the same—these big people with big hearts and big humane urges, doing big things to help their fellow man.

I went to college. I did well enough in communications courses that, leaving school, I had no trouble finding jobs. And I breezed successfully through a succession of them, working in advertising, public relations, and political PR.

Through these job experiences, a pattern was developing. I would tackle a project or a new job, and pretty soon, boredom would set in, along with that vague but growing feeling that nothing was wrong but things weren't quite right, and I would move on again to some fresh endeavor. But these, too, would soon become stale and unsatisfying.

I was looking for… something. What it was, I did not know. I decided, finally, that it must be television. Yeah, that's the ticket. That would satisfy me, scratch that itch and feed that hunger.

And in truth, to some extent, it did. Not completely, but it got me about halfway to "there." Since my résumé was more PR than broadcast, I kind of came in the back door at the prestigious ABC affiliate in Dallas/Fort Worth, WFAA-TV, Channel 8. I took a job in the promotions department.

It was not until I worked on a community outreach program—specifically, a Christmastime toy drive for needy children—that I realized both the full power of the medium and what I had been wanting to do all along.

Because of one brief broadcast announcing the drive, poor people had lined up for eight blocks just to get their kids' names on the list. A whopping forty thousand people had signed up.

Better still, by the time we went on the air with the ten o'clock news, the good people of Dallas and Fort Worth had donated enough toys to meet the needs of every last one of those children.

I realized what I'd been missing all along: those good people. The people with whom I had been surrounded in my youth. Thus my obsession truly began.

I suddenly realized it was my duty, purpose, and mission to find those good people, wherever they might be: the people who are making the world a better place for their fellow man, the people who are making a difference, or, as we say on the show, ordinary people doing extraordinary things.

I did no marketing studies. There were no focus groups—and if the results had been negative, I would have continued with the project anyway. In retrospect, it was a crazy thing to attempt, given my circumstances. I was in the middle of a divorce and had custody of my daughter, then five. It should have been a time of trying to become more stable, rather than less. I should have been trying to create a safer harbor for Bethany.

But in large part, it was for her that I was doing this: I had to do something to make her world a better place in which to live. And, in all honesty, I couldn't have done it without her, because my daughter, Bethany, believed in me unconditionally.

I had no real choice in the matter: This was something I had to do, something I couldn't not do.

In the midst of all the turmoil, with no financial backing and certainly no experience in television production, I simply quit my job, determined that by hook or crook, there would be an "Unsung Heroes" television show and I would find these good people. It was a labor of love.

No bank would touch me because I had no credit history and, moreover, as far as marketing, I was flying on a wing and a prayer. I knew only that I had to produce a pilot and that it would be expensive.

Free-lancers, equipment, and money for travel does not grow on trees—but they do sort of grow on credit cards. I wound up going $30,000 into the hole on my Visa and MasterCard to get my people paid and "on the ground" to chase down heroes all around the country.

I'd get a credit card, charge it to the limit, and get another. I never missed a payment—but I did lose a lot of sleep.

I caught a couple of breaks. First was my connection with Channel 8. What I did would have to be good or they wouldn't air it—but I had a foot in the door, at least. And they liked what they saw when I finally handed them the finished product, so much that they rolled the dice, with the first episode pre-empting the vastly popular "Wheel of Fortune," thus guaranteeing me a large audience for my debut.

I'd always heard "good news doesn't sell," and I'd always believed that sentiment was dead wrong. I held to a belief that when viewers say they want more good news, they really mean it, and I crossed my fingers that they would make their approval of this concept known to the powers that be at Channel 8 in the wake of my broadcast.

They did not let me down. The station was flooded with mail—all of it glowing.

I was, of course, like any mother showing her baby to the public for the first time. I wanted people to like it, and the fact that so many didn't just like it but loved it was thrilling.

But more important, those letters and the universally positive response of the critics told me that that same unscratched itch, that same unfulfilled hunger that I too had felt—the longing to know that there were still good people out there who were still doing good things for good reasons, people who did still "get involved" with helping their fellow man and solving problems in the world—was almost universal among the people in America.

They weren't just hungry for it. They were starving.

In terms of ratings, popularity, sponsors, and the other quanta of the business, our show has succeeded beyond anyone's wildest expectations, even mine. It has allowed us to form the non-profit Unsung Heroes foundation, which allows us to begin helping those who help others.

The television program "Unsung Heroes" brings to its viewers content that is simple, straightforward, and incredibly compelling: Ordinary people who are doing extraordinary things.

We find the good people who are doing good things for others, and then we let the world know about them. The result has been a powerful grassroots landslide.

Some of these heroes are young, some are old. They are black and white and all shades in between. But all have this in common: courage, grit, determination, and a desire to take the wrongs of this cruel world and make them right.

The huge number of requests we get for videotapes of our shows for schools, churches, civic organizations, even prisons tell me that my show has done something good in the world.

I believe that with this book, as with our programs, you'll emerge from the other side with your eyes opened, knowing that there are many problems that need solving, but also that people just like you can help solve them, and that the solution is simply this: caring.

That's what we have here, in a nutshell: people who care.

Meeting them has fulfilled my hunger, which all along was just the desire to find someone I could once again admire, like my wonderful parents—people who would inspire me, and inspire me to believe that the world was still a good place to live and that it could get better.

I found those people in tremendous measure. I'm finding more of them every day.

It is with great pleasure that I invite you to travel along with us on our search for unsung heroes. I believe your world will change as well, for having met them.

As we open each one of our shows:

"You know the problems. Now, meet the people who are doing something about them."

Travel along with us as we take you around the country to show you the people who are making a difference. Meet people, just like you, who are changing the world every day. Ordinary people. Extraordinary stories. "Unsung Heroes."

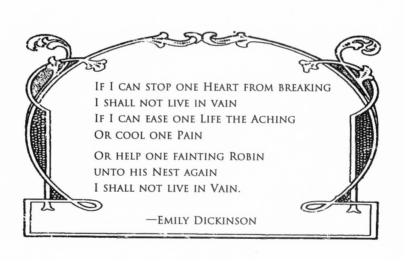

IF I CAN STOP ONE HEART FROM BREAKING
I SHALL NOT LIVE IN VAIN
IF I CAN EASE ONE LIFE THE ACHING
OR COOL ONE PAIN

OR HELP ONE FAINTING ROBIN
UNTO HIS NEST AGAIN
I SHALL NOT LIVE IN VAIN.

—EMILY DICKINSON

PART I

SAVING
THE
CHILDREN

WHAT HAS HAPPENED to our children is an outrage.

What the children are doing to themselves outrages us—leaves us speechless, alienated. Doing drugs. Carrying guns to school. Killing other children in drive-by shootings.

Even worse is what is being done to our children by adults. Child abuse and molestation. Abduction, and even murder. These hit us like punches to the gut.

And the sum of all this chaos is that we feel both alienated and helpless. In this particular *Unsung Heroes* section, however, we'll both quantify the problem and show people who have been highly successful in tackling it.

The "Mad Dads," (l–r) Rev. Bob Tyler, Eddie Staton, and
John Foster, at their headquarters in Omaha.

"We're Not Gonna Take It Anymore"

The Mad Dads

I LIVE IN A PRETTY SAFE NEIGHBORHOOD—and yet I'm afraid to get my young daughter out at night to make a quick trip to the local convenience store. Crime. It's a concern of all Americans—no matter what age, race, or religion... it crosses all lines. Statistics continue to illuminate the problems that exist with regards to youth crime and gangs. We often wonder if there are any real answers. Perhaps there are. I recently met a group of fathers who have banded together to take back their streets from the drugs and the youth gangs with the only thing that will really work: love and commitment.

This is a story of mean streets in the worst sense of the phrase—and "gang warfare" as something that is positive for a change. It's also a spellbinding tale of the three remarkable black men who decided to do something about those streets: These men are working to save a generation, and the idea has caught like wildfire.

I was riding in a van full of angry black men in the middle of the night on the meanest, grittiest, killingest streets that the urban sprawl of Omaha, Nebraska, has to offer—and, believe it or not, the city with the prosaic reputation has them in full measure—past the crack houses and the roving gangs of vicious young men and the hoods selling drugs on street corners, and I was not one bit scared.

Excited, yes.

Scared, no.

The stereotypes tell us that Angry Black Men = Danger.

But the truth is that these black men were angry for the right reasons, as the vast majority of them are. Sure, they are mad, to an extent, over the way "the system" has historically treated them. But increasingly, they are mad about what they are doing to themselves.

3

And the men in this van riding with me through the middle of the night are the ones who've become mad enough to do something about it. Something dramatic, something dangerous, but ultimately, something very deeply caring.

They call themselves "Mad Dads," and they're mad for good reason: Gangs, drugs, and general lawlessness have turned their inner-city streets into meat grinders—places of misery and murder, places where children never have childhoods, where even in broad daylight there is no safety, and the night is a time of terror.

We are on the way to the scene of a murder—a place where, for no particular reason, a young man has shot a fourteen-year-old girl outside a convenience store. And the police have arrived, and an increasingly unruly crowd of nightpeople have gathered as well.

Why are these men—family men, hard workers with day jobs—going to such a place in the middle of the night? Because they care. Because they have finally realized that they can no longer shrug over the crime and the drugs and the misguided youth and say "it's not my problem." They have realized, ultimately, that it *is* their problem, because their homes have become their own prisons, because of the meanness of the streets outside.

The three men—John Foster, Eddie Staton, and the Reverend Bob Tyler—banded together in Omaha, Nebraska, five years ago.

John Foster is, pure and simply, mad as hell. "What is a life worth anymore? I mean, people can't even walk down the street. Women can't walk to the store without the fear of being raped or whatever. All of these things that are happening. Your grandmothers, or your mothers, are so afraid that their homes have become their... their prisons, you know?"

John Foster almost did the *wrong* thing with his anger.

A few years back, his son was back home from college. And, through no fault of his own, got into trouble.

It was Memorial Day weekend in 1987. John's son had a brand new Suzuki "jeep." He parked it outside a north Omaha convenience store and went in to get a soft drink. While he was in there, five gang members spotted the Suzuki and decided that it was worth stealing, and that moreover, it's owner probably had cash on him. So when the boy came out, they jumped him. He fought back. They messed him up pretty bad, beating him and tearing his clothes, but the gathering crowd of spectators ultimately spooked them before they could relieve him of his wallet or his keys.

As John recalls, "I became an incensed, livid father, out of control, trying to demand information as to what had happened to him. And then when I did get enough information, I wanted to retaliate. I wanted to go after those individuals, and I did."

He put all the firepower he had—a .38, a .357 magnum, and even a BB gun—into the front seat of his car and roamed the neighborhood throughout the night, looking for the five who'd violated his son. Towards dawn, he realized what he was actually doing: Looking to kill five *kids*.

A sobering thought.

"It wasn't the right thing to do. And I thank God to this day that I didn't find them, because I know as out of control as I was, if I had seen anybody that even resembled them, I probably would not be talking to you today. I'd either be dead or incarcerated, because that's how out of control I was—and it's... it's scary now, looking back."

In the cold and unemotional light of reason, he knew he'd almost done something very, very wrong—but what was the *right* thing to do in such circumstances?

It was along about then that he realized: He probably needed to apologize. Apologize to those young men, the five who'd brutalized his son. He realized that he needed to apologize to every kid in the neighborhood, and to every single mom struggling to raise them.

He was mad—but he also realized that black men needed to be mad at themselves as well, because to a large extent, they had abdicated their duties as men. Duties to children they had fathered. Duties to their neighbor's children. It was time, he realized, not to exact revenge upon those damaged kids, but to try to break the cycle.

5

Says Foster, a tall, impassioned, and broad-shouldered man who is more than a little dangerous-looking in his own right: "There were some things we had to fess up to, you know? There were black men who had fathered children and gone off and left them. And now we see some of the results of that. But by the same token, we don't want people stereotyping all black men as being pimps and hustlers and drug dealers and streetwise and hyper-sexed who like to make babies but do not want to assume the responsibility of taking care of them. That's just not true.

"I'm going to toot my horn today. I'm a good father. But I just wasn't concerned about that lady who lived next door who's a single mom, you know?

"For the most part, that's the key. And what we're trying to get us to see—and we're speaking specifically to black men—is that we've got to stop skinning and grinning and laughing and associating with the dope man. I mean, there're a whole lot of us in our communities who know who the perpetrators are and who fraternize with them each and every day, yet it's almost an insult for a black man to turn another one in who's, quote, beating the system.

"But by the same token, they're selling poison to our children, holding us back, setting civil rights back, getting the children on a dead-end carousel that's going to continue to be ridden until there's no hope."

It was this growing realization of Foster's that led to the founding of Mad Dads four years ago. He took his anger and frustration first to Eddie Staton, who realized that he also shared these frustrations. Recalled Staton, riding through the darkness that night: "When John came to me and said, 'You know, I want to do something. We've got to get the strong men together; we've got to do something about these kids out here,' it was almost like somebody clicked on a light bulb and said, Right. This is it."

John Foster then went to Bob Tyler. Tyler was not only frustrated, he'd lived the other side, having done time in the pen for drug dealing as a young man. He not only knew the frustrations, but was familiar with the temptations that lead to crime.

Said Tyler: "Most of us bring our own uniqueness to it, too, in that I came out of this. I'd been a part of it. I've been a street hustler, a slick, and part of the dope world. I've lived it, I know it inside and out, I know all of the games they play and the things that perpetuate the participation of all of these young people out here, and I hate it with a passion."

The more they talked, the more they realized that if not them, who? And if not now, when? With almost no budget at all, they set to work challenging the strong black men in their communities to become part of the solution—and preparing them through nonviolent intervention to take back the streets and once again make them safe for their own wives and children.

Since that time, the movement has grown to thirty-one chapters across the country. It's growing still. John Foster believes that is because Mad Dads strikes the same nerve that led him to form the organization: Decent men of every class, religion, and race across the country are united in one passion: Everywhere, they are sick and tired of crime and fear.

Mad Dads is no vigilante group. Nor do they, on their peaceful patrols, try to become substitutes for the police.

But they are turning some inner-city assumptions and traditions on their heads.

Peer pressure is often blamed for ills among young people—but the lack of it among their elders is a problem as well, and Mad Dads is bringing that peer pressure to bear on the adult men they encounter. Says Foster, "What we're trying to do is to get them to see that, 'Hey, brother, if you really are our brother, you've got to help us tell this individual in our community who is selling dope to our children, and who will sell it to your children, and your wife, your sister, or whomever, that he can't do it here no more.'"

Another misconception the Mad Dads are combatting in communities across the country is the notion that the police are "the enemy," when instead, the police are the only ones standing between the law-abiding citizenry and total anarchy.

But angering them most, perhaps, are the cop-outs offered by members of their own race as excuses for their failures and acquiescence to the forces of crime. The perception that black men are nothing more than the passive products of centuries of suppression and racism is an outrage to them and an insult to all African Americans. In a nation of self-pitying victims, they believe that men should instead be men. While they welcome women to participate in Mad Dads, their main thrust is that if they're going to restore peace to their own streets, they have to start acting like men—strong men.

America is a country in which, increasingly, whenever there's a problem, we look for someone else to blame, and someone else to solve it. As Mad Dad Eddie Staton puts it, "The jails and prisons across this country are full of strong black men who somehow were misguided into thinking, Let's blame somebody else and do what we want to each other.

"I think the most frustrating thing is to see how we have failed to understand and to deal with what we're doing to ourselves and to each other. As a people, we've struggled for four hundred and something years, and even before that, we've had to struggle. But we have really gotten caught up in blaming the system, white people, for all of our problems, so much so that we've closed our eyes to what we're doing to ourselves.

"Our biggest headache is trying to recruit the strong men who know that they need to be out here, but for whatever reason, they're not out here. We have a lot of good men who have bought into the concept of Mad Dads and other good organizations who have been successful. But by the same token, we need more men to go to the forefront and deal with a lot of children who are morally adrift."

So night after night these three men and dozens of other committed Omaha Mad Dads take to the roughest streets during the darkest, most dangerous hours. They hope that by their presence as role models and their influence as concerned fathers, they can turn those mean streets around—sweep them clean. Short of meeting violence with violence, these men have vowed that whatever it takes is what they'll do. One-on-one counseling with gang members, shaming the crooks and the drug dealers and the victimizers, whatever it takes.

One of their most useful tools, they have found, are their midnight marches.

Says Foster, "If you're going to march in the daytime, at 4:00 p.m., most of the people that are out there in that night culture, they're asleep. The ones you want to see and have an impact on and get the message, they're asleep. So we came up with the bright idea, Let's have it at midnight, and it worked."

The things they've seen as they travel through the night are heartbreaking. Mankind at its meanest and the family at its most dysfunctional.

"I think the worst that I can remember is about last summer, when a fourteen-year-old girl was shot and killed over a parking space. She was arguing with a guy who had taken her older sister's parking place, and he just point-blank shot her in the head and killed her. And here is a fourteen-year-old girl, slumped on the cold pavement of a dirty street in Omaha, and all for what? It was so devastating when we went up there and saw this, no one could work the rest of that night. We had to go home. We're tired of going to funerals. It's senseless," said Foster.

But the signs of progress are heartening.

Said Bob Tyler, "For example, there's a young man who'd been strongly addicted to crack cocaine, abused his family. Got strung out on crack, started selling it, ended up getting caught, and went to the pen. We worked with him through the whole episode, especially when he got out. He turned out to be a promising young man. Got a college education, and he's now working in a drug counseling center. He's in church, he's back with his family, and he's helping us now, making a major contribution. That, to us, is the payoff."

For Mad Dads, the buck stops right here, right at their doorsteps, right on these streets. The one thing they ask from others is not so unreasonable, when it's a matter of saving a generation: Join them.

They're working hard to get across the message to their fellow Americans that, together, we can make a difference. John Foster said, "We want our message to go into their homes and have an impact, make people say, finally there's a vehicle I can tap into. I can do something. I may not be able to walk the streets, because that's not my forte, but, I mean, I can offer my services by providing them printing, if they need copies. I can do that as a Mad Dad, or I can do this as a Mad Dad. You know, even when the cameras are laid down and the lights go down, you guys are fathers and mothers and aunts and whatever. You have a responsibility, too."

And these men know there's only one alternative to involvement—and an unbearable price to pay if Mad Dads or something like them doesn't prevail to sweep those streets clean again. Because if they don't win, crime will. And it will continue to spread.

These guys aren't joking. Eddie Staton commented, "I'm saying that there is no greater threat to the national security than the youth of this country. I mean, our military, right on through our politicians, our educators, all of it is in danger unless we do something about this generation. I think also, the issue is, Do you wait until your kids are laying on the street, shot and killed? Do you want to wait until it knocks on your door?"

The Mad Dads, they put their lives on the line. They turn their words into action. They are committed to saving young lives, to saving their neighborhoods.

The future looks a little brighter to me, as it relates to the world in which I am raising my daughter, having met the Mad Dads.

Iris Stevenson, director of Crenshaw High School choir

Members of "Food from the 'Hood" at Crenshaw High School

SONGS OF THE HEART

IRIS STEVENSON

AND

PLANTING SEEDS OF HOPE

TAMMY BIRD

SOME OF OUR "UNSUNG HEROES" topics are deadly serious, and justifiably so—but I'm like anyone else. I like a little fun mixed in with my purpose. And I can't recall when I've had more fun on a story than at Crenshaw High, where some truly amazing things are happening: Things that are both great, and great fun.

If you'd told me that a predominantly black high school located right smack in the middle of the south Los Angeles area where all the rioting, the Reginald Denny beating, the fires, and the looting occurred, was one of the best schools in the country to go to right now, I'd have thought you were lying—until our crew went there to be amused and amazed.

After the horrendous riots and fires in economically blighted south Los Angeles, many people believed that nothing good would ever grow back on such severely scorched and bloodied soil.

But those people have never seen Crenshaw High, where the spirit of youthful growth and renewal is soaring as high as the songs the students sing. The young people there are as full of life as the school's remarkable garden.

Some folks say you should sing to your plants because it helps them to grow. If that is true, then Crenshaw can expect a Jack-in-the-Beanstalk–sized season.

Two great teachers, working independently of each other, are making some giant strides.

The experts tell us that the single biggest barrier

standing between young people in the ghetto and success in life is simply a lack of self-esteem. In many of these blighted neighborhoods, the kids are believed to proliferate like weeds and grow pretty much the same way—directionless, pointless. A sign of the decay rather than the cure for it.

There is no shortage of self-esteem at Crenshaw. When we went there, we were looking for good news in an area that doesn't get credit for much.

Riots and rotten race relations dominate the headlines, but that's not the most important story. In fact, we found not one but two minor miracles, both under the same roof.

One is a zesty miracle you can taste, and one is a miracle you can hear, loud and clear. And the two triumphs of the spirit go hand in hand.

The hearing end of the sense range is dominated by the efforts of Iris Stevenson, the choir and music director. We did not find out until later that this big, friendly, effusive woman was the real-life model for the Whoopie Goldberg character in the movie *Sister Act II*. The producers certainly chose well, because Iris is a ton of fun and her class is the most popular on the campus, with hundreds of kids from every walk of life getting turned down because her big classroom is already filled to overcapacity.

This class rocks and rolls and rattles the rafters with hand-clapping, foot-stomping gospel music backed up with drums and Iris's pounding, rolling piano playing. It just blew me away.

Some of the kids in this choir may have once been the kind of kids who probably wouldn't have hesitated to blow someone away—thieves, drug dealers, rioters. Tomorrow's prison inmates and worse.

And today, they're blowing people away by the thousands, all around the world—with their music, their singing, their spirit.

In the wake of the rioting, music teacher and choir director Iris Stevenson looked around and realized that she could offer these kids just about everything that the gangs could. She could offer them something to belong to. A sense of power. A feeling of accomplishment. A framework within which to compete—and in which to be heard. And yet a chance to work as part of a team and to stand out, as well.

These kids only wanted the same thing that everyone wants, in fact: A chance, in other words, to be somebody.

That's all they really want from the gangs. But here in Iris Stephenson's choir, their voices are raised not in a shrill cacophony of anger, but in song.

Where there was heat, now there is light.

And the choir has an international renown, having appeared at the Jamaica Jazz Festival and toured Europe and Russia, performing for royalty. Iris is proud of her kids and their awards—but is quick to tell you: It's not about music. It's about people. It's about healing, and hope.

"They're like my own children," Iris says. "Somebody once saved me out of despair. I feel I am obligated to do that for this generation. I want to show these kids a wider, better community, wider than L.A., wider than the U.S. We truly have a global outlook.

"I want them to get a sense of responsibility, and a sense of community, and the feeling that they've helped to make the world a better place, and can keep on making it better, one by one. I think it works here because the kids want it to work, the school wants it to work, the parents want it to work, and the community wants it to work.

"I've seen these students go from people who are not at all assured of what they can do—they had no goals, they had no dreams—but now they've blossomed like roses.

"Most of these kids have never sung before. They come in very shy, 'Oh, Miz Stevenson, I can't sing, I can't sing.' I just tell them oh yes you can because the song is inside of you. I can't teach anybody how to sing. It's when the heart meets the mind that the song comes out. The song is on the inside, and these people, they rise to the occasion and become leaders."

She's also dishing out a vast volume of love, her students tell us.

As one student told us during a sort of rap session with several of Iris's students: "If she didn't love us, she wouldn't spend so much time with us. You can come in and talk to her after school about things that are bothering you. People who can't have that kind of relationship with their parents, she'll help you with."

Said another, "You can go to her and say, Ms. Stevenson, I need help, I need to get on the right path, and she'll help you get there. Many teachers just don't care. But she goes home with us in her heart. That woman has so many offers to do many other things, but she continues to stay here, and that's why we love her."

Iris admits to that love.

"I want to be remembered as a person who helped many individuals achieve their goals in life. I want these kids to see their dreams realized. That's what I want to be remembered for. I'm about trying to show them a better way—planting seeds now that someone else is going to reap later on."

If Iris Stevenson is speaking metaphorically, biology teacher Tammy Bird is speaking both literally and figuratively.

At about the same time as Iris Stevenson and her students were beginning to rattle the rafters of glory, science teacher Tammy Bird was looking around the neighborhood and the school yard as well.

And what she saw was a patch of raggedy weeds on the school property where nothing much good seemed to grow. And Tammy thought to herself that a garden might give these inner-city kids something positive to do. At least, maybe keep some of them out of trouble.

But from tiny seeds great thing may grow. Next time you're in the condiments section of the grocery store, look for a certain kind of salad dressing. It's called Food from the 'Hood. In addition to being very tasty, it's probably the only salad dressing on the planet with a great saga behind it, and certainly the only one created, mass-produced, and marketed by a high school.

In the summer of 1992, Tammy and her students were discussing ways to heal themselves, their community, and their own relationship with their teacher (she is white; they are predominantly black).

"The kids came together and decided there was a simple answer; grow a garden. Feed the needy. The uprising was about more than just needing food and shelter. It was about ownership. The kids decided that the proceeds of the garden would be theirs to use as they saw fit."

By October of 1992 they were cultivating a full quarter-acre and actually had a surplus, which they sent to local homeless shelters. Then Melinda McMullen, an L.A. public relations executive, heard about the garden and got involved.

She suggested that the students sell the vegetables to build up a scholarship fund. They took the vegetables to the farmer's market where they were surprised to find themselves well received by the patrons and vendors.

But after the first year, they had only $600 in the bank for the scholarship fund and realized that if it was really going to go anywhere, they needed another way to raise cash.

"So out of that $600, we did market research and said, 'Why not salad dressing?' We were already growing parsley, basil, and other herbs real well. Then we did the research on how to make a product and found a mass processor we liked in the neighborhood. We designed the label; one of our kids worked with a graphic artist using his own original crayon drawing. Two years ago, if you'd told me that not only would my students be gardening but selling salad dressing, I'd have said you were crazy, no way. But the garden is bigger than ever, and the program is bigger than ever," said Tammy.

The salad dressing concept was an unapologetic knock-off of the concept behind Paul Newman's line of food products, which has raised more than $60,000,000 for charity since 1982.

The Crenshaw students became the owners of the firm, which they named Food from the 'Hood, and devised a formula for awarding scholarships, with points awarded for academic achievement and volunteer work.

For six months they experimented with various recipes and sent the results to a food chemist for analysis. The first version was too salty. Since heart disease is a problem in their neighborhood and they didn't wish to contribute to it, it was back to the drawing board for one final revision.

The project was attracting some high-profile support. Norris Bernstein, owner of Bernstein's Salad Dressings, provided marketing expertise. And Crenshaw kids met with grocery executives to persuade them to carry their product.

A major shot in the arm came in the form of two grants, totaling nearly $100,000. These financed the building of an office for their fledgling firm and the pre-production R & D, the packaging design, and the intensive business education necessary to run a large, growing company. Here were kids who six months ago didn't know what R & D (research and development) stood for, now talking like forty-year-old marketing MBAs with twenty years' experience.

Suddenly, Food from the 'Hood was bigger than just Crenshaw High School. It now provides employment opportunities for several nearby minority-owned firms.

The first bottle of Food from the 'Hood rolled off the line in April of 1993 and has been distributed through nearly two thousand retail stores in southern California. And they are on target towards selling their goal of thirty thousand cases by 1993.

The salad dressing and company ownership have given these students far more than just money for their scholarship fund. For one thing, it's given them clout and a sense of empowerment. After several early episodes of the television show "South Central," the show's executives approached Food from the 'Hood with an offer to give the salad dressing a free commercial slot. The kids didn't like the way the show depicted their neighborhood. It showed the neighborhood in a light they thought was too negative and despairing.

So the kids gave the company a firm thumbs down.

That got the producers' undivided attention and invited the kids to discuss their problems with the show. And then the producers fixed those problems in order to get Food from the 'Hood's endorsement.

It's given them a sense of pride. Beyond the initial grants, Food from the 'Hood has refused to accept any further charitable donations. Taking things for free takes the fun out of earning them.

And it's given them one other intangible. The ingredients are listed on the label—canola oil, rice-wine vinegar, dijon mustard, garlic, and other spices—but the most important spice of all isn't listed:

The spice that comes from spirit—something that's coming back strong in South Central L.A.

These kids would seem to go against our stereotyped image of urban, inner-city kids. Kids from areas like South Central L.A. are supposed to be tough, mean, cool, uncaring, and headed for a life of crime.

But it's not true to say that they go against the stereotype.

Because the truth is, the stereotype goes against them. It's the stereotype that holds many of them back; the stereotype that pushes many of them into lives of crime and poverty.

Maybe we ought to be thankful not just for the things that we have, but sometimes, the things that others are losing.

Slowly but surely, kids like those at Crenshaw are losing the stereotype, thanks to Unsung Heroes like Iris Stevenson and Tammy Bird.

Elementary school principal Thaddeus Lott

A Whole
Lotta Learnin'
Goin' On

Thaddeus Lott

OUR UNSUNG HEROES are about solving problems.

On the other hand, try to fix what isn't broke, and you break it.

Then try to fix that, and you break it some more.

In a nutshell, this is what has happened to America's educational system. It wasn't broken, but a lot of folks with bright ideas decided it wasn't good enough, that it needed tweaking.

The educational system that was in place in America during the first half of the twentieth century can take much of the credit for making America the leading power in the world—economically, politically, and intellectually.

Educationally, we are now ranked twenty-first in the world, somewhere after Japan, Germany, Korea, and Singapore—and ahead of only Greece.

And while in terms of overall competitiveness the U.S. remained at fifth place, a recent *World Competitiveness Report* lamented: "Most alarming for long-term competitiveness is the U.S. drop in the quality of its people—from second position to seventh this year. This is partly due to the current inability of the educational system to meet the needs of a competitive economy."

A 1992 international comparison of schoolchildren warned that not only were American students performing below average in mathematics and science, but also issued a "clear warning" that even the best schools are not doing a good job of getting our kids ready for global competition.

The survey, which included 175,000 students worldwide, showed that while the top 10 percent of American students "can compete with the best students in any country, the vast majority of American students perform below the international average."

21

The average American thirteen-year-old scored 55 percent out of 100 on a math test administered last March in six thousand classrooms worldwide. By comparison, Taiwanese and South Korean students scored eighteen percentage points higher. In science, thirteen-year-olds in America fared better, scoring an average of 67 percent, but still eleven points below the leaders.

A comparison of various age groups showed that American students fell behind as they got older. These shortcomings became evident as students began being tested on more complicated sciences, such as chemistry.

The survey also challenged some of the prevailing notions in America about what factors lead to academic success. Small class size, a longer school year, and more money spent on books, computers, and teachers did not make a notable difference in student achievement, according to the survey.

Crowded schools? Is that the problem?

South Korea, which along with Taiwan scored at the top, had forty-nine students in an average class, the largest of any country. Hungarian students scored in the top half in math and science, but they go to school only 177 days a year, about the same as Americans, who were near the bottom of those surveyed.

We should spend more money?

The United States is at or near the top of the list on dollars spent on students per capita.

Not that the United States hasn't tried a whole bunch of things that didn't work; by now, after all the tweaking, we have attained an almost encyclopedic knowledge of what won't work—even though a lot of the things that won't work, we just keep on using.

Ask the experts what needs to be done now to fix the American educational system, and, if they are honest, they will tell you: Don't know.

When it comes to what will work: Don't know.

But down in Houston, there is a man who seems to know how to "unfix" what wasn't broke in the first place. Thaddeus Lott wouldn't take "don't know" for an answer, neither from his students nor the Houston Independent School District administration's experts.

If this educator, Thaddeus Lott, gets the audience he deserves and some clout to back him up, he just might save American education and future generations of American minds.

Perhaps "restore" is a better word than save, because Thaddeus Lott has the common sense to know: Don't fix what isn't broke; don't reinvent the wheel.

Thaddeus Lott, the principal of a little inner-city elementary school, is a man with courage enough to stand up and make changes. Because to Thaddeus Lott, when you know you're right, you don't knuckle under to the experts, even if it might cost you your job.

Lott, principal of Wesley Elementary School, himself black—and of course himself a victim of racism since his childhood in the 1940s—knew when he took over this ailing little school that he had two choices: either protest the injustice of unequal expectations—or quietly and patiently shatter the stereotype by doing something about it.

Lott grew up in the 1940s on the very same streets of this poor but self-respecting Houston neighborhood known as Acres Homes. Thaddeus Lott got a college degree and built a career as an educator, first as a teacher and later as a principal. In 1969 he decided to bring his young family back to the old neighborhood—and placed his kindergartener and his second-grader in Wesley.

After four months, he realized that Wesley Elementary couldn't cut it, and saddened but determined to get the best possible education for them, took his two children elsewhere.

But he resolved to someday do something about conditions at the school. And in 1975, a principal's position did indeed become open at Wesley.

Recalls Lott: "I found a situation that was every bit of the challenge I had anticipated and more."

In fact, the situation was appalling. The sixth-graders could hardly read. There was a sense of apathy and decay in the untidy halls of Wesley that oppressed the spirits of staff and students. It soon became apparent to the new principal that few of the teachers cared—and the ones who did were helpless to change things.

Lott soon realized he had inherited a schoolhouse full

of little more than glorified baby sitters, and that if real education were to occur at Wesley, he had to replace them with real teachers. It wasn't hard to get rid of some of the bad apples: Lott's reputation for having little patience with loafers had in fact preceded him.

Lott was determined to fill Wesley with the best teachers possible. He would either find quality teachers and persuade them to come to Wesley Elementary—or just plain create them through intensive, one-on-one training.

But he also realized that even the best teachers could not impart an incomprehensible curriculum to even the most naturally bright children.

Teaching children to read by repetitive oral drilling and intensive instruction in phonics—the sounds of the letters rather than the whole words themselves—had fallen out of vogue with educators in the seventies. But intuitively, Lott realized that the system had attempted to repair something that wasn't broken. In addition to being easier to learn, phonics is easier to teach.

So against great resistance from Houston school officials, Lott took Wesley Elementary against the flow and went back to teaching phonics, particularly in kindergarten and the first grade. And the results were astounding. He made a huge mark his very first year.

When Lott became Wesley Elementary's principal, sixth graders were reading at the second-grade level. Six years later, any sixth-grade class there could read junior high and senior high material.

Test scores were skyrocketing, from among the lowest in Houston to the very highest.

But rather than embracing and rewarding Lott's stellar example, the school administrators under former superintendent Joan Raymond seemed to be doing everything they could to undermine the district's one maverick success story. They denied him funding and materials. They reprimanded him for rewarding his best teachers. They buried him in a blizzard of paperwork. They tried to stop him from using unfashionable phonics.

And here also is where Thaddeus Lott, who'd encountered racism all his life, found it at its most covert and insidious. Even some of the most "enlightened" and "liberal" of the white school officials had a difficult time watching this little inner-city school outperform mostly white schools on the right side of the tracks.

Some of them looked at those soaring test scores and concluded: Why, those poor dumb little black kids just have to be cheating, don't they?

Their fatal error came in 1990, when they made the mistake of publicly accusing Lott and Wesley Elementary of cheating on tests—and then failed decisively (and publicly) to prove it.

Acres Homes parents and other concerned citizens were outraged and descended upon the school board en masse to protest. Superintendent Joan Raymond, unnerved, apologized to the outraged parents, but it was too little and too late.

The newspapers in Houston gave front-page play to the story of the Little Principal Who Could. And soon, every official's worst nightmare came true for Joan Raymond: ABC's "PrimeTime Live" crews looked into the story—and didn't like what they saw. Neither did viewers and voters in the Houston Independent School District, and they made their objections known.

The school board shortly thereafter replaced Joan Raymond with a new superintendent who now not only frequently seeks Lott's advice, but has promoted him to overseer of the principals at other low-income Houston schools. And seven schools in Houston have implemented Lott's phonetic system with good results.

And at the national level, Lott is now a much sought speaker in educational circles. Yet still he remains simply the principal of little Wesley Elementary.

Maybe we should not only be willing to get behind him, but should also insist that he get out in front of us. Because while Thaddeus Lott can't teach every child in the country, it would be good to see him teaching the teachers.

Lou Ann Freas, president and founder
of Grandparents Outreach

A Mature Approach to Child Care

Lou Ann Freas

I FINALLY GOT AROUND to doing my taxes this year, after two extensions with the IRS. It's a time of year I always put off—like cleaning out the garage. But I finally did get around to it. And when I got to the line that lists my child-care expenses, I was shocked to see the numbers there in black and white. At first glance, it may seem like a waste—it's by far one of my greatest annual expenses. Then I decided to look closer at this situation. Child care—the care of my one and only precious child. What could be more important than that? That should be my number one priority—and it is!

The other day, when I picked my daughter, Bethany, up from school, she said, "Mommy, I always know you'll be there after school. And when you can't be, I know I'll be with someone I want to be with—with someone who'll love me until you get back home."

Whew, that put my priorities in perspective. I was reminded of a special lady I met on my travels for "Unsung Heroes," one who understands the importance of good child care.

In the best case scenario, the solution to the kids' crisis (or any other problem, for that matter) solves more than one problem for more than one person. That's the case in San Antonio, with Lou Ann Freas.

Lou Ann has solved the problems of latchkey kids—and a lot more folks' problems besides. Latchkey-kids (kids who go home to empty houses after school because both parents work) face problems a lot more serious than mere boredom or lack of supervision.

Children left unsupervised after school are more likely than others to be depressed. They are also more likely to experiment with alcohol, marijuana, or tobacco. They are more prone to neglect schoolwork as well, according to studies.

Particularly in some of the iffier neighborhoods, these

kids lead lives of quiet terror—afraid to go outside and startled by every noise.

As one of them told us, "Houses get burned down or kids get robbed," which was a sadly succinct summation of the times.

Others react by acting out, rebelling, and running the streets, or joining youth gangs.

San Antonio is not unlike almost any other American city: There, like everywhere else, tens of thousands of children go home from school to an empty house—and many don't go home at all, remaining on the streets after school hours, prey to drug dealers, gang members... and temptation.

And then, at the other end of the age spectrum, another problem. Old age. Loneliness. Uselessness. The feeling that life is over: The boredom and the dull fear of just... waiting.

But Lou Ann Freas, a San Antonio grandmother, came up with a unique solution: Grandparent's Outreach, a unique day-care program that gives latchkey kids, particularly underprivileged ones, a place to go where someone will care for them—and the program gives the senior citizens who participate something perhaps even more precious: Someone to love. A chance to be around children. And, most important, a reason for living.

And in the middle, benefiting as well, there are the parents, who have much greater peace of mind knowing that their kids aren't on the streets but are safe with "granny." Grandparent's Outreach Center volunteers to pick the kids up at the schoolhouse door. They supervise homework, tutor special students, entertain them, feed them—and perhaps most important to the parents, someone knows where the kids are.

Lou Ann, the mother of four and grandmother of ten, got the idea about four years ago. She walked into Santa Fe Episcopal Church and knew she was in the right place—divinely guided, she believes, from that point on to build the Grandparent's Outreach program from there, where she organized the first day-care center staffed by elderly volunteers. The program has since spread from there to other churches throughout the United States.

It's one of those programs that works for everyone involved.

"It gives senior citizens a chance to make a contribution, and to be with kids. The children benefit by having a safe place to come after school. And each of these people loves each other, and knows they are loved. Everyone is helped, all through these senior volunteers.

Five years ago, she'd never heard the term "latchkey kids." Now she and her grandparents' brigade serve kids from more than one hundred San Antonio families.

As one mother said, "She's a saint. She's always smiling and hugging the kids. That's got to be doing something for them. Before I came here, it was very scary for me to have to go to work and leave my child at home. I almost didn't work this year. But I feel comfortable here."

It's been a positive experience for Lou Ann as well—one that she'd like to see spread far and wide.

"I've learned a lot about how these kids think and act. And I feel strongly that the older people should be the ones to pass on what life is all about and tell them what the problems are and how to deal with them.

"And if they have the time and motivation, what better way to spend their retirement? There are 24,000,000 senior adults alive today. If half of them got involved, we could literally turn this problem around all across the nation.

"It costs the government no money; it's people helping people. You've got to know that there are many thousands of kids out there on the street or alone in their apartments. These are the ones we want to reach out to.

"I love children, and I am willing to fight nationwide for these children who are not in any care after school. It is very, very important to reach out to them. People are just moving too fast these days and not thinking about the kids. If they were thinking about it, they would get involved."

It should be stressed that in helping kids in programs like this, they're helping themselves as well. The social isolation that older people find in later life is believed to be the cause of an increasingly serious addiction problem among the elderly.

An estimated 2.5 million older Americans, and by some estimates twice that number, abuse alcohol, prescription medicines, and over-the-counter drugs. A full 70 percent of elderly hospitalizations are caused by alcohol-related problems. Almost 60 percent of older adults drink daily, and at least 15 percent of these are considered heavy drinkers in that they are drinking four or more times a day.

Another increasingly serious depression-related problem is that of elderly suicides. In the 1980s and 1990s, the already-high suicide rates among older Americans rose dramatically—21 percent over six years.

Even before the rates began to climb, they were already the highest of any group in the nation, and well above those for teenagers and young adults.

The increase was highest among white men, rising 23 percent from 1980 to 1986. White men account for almost three-quarters of all the elderly suicides in the nation. The experts point to increased social isolation as the cause, as well as growing feelings of uselessness and being without a purpose.

Lou Ann Freas and Grandparent's Outreach are taking some big steps in the right direction. They are giving some special children back their childhoods—and giving some super seniors someone to love.

Lou Ann has found a way to give of herself, and a way for others to do the same. For several hours every day these senior citizens give the most special gift they have to offer—themselves!

I cannot think of a more important investment we, as parents or as grandparents, can make than in our children, nor of a better place for latchkey children to be than with these super surrogate grandparents!

Nick Molina directs a session at his
juvenile rehabilitation program.

SAVING CHILD HOODS

NICK MOLINA

ABOUT THE LAST PLACE on earth you'd expect to find a concentration of gang-related crime would be in the small towns of south Texas—in a town like Edinburg. But small towns like Edinburg have the same social problems that breed the "wearing of the colors" in their big-city counterparts.

In Edinburg there's rampant poverty. This part of Texas has some of the richest soil and the poorest people in the country.

It's a bonanza for the larger landowners, but a place to eke out only the scantiest income for the predominantly Hispanic migrants and small-farm workers who populate it.

As in the big city ghettoes, social programs are inadequate to meet the need here—and to add to the problem, much of the population is undocumented and thus ineligible for even some of the most basic government services.

There are considerable racial barriers as well. Education is inadequate. Economic opportunity is minimal, and what there is of it is controlled by the Anglo, English-speaking minority. In short, there is anger. There is hopelessness. There is inequity.

And thus, there are gangs.

Nick Molina hasn't been much luckier than any other Hispanic man in south Texas. His job doesn't pay much and his standard of living, compared to more affluent middle Americans, is low. His is not a life of luxury.

Nevertheless, Nick Molina was able not only to have a family, but to keep it together. He's a father and a grandfather. But perhaps most important, Nick Molina sees himself as part of a larger family—the family of Man.

And he didn't like what he was seeing happen to all those sons and brothers and grandsons. The difference with Nick Molina was he decided to do something about it.

First was his choice of occupation. He chose to go to

work as a counselor in Edinburg's department of juvenile corrections. Day after day for more than twenty years now, he's worked with the kids one on one and one day at a time trying to steer them off their self-destructive courses on these dusty Texas streets and back onto a path that will take them somewhere worth being—to a good education, a good job, and a better life.

A good start—but for Nick Molina, it was *only* a start.

One on one, one day at a time wasn't enough. He knew he couldn't do it all by himself. So Nick went out into the larger family of Man and found his better-off brothers.

He buttonholed them and cajoled them into what he sees as their responsibility to the larger family: To reach out to its troubled sons and daughters and give them a helping hand. To pull them back into our larger family.

Each member of the growing group of unpaid "big brothers" and "big sisters" that he has put together acts as a sort of volunteer probation officer. But not the kind that people merely have to report to. The kind that genuinely care.

And Nick realized that there was another step he could take. As a probation counselor, Nick realized that he was seeing those kids only *after* they were in trouble, already well along on a road that could lead them to lives of misery and maybe to prison.

Nick decided to go closer to the source—those streets, those gangs—before they led those sons, daughters, brothers, sisters, grandsons, and granddaughters to greater ruin. Every day when his official workday is over, Nick "clocks in" on his second job, out there on those streets, talking to those kids, those gangs.

Nick doesn't lecture; he *listens*. And so they trust him. He doesn't tell them what to do, but finds out what they *need*. Where they are. What is missing in their lives. What could be done to make their lives better.

Then he fights to see that they get it. And before you know it, some of these kids begin to look more to this father and grandfather for guidance—and perhaps a little less to some poor kid who's only bluffing, a kid who is no smarter and every bit as scared and confused as they are themselves. In other words, Nick becomes the leader of the gangs. So far, it's working.

Some might think that Nick Molina is an exception, contrary to the norm. Nick doesn't see it that way though. As far as Nick is concerned, spending his time—and sometimes risking his life—out there on those streets is only part of the job description, the one for the title of Father and Grandfather in the family of Man.

John Peter, president and CEO of KidsPeace,
with children at the National Center for Kids in Crisis
in Allentown, Pennsylvania
Credit: KidsPeace

KIDS' PEACE

JOHN PETER

THERE EXISTS THE ERRONEOUS PERCEPTION that so-called corporate types, which is as bad a stereotype as any other, are not inclined to do things for others.

You take one look at John Peter and you are tempted to apply the sobriquet. Healthy, dignified, and happy, he looks very much the part of the CEO.

And he is the CEO, but of an organization that is doing a great deal of good in the world for some people who need it the most, since they will be the world of tomorrow: America's troubled kids.

Behind these headlines, there is an even broader and more insidious problem, though it's one that's far less high-profile: For every mother and father who are raising children wrong, there are probably another one hundred that are simply failing to raise them right. And the sum of all this is that we feel both alienated and helpless.

There is nothing more innocent than the face of a child—full of life, wonder and hope. And there is nothing more despicable than the abuse of a child.

On any given day, in any given community in this country, a child is being robbed of his or her childhood. Kids and families by the thousands are suffering the effects of abuse, neglect, and emotional distress.

But John Peter is doing something about it, both one to one and on a national scale. "One of our missions is to try to help the family itself. Our goal is to reach out to every family in America with materials and a message as to how they can help themselves. We think the family needs some help. We don't want to write academic papers, but we do want to talk to every family in America."

John Peter believes the answer to America's family problems lie in an apple orchard atop a mountain in Pennsylvania. That is where KidsPeace is located, on one of the highest peaks in this part of New England. This place is where children from all across the country come to reclaim their childhoods. Under John Peter's guidance,

37

the buildings have become home to one of the most innovative treatment programs in the world—a safe place for kids in crisis. KidsPeace is a safety net for America's kids. It offers the most comprehensive series of programs ever developed in one place for kids in crisis, ranging from prevention and early intervention, foster and residential care, to the establishment of a national children's hospital. KidsPeace has created a unique system to treat children, all in one compassionate, consistent, and medically effective setting.

John Peter's success record is a testimony to his determination. But it's also testimony to the growing numbers of children in crisis across the country.

In 1993, flanked by leading child experts, he began creating a wave of support and awareness nationwide. Because millions of parents lack the ability to effectively raise their own children, he took his message to the nation's capital, to announce that KidsPeace is attempting to reach out to every family in America. KidsPeace is in fact the most comprehensive program ever developed for children in crisis.

KidsPeace now helps more than two thousand children a day at twenty-five locations around the country.

John Peter is an entrepreneurial genius—KidsPeace hospitals and centers have expanded one-hundredfold over the past twenty years. He's got the kind of public relations skills that allowed him to persuade the voters of Pennsylvania to give him $45,000,000 to create the National Center for Kids in Crisis. He's that rare person who puts his business acumen into a selfless venture—saving kids.

John Peter, with guidance from Dr. Lee Salk and other noted authorities like Dr. Alvin Poussaint, Dr. Lewis P. Lipsitt and others, has created the most successful intervention program in the country, with a residential completion rate of eighty percent (nation's highest).

It operates an 800 number connecting community-based professionals with a network of twenty thousand emergency care providers.

Then there's the national public service announcement featuring Trusty the Goldfish. Sounds insipid, but it's effective: It aired nationally more than two hundred thousand times over four hundred stations and cable systems, making an incredible 1.63 billion viewer impressions. It set a record for responses, getting three hundred thousand of them through the 800 numbers.

But one of the most important operations of KidsPeace is the Salk Center. It began when John Peter took a walk in the New England woods looking for an answer and found it in an apple orchard.

Here, amid the peace and quiet of New England's crisp beauty, he began to build a three-hundred-acre campus nestled amid plenty of natural forest, open spaces, and seventy acres of orchards, on one of the highest peaks in New England.

It is to this modern facility that thousands of kids have come to reclaim their childhoods—their kid's peace.

When the crew and I first arrived here, we kept discussing our feeling that there was something wrong— that it was too clean, too nice, too... expensive.

Because we had lived with the notion for so long, like everyone else, we had the idea in the back of our minds that institutions for troubled kids were supposed to be exactly that—institutional. Cold. Punitive. Unfriendly.

And of course we realized that *we* were the ones who were wrong.

Because John Peter long ago recognized that, in addition to needing to get the word out, there was also a great need to offer children help in a facility that didn't make them feel like throwaways or second-class citizens or "problems to be solved."

In other words, he believed what all of us should know instinctively: Nothing is too good for our kids. And it was only practical.

"We started out with very meager facilities," he said, "but we found out that in better facilities, kids get better faster."

In 1974, they were helping thirty kids. The KidsPeace program now comes to two thousand a day in twenty-five facilities across the country with programs that range from prevention and early intervention to providing foster care and treatment in the national hospital. It is almost as though John Peter is single-handedly trying to save a generation.

"When they come in and I see their pain and their struggling with issues, and I see them begin to get some security and comfort and some help developing skills in handling problems—when I see them develop, learn, and then when I see them walk out that door knowing that they are going to succeed, it means a lot to me."

His success record is testimony to his determination, but it also documents the fact that the problem is too big for one man to battle alone.

Because on any given day at any given moment, hundreds of thousand of children are being robbed of something most precious—a childhood. Families by the thousands are suffering from abuse and neglect.

In the quiet foothills of Pennsylvania, a very special place with a heartfelt mission is listening to the desperate cries of children.

KidsPeace is issuing a clarion call to all Americans to bring peace to all our children—and maybe you can help. If you know of a child in an abusive situation, please make a call to someone in your community who can help.

If your child is experiencing emotional trauma that you cannot handle, call KidsPeace at 1-800-KID-SAVE to find a qualified child expert in your area, and to learn about KidsPeace treatment services.

Joe Marshall, founder and director of the
Omega Boys Club
Credit: Omega Boys Club

BE SOMEBODY

JOE MARSHALL

WHEN WE ARRIVED IN SAN FRANCISCO that chilly and damp day and drove to the Omega Boys Club in one of the city's rougher neighborhoods, we were in for a surprise.

It turned out to be a pleasant one, but only after no little amount of misunderstanding.

At first, we thought that Joe Marshall's apparent attitude was going to pose a serious problem. He was distracted, quiet, and uncommunicative—not exactly an ideal subject for a television show. And I must admit, the crew and I felt a little insulted. While, true, we weren't Barbara Walters and "20/20" come to make him famous, we did believe that on the other hand we weren't exactly chopped liver, either.

Joe continued to answer our questions off-handedly— yes, no, maybe, with little elaboration and elucidation.

We'd come quite a ways at a not inconsiderable expense to do his organization a not inconsiderable favor; with every organization we've ever covered, there is an almost immediate increase in both funding and visibility. That is what I felt we were bringing him, and I wondered why he didn't seem to want it.

Finally I could stand no more. The way he was acting, it looked like all our effort was going to come to nothing. We are only human, and there are few things more frustrating than trying to help someone who doesn't seem to care.

I'd never had to pull the plug on an "Unsung Heroes" "mission," but I was resigned to the inevitable fact that someday that day would arrive, and it looked like the time had finally come.

I had about reached the point of saying, "Thanks for nothing, pal, we're outta here." I said instead, "Excuse me, Joe, but you don't seem very interested in what is happening here. If you don't want publicity, say the word and we'll be gone."

Joe kind of froze for a moment there, wide-eyed with surprise. Then his handsome features softened and he chuckled pleasantly. He picked up a letter from his desk and handed it to me to read.

I read it and was stunned. And understood why Joe had been stunned as well. He wasn't being rude or disinterested; fact of the matter is that he was in complete shock. After years of struggling to make ends meet, after years of begging to maintain even minimal funding, just a few minutes before our arrival, Joe had gone from zero to sixty in about four seconds—from Unsung Hero to Sung Hero in about the time it takes to open the mail. He'd been officially notified that the "bad old days" were now over.

And there had been some bad old days indeed.

Even before Joe Marshall had decided to both care and take action, his life had been no bowl of cherries. He was a popular high school math teacher trying to support himself, his wife, and his two young children on a teacher's pay, itself no small task. Then, of course, there was the matter of the 'hood. Most white middle-class people think of these places, these Southsides, as simply places where they hope their cars don't break down on the commute between safe home and safe office—never for a moment realizing that these neighborhoods are by and large composed of decent, hard-working, law-abiding people like them who, only by reason of the color of their skin haven't had access to the same breaks and advantages that pave the way for Middle America to enter into the American Dream. People, in fact, like Joe Marshall.

"Nonsense!" the comfortable and contented may reply, "A black kid stands a far greater chance of being accepted to college than my own daughter," which, strictly in terms of affirmative action, might be minimally true.

But that being granted, ask yourself the next set of more important questions.

This black kid—how's he going to support himself and pay tuition? How's he going to get to school if he doesn't have a car—or even know how to drive. How's he going to deal with coming from a culture and a distorted value system where those who try to improve themselves are ridiculed by their peers?

The list of barriers in such an environment is almost endless—and it is, in fact, probably debilitating. All too often, deadly.

So many times, Joe Marshall would find himself outraged. His former students would write to him, to tell him that he was the best teacher he ever had—and the letter would be on state prison stationery.

Or one would walk up to him in public to say pretty much the same thing—only through a crack-cocaine-induced haze.

Then, there were all the funerals Joe Marshall found himself having to attend. The national epidemic of violence kills 55,000 young men a year—as many as all the deaths from car accidents, cancer, and heart disease combined.

And the graduates (and, more often, the dropouts of San Francisco's Potrero Hill Middle School) were by no means immune.

Marshall decided that it simply had to stop, that enough was enough. Too many of his own most promising students—too many young men who should have gone right—were going wrong, or were simply gone.

Joe set out to reclaim a generation of young black men who are ever-increasingly lost to drugs and violence. Joe and Jack Jacqua, a white retired teacher who is equally concerned, decided to fight back by establishing the Omega Boys Club, an organization which takes a fresh new approach to unraveling young men from the snare of street crime.

Omega is part rap session, part community center— and an increasingly big part of the war on youth crime, because at its heart is the one thing many of these boys and young men lack and desperately need: a sense of family. Someone a little older and a little wiser who'll listen to them.

Joe believes in these kids. And he knows what they need in their lives—what they are actually searching for down all those wrong avenues of drugs, crime, gang membership.

They are looking for a little love, someone who believes in them, and some respect. Joe gives them the love for free and then teaches them how to earn respect. He believes that it's not they who have given up on us, but that we have given up on them. And he's trying to change that.

Most amazing is the attendance at his evening "study hall"–type tutoring sessions, where these kids can get help and guidance on their school course subjects.

It's full every night. These kids want to study. They want to learn. They want a way out, but don't know how to find it. Omega Boys Club takes them off the streets and puts them on the right road.

Joe Marshall and Jack Jacqua run the club as if it were a family, providing for the kids whatever a loving and concerned family would provide—shoelaces to scholarships. In fact, one hundred of the Omega Boys Club's members—many of them former street thugs and criminals—have gone on to college as a result of Marshall's efforts. He has paid out of his own pocket for TV spots to ask the public for help with his scholarships.

The parents of these children who are growing into productive citizens describe their offspring as miracles and dreams come true.

One symbol of the organization is a young man named Joe Thomas, once upon a time a good kid gone bad. His first victim was an elderly San Francisco woman he decided to rob on the street. He knocked her down and broke her arm while snatching her purse.

And, remarkable since this was truly his first offense (they usually are not caught until well into their criminal careers), he was caught and sent to juvenile hall. Juvenile authorities didn't do him much good, though; by the time he was eighteen and old enough to be tried as an adult, he'd been back to juvey hall twelve times.

He supplemented his living hustling dope by working as a custodian in a building near the Omega Boys House, and he would eavesdrop on the meetings. Finally he approached Joe Marshall one night. He said simply, "Can you help me?"

And Joe Marshall could. He simply welcomed Joe

Thomas to the family. In May of last year, Joe Thomas stepped up onto the stage at Morris Brown College in Atlanta, Georgia, and got his diploma.

The nationally recognized club works with African Americans aged eleven to twenty-five, trying to turn them away from drugs and violence by instilling pride, teaching academic skills, and promising a college education to those who dare to succeed.

Joseph Marshall has also taken his message into a wider arena—the airwaves. He hosts a popular talk show called *Street Soldiers* on KMEL, a popular San Francisco station. He reaches two hundred thousand listeners a week. *The New Yorker* magazine called the show an electronic parent. These kids call for one big reason; they want adult advice.

It's a show with heart, and it gets down into the nitty-gritty of life on the San Francisco streets. People open up to Joe and his street soldiers, because they talk straight, using hard-core, streetwise logic with no sugar coating.

And when necessary, they talk tough. Many times, street soldiers have been able to stop a gang retaliation or a drug sale simply by convincing these young people that there's someone who cares about them. And that there's someone who is willing and waiting to help and that there are alternatives.

Joe feels that these kids get into trouble simply because they are, in a sense, orphans. Orphaned by their families, their communities, the government, and the media. Thinking that no one cares can make you quit caring about yourself.

Joe used his radio talk show to organize a massive meeting of two thousand young people and concerned citizens—gang members and gang victims, drug dealers and their victims, rap artists and their listeners—to talk about ways to save both our kids and our streets.

The talk was tough there, too. Congresswoman Maxine Waters had some straight words for the gang members, hitting them right in the macho.

Joe's growing success in helping solve the problems of youths resulted in an invitation to testify before the U.S. Senate. He told them the problems. And the senators had, of course, already heard all that before.

But he also told them the solutions—what clearly works, because Joe has proven it works. And then he told them why we have not been successful before. And he didn't leave them much room for excuses.

Joe Marshall is solving a problem that a lot of people think has no solution. Joe is using love to take back the streets. He's making a home for these troubled young men, these orphans. In fact, he may be the only man in America who can say he put one hundred of his kids through college.

There are, in this great big America of ours, so many of these kids—kids who don't want to be dangerous, kids who are looking for a way out. And there's only one Joe Marshall.

But then, there are also a whole lot of us.

Why, though, were Joe Marshall's bad old days finally over?

The letter was from the John D. and Catherine T. MacArthur Foundation, informing him that his organization was to be the recipient of a $300,000 grant to sustain and expand their good works.

John D. and Catherine T. were heroes in their own right—rich people who felt their money could make the world a better place.

It was really kind of wonderful, being there at the moment an unsung hero finally got "sung."

Sharon Cox, editor of *Class Acts*

A CLASS ACT

SHARON COX

SOME MAY HEAR ABOUT OUR NEXT HERO and say, why, she's only doing her job. The larger picture, however: That every opportunity—every job, every relationship, every single day—provides a chance to be a hero. Or, like Sharon Cox, the woman you're about to meet: a class act.

Once in a great while an American business organization makes a decision that results in a win-win situation for everyone: the organization makes money, and the public is done a great service.

That was the case five years ago at the *Fort Worth Star Telegram,* a respected north Texas daily newspaper with a circulation of 300,000. Publisher Richard Connor knew his staff had a good idea, but he had no idea just how far they would take it.

Conners told me, "We had a group of employees make a recommendation that we needed to start a special publication aimed at children. Our interest was to help them deal with their problems and also to start to build newspaper readership at a young age. We are absolutely stunned by the success of it. There's no question why it's successful. The staff at *Class Acts* is constantly in touch with the audience we're trying to reach."

At the center of that staff is Editor Sharon Cox, a former educator who took what could have been just another nine to five newspaper job and turned it into her life's work.

Richard Connors sings Sharon's praises: "It would be hard for anyone to understand how much time she dedicates every week and every day to making certain that we are in touch with children and adolescents in the community so that we can communicate with them and so that they can communicate with each other."

Sharon is a person who really just takes her work with her wherever she goes, seven days a week, twenty-four hours a day. She's the mother of three children, she is a busy wife, and she's a busy executive editor of this

51

publication. She has a staff of people who are responsible to her, and she is responsive to them. She is constantly working with her staff, with her own children, and then with all the the people whom *Class Acts* reaches.

Sharon's commitment to young people is unrelenting. "The focus of the main goal of *Class Acts* is to get students to read the paper first, and second, to not only get them to read, but also to get them to write. We try to get as many students involved in *Class Acts* as we have readers, and there're a lot of different ways they can do that. We have letters to the editors, we have an advice columnist, "Dear Mora," we have student reporters who review movies and video games. Student reporters do school news, students submit jokes and raps and rhymes and riddles. There're just a lot of ways students can get involved. We also have hotlines and viewpoints where they can call in and express their views on a certain topic for that week. I mean, our whole philosophy at *Class Acts* is that we love kids. This is not just my paper, and it's not a paper for parents and it's not a paper for teachers. It's strictly a news magazine for children and young adults. The whole staff is part of *Class Acts,* and the entire staff, whether it's a twelve-year-old student reporter or a twenty-five-year-old full-time staff member, are all dedicated to getting young people excited about reading and writing and to learn more about the world and the community in which they live," said Sharon.

Sharon Cox feels rewarded by her job, partly because, like any parent, she likes to see young people grow, blossom, and bear fruit.

"What's really exciting is when I see letters and articles coming in. At the beginning of the school year, I go out and talk to those kids and get to know those kids, and what's exciting is actually seeing their spelling improve, their grammar improve. It's exciting to see their writing improve and to see that we are helping them with their communications skills," commented Sharon.

Another source of the energy and dedication that Sharon Cox brings to *Class Acts* comes from the fact that she's learning as much from the kids as she's teaching them. Some of it isn't pretty—but at least she's getting a clear idea of the world that our children are growing up in.

"The topics have changed, and it's sometimes frightening and sometimes exciting, because kids are extremely fickle; what's hot today is cold tomorrow.

"When we planned our stories five years ago, we had no idea that we would be writing about a twelve-year-old student stabbing a teacher on the steps of the middle school or a five-year-old child being gunned down in her home at two o' clock in the morning in a drive-by shooting. We had no idea that we would be covering that type of violence," explained Sharon.

If this sounds like rough stuff to put before a so-called "kiddie" audience, keep in mind that kids are already fully aware of the dangers in the world in which they live. In fact, they may know more about this dangerous world than adults do. Sharon makes it her business to learn to navigate this world.

"I did not know until today when I talked to some of these kids—and I've known them for a year—that kids are taking guns to parties. We should know, because just in the last ten days, two young teenagers were killed by guns at parties. Yet we don't realize this is actually occurring."

It's our job as parents and citizens to bring a stop to the violence. But in the meantime, *Class Acts* gives the young people a serious forum to help them deal with it, both now and in the future. *Class Acts* takes its responsibilities deadly seriously.

"The *Class Acts* readers of today are not only newspaper readers of tomorrow, but are politicians, community leaders, and hopefully, they're the key to solving today's crime problems and other problems that we're having today, whether it's the environment, pollution, violence in the schools, teen pregnancy, or AIDS. One of them may discover a cure for AIDS."

But the bottom line may be that the kids who are involved with *Class Acts* may be learning the most important lesson of all—that with an education and some self-confidence, the sky's the limit.

"I see a lot of kids who, a year ago, before they got involved in *Class Acts*, may not have ever thought of college as a goal. But by working with some of our staff members or me, they realize that anything is possible if they'll just work for it."

Richard Connors's praise continues: "Role models are really important, and Sharon Cox is a role model, not only because she's a good editor and because she's a good businesswoman, but because she's a good person."

No matter what her job title or who pays her salary, Sharon Cox is clearly one of those people whom our society should once again value most: She's a teacher, and a good one. She leads by example. She doesn't just instruct; she gets our children involved.

Lo Andrews and participants at
Visions Basketball Camp, Dallas, Texas

Hoops and Hopes

Lo Andrews

THE LATE CIVIL RIGHTS LEADER Bayard Rustin once watched a bunch of poor inner-city kids playing a fierce game of basketball on a ghetto playground, and it broke his heart.

Why?

There was no fun in it. It was no longer a game, for them. There was no joy, no frivolity, only a deadly earnestness; these young men believed that they were preparing themselves for a career. And the only reason they were doing so, Rustin realized, was out of sheer desperation and a lack of alternatives.

It is perhaps one of the biggest betrayals of the underclass—the seeming collusion between the networks and the advertisers to come together in that talking box in all the millions of American living rooms to create and perpetuate a myth that simply is not true.

The myth: That professional basketball offers these young ghetto-dwellers a quick road to riches. That if they buy the right shoes, see commercials starring basketball players who, thanks to high-dollar special effects, can actually fly, then their futures are secure.

The myth also tells them that they will go to college no matter how bad are their grades, because they can run and jump and shoot.

The damage: Many of these kids not only believe it, but make it the centerpiece of their means of assessing their own self-worth. It becomes their only goal, to the exclusion of all others.

And that is well nigh a fatal mistake, if not in the physical life, then at least in the life of that soul.

The scary statistic is that less than one percent of the half-million high school roundballers will get even Division One athletic scholarships.

It is on a par with a lottery—but then, where most of them come from, the only good shot is the long shot, because there seems to be only two routes to success, to fast cars, fine women, and the good life—three, if you count the lottery.

Otherwise, you can play basketball. Or you can sell drugs.

And when they fail to make the grade, not only do these young men feel worthless, but, having so totally believed this myth and bought into it, they have excluded all other avenues to success. They have neglected their education, their communications skills, even their manners.

And in their own eyes, they become what the myth of professional basketball was supposed to allow them to surpass and overcome: They ultimately must enter the grinding cycle of poverty and the fear of becoming just another nothing who, in order to be Somebody, has to pick up a gun or a knife because it feels like the only way they can get respect or make a difference.

Otherwise... just another unskilled black man in a still mostly white world.

Just another dumb... pick your epithet. They've heard them all. Nothing new. If you listen, you'll hear that they call each other these names the most.

The descent into hell of the underclass truly begins the moment they stop dreaming about an achievable future. It begins the moment they actually believe the names and the stereotypes and internalize them, and that moment, for all too many of them, comes the minute the Basketball Dream finally dies.

They don't think of the numbers, of the odds that are so decisively arrayed against them. Michael Jordan, Kareem Abdul Jabar—those guys aren't one in a million. They are each more like one in two hundred fifty million. There are more lottery winners than top-flight pro basketball players.

Yet amid the horrors and decay of the Cabrini-Green Housing Project in the southside of Chicago, a kid can look out a window and see the arena where Michael Jordan made millions.

Put on those Air Jordans, and fly...

Lorenzo Andrews was, once upon a time, one of those black kids, in many respects.

He was counting to a degree on basketball, and, truth be told, the game carried him a lot further than it does most of those who count on it. He got far closer to riches and fortune than the vast, vast majority of these black boys and young men ever will.

Despite his hardscrabble background in the "inner city" of Oklahoma City, he earned All-America at Millwood High School and then went on to play at Oklahoma State, where he led OSU to the Big Eight title in his senior season.

Lorenza "Lo" Andrews was a young black college basketball player with lots of promise, and the scouts came a-sniffing. They liked what they saw.

And then he was the Kansas City Kings' fifth-round draft choice in 1983. He made the team, and the visions of sugarplums danced in his head—the same visions that dance in the heads of every kid bouncing an orange ball on those gritty concrete parking lots and throwing that ball through a basketless, chipped yellow hoop. It's the same dream that infects the imagination of every kid practicing layups and jump shots far into the autumn twilight, while the schoolbooks he should have brought home moulder in the lockers lining the high school's darkened halls, their lessons forever unlearned.

Lo Andrews imagined the expensive cars, and flying first-class from city to city, and the fine women, and the restaurants, and the headlines, and the acclaim, and the world lying adoring at his feet.

He saw the multimillion-dollar product endorsements, and those million-dollar commercials showing Lo Andrews flying through the air with wings on his heels, a winner and a hero... and then, he got cut.

He didn't make it.

He didn't quite have what it took.

He was a very good basketball player, but in the competition for the majors, "very good" doesn't cut it. "Excellent" isn't even good enough.

Fantastic might make it. One in twenty million might make it. But good, very good, and excellent are all just fancy ways of saying, "also-ran." The Kansas City Kings gave him his walking papers. Bye, write if you find work.

The basketball dream was over. *Finis*. Wake-up call, time to smell the coffee.

And that could have been Lo's low point, and maybe the end of all of his dreams. Maybe a man headed for menial labor, or a dead-end job, or a life of petty crime. Or even homelessness. Maybe a man forever feeling bitter about the vicissitudes of life and of birth.

The promise of a multimillion-dollar pro career was slam-dunked, gone.

But Lo Andrews had understood something that many of the rest of these kids don't get; that basketball could buy him an education, at least, and that he should take the fullest advantage of that, which he had. Lo went on to fulfill a greater promise. He didn't foul out, but completed his marketing degree.

Says Lo: "I grew up with both a mom and a dad, and they had their own version of 'no-pass, no-play.' If I didn't hit the books, then I couldn't play sports. I made up my mind to do the best I could, no matter what it was I was doing."

And then after school, after he was cut from the Kings, he spent a few years proving not only his education but his talent and his people skills to his employers. He is still a young man—and he's already a vice president at a Dallas bank.

He's a success. A wheel. But he was determined to give something back to the community.

So he opened an annual two-week camp to teach inner-city kids how to... play basketball?

Yes, given the above, that would appear to be, at the least, hauling coals to Newcastle or, worse, throwing gasoline on a dangerous fire that is already blazing very nicely, thank you very much.

It would appear to make that situation that much worse, when you consider that Lo Andrews actually arranges for these big stars of the game, the Mark Aguirres, the Isaiah Thomases, and others who have made it big in spite of the odds to actually come teach the game to these kids and give them some pointers.

But there is more to the program than meets the eye. Lo realized that, so pervasive is the "hook" of basketball for these kids that there was no way to counter it: A former basketball player who went around saying "Basketball is bad" just because he didn't make it to the pros would find himself preaching to some pretty empty halls.

Basketball in and of itself is of course not a bad thing. Even the dream of it isn't bad—as long as it is not the only dream and the only perceived avenue for success and progress in these young lives.

The problem is that these kids in the ghetto often have only two role models: The flying superstars they see on TV and the pimps and the drug dealers in their big cars and extravagant clothing living a high-life based on the import and sale of human misery. These guys are all too real. You don't need a TV to see them.

And Lo Andrews realized that he could make a difference.

As an example, he himself is not a bad one. A man who, it is true, played basketball and strove for the pros—but who meantime also made sure that if it all came to a halt the next day, he'd have not only a piece of sheepskin in his back pocket, but all the knowledge it represented and a knowledge of how to use that knowledge.

But he also brings in other black stars, other heroes, as role models—stars in the world of business, of public service, of the media, of politics. Stars in the worlds of education, research, you name it.

"We call it 'Visions' because I want the kids to dream," Andrews said. "We want them to realize that whether they want to be Michael Jordan or banker or astronaut, they need to work and strive and dream for that goal. If you don't dream, you don't have anything."

And the same is true of an education: Without one, you're toast.

So just a few feet off the court is a learning center to help the kids get back on track scholastically, and understand why it is important that they do.

And Andrews decided also that the very same American corporations that fuel the dream—that buy the airtime to show the games—and the sports equipment manufacturers, and so on, have a duty to these kids to give them alternatives. He took that message to Corporate

America, and Corporate America, to its credit, agreed.

Thanks to underwriting from people at the Coca-Cola Company, Gatorade, Kraft—and, yes, Nike—the kids, for the two weeks of training plus all materials and meals, pay only twenty-five dollars.

And since these kids are by and large poor, there are ways around that as well. Men like Buff Parham, general manager of Dallas's lead television station. Or Alphonso Jackson, head of the Dallas Housing Authority, or banker Fred McClure, who also served twelve years on the White House staff.

These men—both athletes and nonathletes—don't just stand up in a roomful of kids and talk. They get to know the kids, counsel with them.

Andrews himself, when not planning the next year's camp, serves as a big brother and mentor, for example, to Courtney Williams, a Dallas high school basketball player who is showing some promise.

Thanks to Andrews, that promise doesn't have to be pro basketball. They don't even talk about basketball, in fact.

When they first met, Williams wasn't doing well in school. Andrews helped him to believe in himself, with the results that the grades rose from the sub-basement of D's and F's back up to B's and C's.

The bottom line of the camp is, in fact, instilling that belief in oneself, that self-esteem so necessary to the courage to venture into new arenas, to dare to succeed— and feel that success is deserved.

These kids—four hundred of them come through the camps every summer—have been deprived of much by circumstances, race, and the economy. There is something very stirring and uplifting about a whole gymful of them lined up in orderly rows, chanting the chant that Andrews and his staff of aides drill into the kids over and over until it finally soaks in and they believe it:

I'm a winner and I know it.

Nothing less, oh yes.

I'm a winner and I know it.

Oh yes, oh yes, oh yes.

Oh, yes.

Former Hell's Angel, Barry Mayson

HECK'S ANGELS

BARRY MAYSON

WHOEVER YOU ARE, wherever you've been, whatever you've done, you have something to offer. Take the case of Barry Mayson.

Kids want someone to look up to. And for some strange reason, some kids want to look up to someone baaaaaad. And Barry Mayson and his band of bikers fit the bill nicely. They've been down a road or two.

Some of the men wear their hair in ponytails and most sport scruffy beards. They all ride Harleys and have tattoos up and down their arms.

They look baaaaaad. But they're not. They look like Hell's Angels—and some once were—but they've turned those big bikes onto a higher path.

In their current incarnation they are youth ministers, called to help Hell's Angel-turned-evangelist Barry Mayson with his anti-gang efforts.

The men are former gang members themselves, but they preach nonviolence and abstinence from sex and drugs. They also stress staying in school, keeping grades up, and standing up to peer pressure.

Mayson, whose Light Club in Plano, Texas, has targeted young gang members and candidates for gang membership for more than a year, wants to export his message to other communities. He speaks to young people at schools and community events throughout the country.

He's providing kids with a place they can go rather than leave them to congregate and get into more trouble. It's the kind of supervision a lot of them aren't getting anywhere else. "It's not like the usual church," said one fourteen-year-old who spends most of her evenings at the Light Club. On Wednesday nights, she and twenty-five to fifty other young people sit for an hour or more listening to Mayson and the testimonials of the other reformed bikers during a weekly Bible study.

The centers also provide a place where youths can

gather to play pool, ping-pong, and other games.

The young people often hear dramatic messages from the former gang members. But perhaps none of the bikers have a hairier history with which to regale youthful listeners than the white-maned, leather-outfitted Mayson, who roars around on his big red and white Harley-Davidson, spreading the good word about a better life by comparing it to his bad old days.

He knows about the dangers of negative role models imparting negative messages.

"When I was a kid, I saw a movie about the Hell's Angels. It turned me on. I thought this has got to be the life—freedom, jamming down the highway with the wind in my face, and doing what I wanted to do. It became my goal—to become a Hell's Angel."

He succeeded beyond his wildest dreams, he says, by becoming not only a Hell's Angel, but one of the "best," which means, by normal definition, that he was one of the worst.

He was president of the down-and-dirty South Carolina chapter—an honor one does not attain on the strength of one's civic-mindedness. He had a death's-head tattoo and so many teeth knocked out or loosened in dozens of brawls that the dentist decided to just go ahead and pull them all out.

He ran a string of prostitutes and beat them up when they didn't make their quotas.

"I was the worst of the worst. When I was with Hell's Angels, I thought power was a .357, my bike, and more money. For the last six months, I was trained to be a hitman inside the organization.

"I had explosives buried in my back yard. I was dealing in drugs and stolen goods. I didn't think anybody knew what I was doing. But I got to noticing I was going to more funerals than parties.

"I'd see them laying in those caskets, and I'm wondering if that's where I'd be five years from then. Dead? In prison? Would my kids grow up without a daddy?"

In 1976, this bad, bad biker was given an order to kill "a bunch of people" inside the organization who had strayed from what passes for the Angels's "code of ethics."

"It was then that I made my decision. I wouldn't do it."

Shortly after that, Angel leadership called him out to San Francisco along with the rest of the state chapter presidents to attend the funeral of a member who'd been shot in the back. According to the rumors then in circulation, he'd been "taken out" because he was soft.

Barry says he got the strong impression that his fellow presidents held the same opinion about him, since he'd refused to perform the earlier killings. He looked at the man in the box and figured he'd be in there himself if he didn't get out of there quick.

Mayson says that he holed up in a downtown restaurant. The other gang members were forced to wait outside for a while, hoping not to attract unwelcome attention. But they finally realized Mayson wasn't coming out, so they went in.

Mayson figured his number had finally and inevitably come up. He went to a phone in the restaurant and called Atlanta, Georgia, to talk to the only two people in the world he felt he could still trust: His mother, Mary Carder, and his wife, Frances, who was staying with her.

He called to tell them goodbye and that he was sorry for the many bad things he'd done to them and to others in his life.

"Mom said she had hope, and the hope was in God, and if we asked God to forgive us, he would."

The emotional pressure of having people sitting in a restaurant waiting for a discreetly opportune moment to kill him was enough to put the biker on his own "road to Damascus."

Then and there, he said, "God, get me outta this mess. I'll get to know you and do whatever you want me to do. All I ask is to be able to live long enough to see my kids grow up and get out on their own." And he and his wife began to pray on the telephone with Mrs. Carder.

And then and there, it would seem, his prayer was answered. Barry gave Fran some telephone numbers— numbers of San Francisco churches, of all things. Fran ran next door to use the phone to call them.

The first preacher to whom she explained the situation did not, understandably, wish to get involved.

The second minister agreed to come to the restaurant to see what he could do.

Six foot five and well dressed, the minister smelled like a cop to the Hell's Angels. They decided to deal with Mayson some other day—and split.

That was over fifteen years ago—though he believes that the Angels are still after him: "I was told some time back that I was on the top of the Hell's Angels's hit list. I don't know if they're still after me, but I do know they'd like to see me buried. It's by God's grace that I'm here today."

Mayson says that in exchange for that spiritual and physical salvation, he believes God told him to lead others out of the darkness. Mayson, however, knew only one life—the biking life.

So when he left the Angels, he kept the look. One by one, he was able to persuade other tough guys to leave the pack and come into the fold.

Some aspects of their ministry remain pretty frightening.

Imagine this: You're on a lonesome highway, at night, all alone. Your car breaks down. You're sitting there on the shoulder wondering what in the world you're going to do. And in your rearview mirror, you see eight or ten motorcycle headlights jouncing along... and all of them slow down, then pull over to the shoulder, and stop behind you. In the red glare of your taillights, you see eight or ten leather-clad men dismount.

You lock the doors. You roll up the windows. A big rough-looking guy with long crazy white hair ambles up to the window and shouts through it: "What's the trouble?"

By this point, you have no presence of mind left at all, and, moreover, not many choices, so you tell him: "Think it's my alternator belt."

Whereupon Barry Mayson goes back to the toolbox he keeps on his bike, finds an alternator belt to fit your make and model. He and the guys lift your hood and begin repairing it.

While Mayson is working on your car, you may notice with some relief the words on the circular patch on the back of his jacket: "Jesus is Lord, Full Gospel Motorcycle Association International, Church of the Highway," and the picture of a man on a motorcycle with the words, "Holy Rollers."

And since you've already had something of a religious experience, when the boys are finished and they come back around to your window and ask you to pray with them, why, you're more than ready.

As Mayson tells both his youthful audiences and his roadside converts: Every angel has a past, and every sinner has a future.

They believe him, because they can take one look and see that he's not kidding.

A prominent preacher in Plano said about Barry Mayson: "Some young people don't feel comfortable opening up to and asking for help from people who don't understand misfits, who don't understand troubled teens. But the neediest, most confused of young people will go to Barry Mayson. Barry's reaching out to and 'reaching' some young people who cannot be reached by anyone else. Young people who don't fit in with the popular kids at school, young people who need someone who can understand them."

In Plano, Texas, where high school suicide has been on the rise, Barry Mayson is making a difference. As a result of his efforts, Light Clubs recreational facilities are popping up across the country.

PART II

THE WORST
IS OVER—
STORIES OF
OVERCOMING

EVERYTHING THAT the fully-functional consider truly the "end of the world," perhaps even just cause for suicide, has happened to the people in this installment in our series of "Unsung Heroes" compilations.

These are stories of people and families who have faced challenges that most of us can only shudder at as we imagine: disfigurements, mutilations, crippling birth defects, brain damage, horrible fires, congenital blindness, and drug addictions.

In other words, the harsher slings and arrows that thousands of human beings, the little people who populate the real world, must live with every day in this rough old life.

And yet this segment is by no means a downer. Because not only did these people survive, they went on to *live*.

The little people?

They're almost always bigger than we—or even they—think.

Robert Allen (left), receiving his diploma
from President Bill Odom, 1984

THE MAN WHO FELL
TO EARTH

ROBERT ALLEN

THERE'S AN OLD SAYING often repeated in Robert Allen's neck of the woods that goes "the Lord helps them that helps themselves." The Robert Allen story is that— and a whole lot more.

In fact, it's a lot like what you'd get if William Faulkner had written science fiction—except that this one is fact.

Every time I think about Robert Allen I am somewhat embarrassed for myself over how great were my advantages and how little I made of them.

When we finally arrived at the home of Robert Allen, way, way, way deep in the boonies of Tennessee down an overgrown and bumpy dirt road that wasn't much better than a cattle trail, I saw Robert Allen coming out the front door of that old ramshackle home, and I thought to myself: "Oh, Lord, please don't let this be the man we've come all this way to do a story on." Because I thought surely no human being would dress that badly— especially one who was about to go on nationwide TV.

That marked the very last time I'd ever judge a book by its cover. I'll never be that judgmental of anyone again.

"Sometimes," Allen muses, "I do wonder where I came from. Maybe I just fell out of the sky."

It certainly seemed that way to the administrators at Bethel College in McKenzie, Tennessee, on that day in 1980 when this strange figure appeared seemingly out of nowhere, the portrait of an ignorant and impoverished backwoods hayseed.

Robert Allen was, at this point in 1980, thirty-two years old. He was a lanky six feet tall and wearing a sweater held together with safety pins. There were holes in his shoes, and his front teeth were gone.

In fact, given the fact that he does indeed play the banjo, Allen looked pretty much like the grown-up version of the kid on the bridge in *Deliverance*.

He had never been on a bicycle or inside a movie theater and had never had a date. He could not drive a car. He was soft-spoken and shy to the point of painfulness; as he made his way through the bureaucratic maze of this small Kentucky college, he had the air of a man who hadn't been around people, maybe not in years.

And it was true. He hadn't, and thus his social skills were about on a par with the raccoons in the woods from which he'd materialized. But Bethel takes all comers and so were ready to try to help this feller.

He told placement officer Cathy Emory, "Ma'am, I think I'd like to go to college."

"Fine," said Ms. Emory. "Do you have your high school transcript?"

"No ma'am," he offered, stammering.

"Well, that's okay, we can get it for you. Where did you go to high school."

"Ah didn't."

"You didn't go to high school?"

"No ma'am."

"Well," she asked, increasingly curious, "what about junior high?"

"No ma'am."

"Elementary?"

"No, ma'am." She didn't know whether to laugh or cry.

Setting, in the past: One of three ramshackle little backwoods houses that compose the tiny little Tennessee town of Ross. There is no plumbing.

It is the early 1950s.

Hazel Jones marries a man named Allen. He is not germane to the story, because, several months before Robert Allen was born to much-too-young Hazel, Mr. Allen took a powder, leaving the expecting child bride to the care of the Joneses—rustics in the strongest sense of the word.

The highest aspirations of the young boy's male relatives: to be part-time local handymen, work their hardscrabble land only to the extent that it provided subsistence, and hunt. If you are picturing Jed Clampett pre-Beverly Hills, you've got the picture, only these hill people never struck oil.

Hazel worked for a while as a waitress in the nearby town, but it is evident that she didn't much care for the responsibilities of motherhood. At the age of sixteen, she ran off with the proverbial traveling shoe salesman.

She left Robert to be raised by elderly relatives—his grandfather, three great-aunts and a great-uncle—all living pretty much hillbilly style, piled up in that rambling, crowded ramshackle house with no indoor plumbing or electricity. And Robert Allen never went to school a day in his young life.

His uncle Eddie Jones, legally his guardian, concluded that readin', writin', and cipherin' and so forth were "a waste of time" and blocked authorities from enrolling Robert Allen, then only seven, in public school.

And they kept him isolated on the home place by telling him that if he strayed too far from the nest, his father would return to kidnap him.

He believed them.

Maybe they believed it too.

He did have an aunt, Aunt Bev, who could read. And she read him comic books. The family was dirt-poor and such commonplace items were, for them, difficult to afford. So they didn't have many.

As Robert Allen recalled: "My great-aunt Bevie (herself possessed of no more than an eighth-grade education) would just lift me up onto her lap... every night Bevie read me the same comics. Comics were the only books we could afford; they cost only ten cents each. Hearing the same stories over and over, I'd memorized every balloon above the cartoons, and by age six I was beginning to sort out the words.

"One night, Bevie lifted me off her lap to put a piece of wood in the stove, and I picked up the story of Uncle Scrooge where she had left off... Blind Aunt Ida, listening across the room: "You're *reading*, Robert!" I had some favorite ones that she would read to me that I learned by heart. So I was putting together what I could remember from the page with what I could spell out. And that's how I learned to read and write," he says, matter-of-factly.

Ida soon had Robert reading to her a great deal to pass the time.

"She had me read to her the entire Bible, cover to cover, five chapters a night before bedtime, no matter how long or short." Soon he turned from comic books and the Bible to the classics and became a familiar figure at garage sales, trying to build his collection of books a nickel's worth at a time. His mind proved to be remarkably absorbent; perhaps, after that long, hungry childhood, he was as an adolescent literally starving for knowledge.

Then, wonder of wonders, after purchasing thousands of books, he finally stumbled upon the public library at Huntington.

Librarian Claudine Halpers was amazed at the young man who came each day to systematically devour everything on the shelves, while the kids from the local schools just came in, grumbled, did the minimum necessary to complete their classwork and left.

And they were equally amazed that he committed these thousands of volumes to memory.

"The other kids thought I was kind of weird," Robert concedes. Neighbors back in Huntington said it was worse than that: Many people believed the poorly dressed young man was retarded.

Hence, those books became both his pastime and his playmates—and one by one, as these older relatives who'd surrounded him with this circle of misguided love each themselves passed on, the books became even more central to him.

With them, he taught himself history, poetry, literature, and foreign languages using borrowed and half-price books, and as a boy, he was already reading Shakespeare, Milton, and Wordsworth.

He took time away from them only to support himself and his Aunt Bevie with a variety of hardscrabble jobs, making his living with his hands as a construction worker, carpenter's assistant, upholsterer, you name it.

Reading whatever he could get his hands on, this backwoods boy was suddenly free to roam time and space; from great antiquities to current events, he travelled through the world of the mind, meeting the world's great poets and philosophers by studying the pages they'd left behind.

He became as "at home" in mythological Babylon and eighth-century Judea and Renaissance Europe as he was in that ramshackle farmhouse.

Will and Ariel Durant's massive and daunting ten-volume *The Story of Civilization?* Robert Allen knows it backward and forward. The classics, which correspond to each of the periods of human history that the Durants fleshed out? He's read them in their original Greek and French. The complete works of Milton, Burns, Keats, Whitman, and Wordsworth? Tolstoy? Knows them by rote—and not as something to cleverly parrot, as with so-called idiot savants. He knows them—and knows what they mean.

Imagine the mind of a man so socially backward that he never knew there was such a thing as "an education," and yet so powerful a genius that first he taught himself to read... then taught himself to read music, and then, to compose it.

He might have forever remained an undetected genius if that Carroll County librarian, Claudine Halpers, had not recognized him for what he was. Robert Allen didn't know how remarkable he was because of his own isolation. He had no doubt familiarized himself with René Descartes's "I think, therefore I am," but in Robert Allen's case, that had to be amended to read "... whatever that is." Living so solitary a life, he had had no one else with whom to compare himself. And the years rolled on, years of manual labor and reading, and one year he woke up to find himself thirty-two years old.

Recognizing that he had gobbled up all the Carroll County library had to offer, librarian Halpers urged him to try his hand at higher education.

"Robert," she said, "When you gonna take your GED?"

"Dunno," he says. "I dunno if I could pass it."

"'Course you could."

"What if I take it and fail? Then I'll have lost the five dollars you have to pay to take it."

"Tell you what," she said. "If you pass, you pay it. If you fail, I'll give you the money back."

He could have passed it in his sleep. And he got to thinking that maybe he could go to college after all.

He arranged to take a series of CLEP (College Level Entry Placement) exams, which would allow him to skip levels he had already completed through his own study.

He thus had no high school diploma and no transcripts of any kind, but when an amazed Cathy Emory asked this seeming bumpkin what made him think he could get through college if he'd never been to school, he handed her the CLEP results.

He later recalled that she took one look at the results and her eyes "came out on stems, like a cartoon Roadrunner." He had placed in the ninety-seventh percentile of every subject in which he was tested—an almost unheard of score, and especially for a man who'd never had a day's schooling in his life. He was better read than most of his professors.

It didn't take Ms. Emory and the faculty long to realize that a genius had just kind of bumbled up into their midst, and they did everything they could to make the transition from living an 1800's style of life in the woods to moving onto a twentieth century campus easier for him.

They arranged financial aid.

Allen took a full course load his first semester when he entered college in September 1981, signing up for the full fifteen hours' credit.

Three years later, the man who'd never been to school a day in his life graduated summa cum laude. He graduated in 1984 with a 3.91 grade-point average, getting As in everything except typing.

Aunt Bevie, then seventy-two, was able to be there for graduation. She was the last of the previous generation to go, dying in 1988, leaving Robert alone with his books—but, thanks to his having finally begun to move out into the larger world, he was not as alone as he might have been.

The day he graduated, the faculty, which by then had come to love this eccentric reminder of the tenacity of the human mind, rewarded him by buying him a new suit and some front teeth.

With the help of a fellowship and the support and encouragement of friends, Allen went on to Vanderbilt, in Nashville. It was the farthest he'd ever been from home. In Nashville, now in his mid-thirties, Robert Allen had his first elevator ride.

To the relative sophisticates of Nashville and Vanderbilt, Robert presented an even stranger sight. It was his first venture beyond the green and isolating hills of Tennessee.

Yet in spite of all the newness and the strangeness, by paring expenses so that he could afford to live in a one-room garage apartment (which he shared with his cat, Sparkplug) and studying constantly, he earned a masters and then his doctorate there. For his doctoral dissertation, he got high marks by simply presenting his own poetry about those green hills.

He came back to teach at Bethel, then got a better offer from Murray State College at Kent.

He continues to write his poetry. He is working on a history of his family. And he teaches.

He can give an entertaining speech and read some of his original poetry—but in truth, it would be almost as good if he stood at the podium saying not a single word, letting his record speak for itself.

Let it speak to the kid who says he can't learn because he hasn't got a very good teacher.

Let it speak to the educator, as well, who believes these kids need to be coddled.

Let it speak to all of us, to remind us that how much we can learn and master is, ultimately, something only we ourselves can determine. We can take it as far as it will go. Or, on the other hand, we can just stop—just lie down and say that's as far as life is going to take me.

Robert Allen, under circumstances a lot rougher than those facing most of us, and with far fewer advantages, just didn't stop.

In a small farmhouse where electricity and plumbing were an unattainable luxury, Robert Allen and an aging aunt battled ignorance with a kerosene lamp and tattered old books.

Reading is what saved Robert. Writing poetry about his family carries him on a bold journey of personal evolution. He read and read until he was a citizen of the the world, never having left west Tennessee.

Robert has proven that reading can transform an individual life. It is this lesson that he passes on to the hundreds of students he touches each semester as Professor Robert Allen—that knowlege is a most precious gift.

Lieu Lai at her high school graduation

A LONG, LONG
JOURNEY

LIEU LAI

I COULD BARELY UNDERSTAND about every third word Lieu Lai said to me, a fact that makes her achievement just that much more remarkable.

Like Robert Allen, Lieu Lai came from a different world—different from mine, different from Robert Allen's, and different from yours. It is one we've all heard a lot about, but which many of the lucky among us only have to visit in our imagination—Vietnam. Not North, and not South. Just plain old "reunified" Vietnam, and the one that people by the hundreds of thousands have been so desperate to leave.

Whereas Robert Allen's longest journey in his quest for education took him only a few score miles to Vanderbilt, Lieu Lai's journey to enlightenment began ten thousand miles away when, nearly ten years ago, Lieu Lai and members of her family escaped from Vietnam with their lives. Finally free, they chose to come halfway around the world to America.

What is the value of freedom? For people like the citizens of the U.S., where most of us have had it all our lives, it is too frequently taken for granted.

It is difficult for us to fully comprehend the horrors that that small country went through—the paroxysms and spasms of war. We saw it, through the medium of television, up close and more personal than any war ever fought in human history.

Our nightly newscasts were a nightmare melange of rockets and bombs, napalm and mayhem, Agent Orange and booby-traps—but we who did not serve there had the consolation that it was, after all, halfway around the world; that when it was night here it was day there, and it was all far, far away.

Lieu Lai was born, on the other hand, right in the big middle of it—an unwitting infant witness to the fall of

Saigon and the collapse of the South, and who grew up thinking that the North Viet soldiers' supervision of every aspect of life was just the way life was.

Not so with her father, who had seen a taste of life under a freer flag. In the midst of the turmoil and upheaval, his dreams were dashed, like those of thousands of Vietnamese, left to fend for themselves after the U.S. pulled out.

Where before there had been a corrupt government but essentially a free-market economy, there was now the New Thinking of the North. In the New Vietnam, the individual was not a person, but an organ and a tool of the larger state, and the family was only the means of replenishing these tools.

Lieu Lai's father made a brave decision.

As Lieu told me, "My dad wanted us to have freedom, education, food, nutrition. He wanted freedom."

The more he saw of the North Vietnamese as they busily "consolidated" the country through "re-education," the less he wanted to do with them, and the more determined he became to get his family out.

One night in 1985, he decided it was time to go. He divided the family into two teams, with half the children under his care, and the other half under Lieu's mother's.

Lieu and her younger brother, Nam, went with her father. Under cover of darkness, they set out from their little house, heading for the coast where he had arranged for a boat to meet them.

Lieu, then only eleven years old, remembers it as if it were yesterday—the night spent hiding in the coastal jungle avoiding patrols. She remembers the mud, the mosquitoes, the lack of sleep. She remembers her anxious father keeping vigil through the waiting period. And, finally, she remembers spotting the little fishing boat that would ultimately take them to freedom.

Lieu and her father and one brother made it to the boat off the Vietnamese coast. The next day, as Vietnam began slowly disappearing over the stern and the boat took them ever farther into a new and unknown life, she realized that her mother and her two sisters and another brother had not made it.

Lieu's mother and her siblings are still alive. They are allowed to write back and forth—but not to leave the country.

Lieu is most heartbreaking when she talks of her father. "My mother was almost crazy because my dad leave. Dad is hurt a lot. I have to give him something to warm his heart."

She knows that whatever rough knocks America has handed the little far-flung family, it's better than where they came from. And out of gratitude to her father, Lieu is trying to live the dream that he'd had for her, and had sacrificed so much to attain.

Mr. Lai, a fisherman by trade, with very little English and no other marketable skills, headed for Houston, Texas, and the coast, where he hoped to be able to make a living for his children and to reunite his shattered family. But economics ultimately scattered them farther apart.

Lieu and Nam moved instead to Dallas five years ago to join two older siblings who'd already escaped to America, made it to the Dallas area, and managed to become established there.

Lieu enrolled in public schools in Arlington, where she soon realized that her journey was far from over.

Lieu Lai spoke barely a word of English. She could barely read and write, understandable at that age and considering the interruptions in her education.

If you've ever been to a place like Japan or India or Russia, or even to nearby Mexico, you can perhaps begin to imagine her predicament. Imagine that every advertisement, street name, warning sign, and uttered word, whether it be in the reassuring voice of a friend or the short sharp bark of a traffic cop, is a total mystery— a meaningless sound, or a squiggle of some foreign alphabet linked to other squiggles in a manner that only has full meaning for the natives. And then, imagine that you are going to have to live in that strange place for the rest of your life.

Imagine further: You are, after all, just a little girl, and you are transported ten thousand miles and tossed into a school where people do not understand a word you say, and you do not understand their language either—and you have to not only learn the language, but the new and amazing things they are trying to tell you in that tongue.

Daunting, is it not?

And Lieu did feel daunted—confused, dismayed, abashed, and overwhelmed. But only at first.

Because at some point, a quiet, fierce determination came to the fore to take its place. She is, per the Oriental tradition for women, self-effacing and shy. But talk to her long and you can feel the steel and the strength of her people in the face of adversity.

Lieu struggled with much more than the difficulties that face a typical American student, the American-born, native English speaker. There were three whole new worlds to learn. The world of language, and the world of custom, and the world of ideas her teachers were trying to transmit to her across that language barrier and that cultural gulf.

She was truly a stranger in a strange land: All of a sudden she's having to compete in the third grade of an American school.

Lieu had more than her share of fairly good excuses for giving up, and certainly for accepting mediocrity. Many of us would have thrown in the towel under similar circumstances.

Lieu rose to the challenge. Part of it is her nature, that steel. And part of it was her feelings and her respect for her father and mother and what they had sacrificed, risked, and what they had lost to remove her to a land where at least she stood a chance—to a place where she was not predestined to be a landless peasant or a cog in the wheel of some low-tech industry.

And despite her youth, Lieu Lai realized the extent of their sacrifice. For whatever the reason, she, as we say in the U.S., "got on the stick."

Lieu Lai credits the teachers and counselors at Pinkston, whom she termed her strongest support system, at helping her to overcome the barriers.

But they in turn recall when the turning point clearly came in her. It was during her junior year, when they told her that out of her entire class, she was second.

Which, given her background, was incredible. They were all quite proud of her. But for Lieu Lai, it wasn't good enough.

Teachers and counselors say that something just suddenly came over her, after she realized that she indeed had a chance at graduating at the top of the class. She made a deep commitment from that point on. Once she realized that she could do it, she decided to go for it.

Teachers say that she exhibits one of the strongest drives to succeed that they've ever seen.

So Lieu Lai made herself a promise—and it was a promise she kept. English was the problem; the solution: to learn it, and learn it well. Though she still speaks haltingly and with an accent, the grammar is, unless she's excited, usually perfect.

And, having learned it, she made herself a promise to learn everything else as well.

She told her friends at school, "I've always wanted to thank my father for his courage. I've had nothing to give back to him—until now. I want him to know that the dream he had for all of us has come true. If I could somehow wrap my success in high school into a big bow, I'd give it to him."

It was, in fact, a pretty big bow that she gave him, because, as she spoke to her friends in those carefully composed words, her father was also in the audience. Because she was standing on the stage in front of the entire school—the valedictorian of Pinkston High.

It may be that Mr. Lai, the father, will always remain a simple fisherman, a man displaced by history, and perhaps too old to overcome it. At great risk, he left behind a world that war had shattered to save her.

Lieu Lai has enrolled in the University of Texas, where she intends to major in accounting. She's come to a brave new world and is taking advantage of it.

Who can say which one is the hero?

Tom Clark and daughter Brookanne after a horseback ride

The Clark family taking a stroll near their home

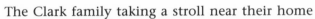

The Littlest Angels

The Clark Family

I AM A MOTHER. And I love children.

So I approached the Clark family with, frankly, quite a bit of trepidation.

I was very afraid of having my heart broken. It's happened before, doing other stories on children with serious problems—those children who are ill, or are crippled, or are in serious trouble. It's great that we find so many to help them, but sad that there are so many who need it.

Nobody on earth should have to face these kinds of problems—and the fact that they are imposed on our young and trusting children compounds the problems, stirs our hearts even more to reach out, to help somehow.

I expected that this family would give my heartstrings a real workout. And they did—but in a way that was totally unexpected. In fact, by the time I left, I was almost feeling sorry for myself—wishing I had a tenth of their character.

And no, this is not one of those tales of nobly and quietly suffering through horrendous duress. It could very easily have been one of those; it has all the ingredients.

The fact that it's not is what makes the Clark family so wonderful.

This is a house that has every excuse to be filled with doom and gloom and dire foreboding. It could be a very depressing, misery-filled environment.

I am ashamed to admit that, if it were my home and what happened to them had happened to me, that is what it would be. Miserable.

The Clarks had had a run of what can only be described as astronomically rotten luck.

Their lives, in the beginning, were storybook enough.

The Clarks started out like most of us. Before they married, before they started out, they considered themselves normal in every respect. Young and in love, both with successful careers. It seemed that "normal" was something that came naturally—almost like an external force that had been bestowed on them and settled and stabilized their lives.

Tom and Olivia got married, and, after they became more settled, like any young married couple in their early thirties with the tick tick ticking of what they assumed was their biological clock, it seemed that normality dictated that it was the appropriate time for them to begin thinking about raising a family—a family that they presumed would, of course, be normal.

But it wasn't a biological clock. It was a biological time bomb set to blow up their lives.

Both carried the abnormal gene for a disease called SMA—spinal muscular atrophy, a disease that destroys nerve cells. And it's inherited, progressive, and incurable.

Only one couple in 12,500 will have an SMA child.

And normally, even when both members of a couple carry this rogue gene, the odds are one in four that any child born to them will have SMA. Unknowingly, the couple beat all the odds. Their first child, Brookanne, was diagnosed at one year of age; doctors gave her at the most two years to live.

Horrendous enough for this perfect, normal couple to learn that their pretty blonde baby would die. Add to the stew of their misery and grief this ugly ingredient: At least in most couples faced with the life-shattering fact of a severely disabled child, there is the cold comfort of the fact that there is only one "guilty" party and only one who has to deal with blaming the other.

It would have been easy for each to wish they'd never met the other; equally easy to say "I would have been better off without you—and you without me." And easy to regret both the fact and the fruits of their union.

And now, add this:

At the time of little Brookanne's diagnosis, Olivia was already pregnant with their second child, Tommy. After he arrived and he too was diagnosed, Olivia and Tom were carefully using birth control and seriously looking into sterilization when—bingo—in spite of her best precautions, out of a clear blue sky, she became pregnant again.

And Baby Jeffrey made three: He, in spite of the odds, also had SMA.

But Brookanne lived. And so, lo and behold, did Tommy.

The disease continued to eat away at them—but only at the visible, exterior parts of them. In their hearts and minds, these kids were growing like any other child. In spite of increasingly reduced ability, in spite of the motorized wheelchairs that, one by one, they were put into, these children were living.

And these children have taught Tom and Olivia a lot about life. Several years back when Tommy was in intensive care with pneumonia, the doctors said his heart was about to give out. Olivia held Tommy in her arms as he struggled to breathe. She was at her wits' end.

Tommy sensed this. And though he was only four, he sagely told her that everything was going to be all right, because an angel had visited him and told him so.

And then he proceeded to fight his way back to what was, for him, normal health.

The Clarks began to realize they could look at the proverbial glass either as half-empty or half-full. If they wished, they could see their children as dying or doomed. But then all God's children are dying and doomed from the moment they are born, aren't they?

Or they could see their children as living, growing human beings, and try to help them the best that they could.

This is a story about a family that is confronting a life-threatening illness. In their short lifetimes these children have learned to seize life, to magnify it, glorify it, and be grateful for its gifts.

Tom and Olivia Clark say they are no different from any other couple working together to raise three children. Except that Brookanne, Tommy, and Jeffrey suffer from spinal muscular atrophy, the rare and deadly form of muscular dystrophy that robs the children of their muscles. It is inherited, progressive, and incurable.

Olivia offered, "When Brookanne was first born, I kept wondering, Is this the day I'm going to lose her? Then I decided that living that way was for the birds. I couldn't live my life that way anymore. And so I said a prayer. I said, God, we waited too long for her. We wanted her too badly. You're going to have to fight to get her back. It's been a major battle ever since, but we're winning it."

Tom went on to say, "We just take each day, one day at a time, and just enjoy the time we have with them."

The way Tom and Olivia live their daily lives seems almost beyond human capability. These are full-time teachers and coaches who spend their workdays strengthening the bodies of healthy children and who return home to the rigorous routine of working to strengthen the fragile bodies of their own children.

"People say, How do you do it, Olivia? I say, God gives you the strength you need."

The Clark family motto is that whatever can be done on two feet, can be done better on wheels.

"We love them so dearly, we just raise them just like anybody else would raise their children. We don't see ourselves any differently from any other family, but we do get around a little differently. We just love them. I don't see how anybody's life couldn't be blessed from having them. They're blessings. I don't know what we did to deserve them, but I'm glad we've got them. We used to wonder, why us? Then it dawned on us one day—it's because we love them the way we do, and maybe someone else wouldn't," said Olivia. Tom continued, "They make you appreciate life and everything you have."

Olivia went on to say, "We don't feel sorry for ourselves. We feel blessed. We do the best we can. The kids say their prayers: 'Thank you, God, for the strength you gave me today. Please give me more tomorrow.' And then that's it, they don't dwell on it."

Tom added, "Everybody has their ups and downs, but we'll get through it, we'll be better for it, and we'll just be that much stronger. That's kind of the way we live our life from day to day. Enjoy your day. It may be the last one God gives you, you never can tell."

It is hard to explain how a home with seriously ill children can be one of the happiest places you've ever been. But at the Clark residence it's all about love—the precious gift Tom and Olivia give to their children. Brookanne, Tommy and Jeffrey—the littlest angels, whose magic touches the earth but for awhile. Their bodies may tire, but never their spirits.

"We just always believe that they'll find a cure, that something will happen and they'll turn it around and the children will be okay. We still hope they'll come up with a cure and be able to help the kids. We always have that hope," said Tom.

What is normal?

It's all a matter of perspective. And from the viewpoint of Brookanne, Tommy, and Jeffrey, normal is living life in a wheelchair—but then it's so much more.

For Tommy, eleven, it's life in a wheelchair—but it's also friends at school, football fanaticism, and whatever is the current TV-induced craze—Mighty Morphin Power Rangers or whatever.

For Brookanne, thirteen, sure, there's the wheelchair, and some tough physical problems—but it's also school and giggling with the girls and parties and the same concerns that confront any other girl on the brink of being a teenager.

"For a long time," Olivia says, "Tom and I wondered, Why us? And why all three of them?" The answer was, it turned out, pretty simple: Because they'd been hoping and praying to have a normal family.

And sure enough, they did.

W Mitchell's motto is, "It's not what
happens to you; it's what you do about it."

The Man Who Would Not Be Defeated

W Mitchell

OF ALL THE PEOPLE I've met in connection with "Unsung Heroes," the only one who remains truly a mystery to me is W Mitchell. Like all the heroes I've been fortunate enough to meet, of course I admire him; in his case, considering how much he's been through, it is impossible *not* to admire him.

I've done stories in the past on burn victims who've overcome their pain and disfigurement and gone on to do good. "Unsung Heroes" has done stories on handicapped and mentally challenged people before. By the end of the production phase, subject and crew had all become old and familiar friends. Ditto for motivational speakers who turned tragedies to triumphs, as has W Mitchell.

In every case, with the passage of time, the "differences" that make our heroes initially unique have receded in my mind until they finally become just one more influence in my life. I can manage to finally imagine that I might possess sufficient nobility and strength to follow their examples, to resume my life after great misfortune and maybe even someday manage to be happy again.

However, W Mitchell transcends the human. Though he insists otherwise, I cannot help but believe there may actually be something superhuman about him. He would insist, in fact, that this is the exact opposite of his message.

But I know this only intellectually. I can't incorporate it into my intuitive feelings. When I started the interview process with W Mitchell, I was feeling intimidated, awed, and nervous. When we'd finished it a couple of days later, I *still* felt that way—awed, intimidated, and nervous.

I don't have any personal knowledge of what he was like before his transformation; I can only assume that he was, as he says, pretty much like the rest of us, with the same needs and aversions, hopes and fears, talents and shortcomings that make us all human—until the transformation.

Then there is Mitchell now, no longer human—but beyond human, in a way. If I let my imagination run a little wild, I think that the gods may have been testing him severely before allowing him full membership into their ranks. The truly cosmic "bad luck" that saddled him with the misfortunes he so completely ignores would tend to support that musing hypothesis. Though he refuses to see himself in that light, a case can be made that W Mitchell is the Unluckiest Man in the World.

Before that fateful day—the first one, anyway—he was, by his own account, a young man completely in love with the world. On that clear and balmy June 19, 1971, he couldn't have been flying any higher, both figuratively *and* literally; the day before, he'd fulfilled a lifetime dream by successfully completing his first solo flight toward obtaining his pilot's license.

He had a dream-job as a brakeman on a cable car, a job he shamelessly and unapologetically used as a means of meeting beautiful women, both tourists and residents of the romantic city by the bay. After he'd worked out a deal with a streetside flower vendor to sell him a gross of day-old roses for ten bucks, there was no shortage of female companionship for this brash young twenty-eight-year-old man of the world. He was swimming in girlfriends, and the world was his oyster.

And then there was the brand new motorcycle. A Honda 750, which at the time was the hottest road-rocket on the street and upon which he was zooming down South Van Ness Avenue when the laundry truck cut in front of him. He hit it squarely on the side. And the lid on the motorcycle gas tank popped open, pouring nearly three gallons on Mitchell's clothes and the red-hot engine. The resulting fireball was visible for blocks.

By the time a quick-thinking car salesman could grab a fire extinguisher and put him out, Mitchell had been burned over 65 percent of his body. The leather motorcycle jacket had saved most of his torso, but not his hands; the helmet saved his scalp—but not his face.

He was in a coma for two weeks. When he awoke—a tracheotomy tube in his throat and his eyelids stitched shut to keep them moist—he was literally just a hospital-bed full of red and black charred meat. Grown-men friends who came to visit would take one look at him and faint. And long after the eyelid sutures were removed, doctors and nurses were especially careful to keep him away from the one thing they thought might kill him for sure: Mirrors... and he was glad to have them do so.

The psychological pain would seem unbearable—but was nothing next to the physical pain of both the burns and, worse, the treatments. Almost every hour of every day, skin was whirlpooled or scraped away, grafted back on, stretched, squeezed, lubricated, or poked with needles for intravenous feedings.

It was after about a month of this that he turned to a nurse and said: "I've died. I'm dead. This is all a fantasy. I didn't survive the accident at all. I'm actually dead." The pain and the damage and the unending agony all told him that there was no other answer; his mind told him that there was no way he could have actually survived.

Having seen that same syndrome in other survivors of massive trauma, she loaded him onto a gurney and wheeled him outside into the fresh air and sunshine of San Francisco to force him to look at the skies and the trees and the living people of San Francisco. The nurse had also made an understandable mistake; she'd called Mitchell's girlfriend, June, and asked her to bring his Great Dane, "Puppy," to the hospital grounds. It was a mistake because when Mitchell called his old friend's name, the dog recognized the voice—but not the face. If you could call it that. The dog became so frantic that June was afraid that the dog would jump up on the gurney and dig down through the pile of bandages and charred flesh, trying to find his master.

It was only one of a seemingly unending succession of daunting, horrendous moments that were to continually barrage the reeling burn survivor over the coming months and years as he learned to come to grips with each new horror one day at a time.

Mitchell was pleased that the doctors had been able to save his hands, which he could still feel underneath the bandages. They removed the huge wads of gauze: Phantom limbs. Nothing of his fingers had survived the surgeries to save them, only the stumps of his hands remained.

His resiliency and sense of humor were growing even then; he took one look at those stumps and said, "Wow. This is going to destroy my pool game."

When he finally, by ruse, got a chance to take a look at himself in the mirror—only his eyes recognizable, the rest of his face a nightmarish parody of a human being:

"Woooo," he said. "That's an interesting-looking guy."

He was beginning to take life's lemons and turn them into lemonade. Once he had a face and fingers; now he didn't; he could see that as catastrophic and debilitating, or he could see it as a challenge. He chose the latter. But still the gods were not through testing him.

After months of agonizing surgery and physical therapy, he learned to walk again—but still the list of "couldn'ts" were seemingly endless. A stiff breeze on what was left of his hands was enough to produce almost unendurable agony. He couldn't feed himself, answer the phone, turn on the TV, or even relieve himself unassisted.

He tells of his frustrations—and the victories to which they led him. He couldn't open doors with his hands, so he learned to open them with his feet.

And even though it made his face hurt, he was once again learning to laugh. When it came time to reconstruct that face, his doctor asked him for a photo of himself, pre-fire, so the doctor would know what he'd looked like.

He laughed, even though it hurt. Mitchell says he believes that from that moment, he began gaining the needed perspective to go on and live his life. He would need it.

At first, as he slowly began going back out into the world, he would not meet other people's eyes, thinking that he was doing them a favor; if he didn't look at them, maybe they would be spared the shock of having to look at him.

It was a rough world, but he was once again learning to live in it. There was the drunk who wandered up to him and told him that he was the ugliest thing on earth and offered to beat his face in. Mitchell said he was in no condition to fight and suggested maybe the drunk would like to fight his friend—Puppy, the Great Dane.

Because his hands were in greater pain if they were allowed to brush his trousers, he frequently walked the streets of San Francisco with his hands out in front of him. People mistook him for a beggar and tried to give him money.

Then there was the schoolhouse he walked past: "Monster, monster, monster," the children chanted.

This made him sad. He was not offended—but suddenly wanted to share what he knew: that you could look like a monster on the outside and still be a good person—warm, funny, and caring—on the inside.

It was in that moment that he decided his life's purpose would be sharing that message with people, especially kids.

And he decided that he wanted to do more than survive. He wanted to thrive. That meant never telling himself the list of things he couldn't do and instead setting about finding other ways to do them.

Six months after the burns, Mitchell was actually flying planes again. The owner of the laundry truck settled out of court, writing him a check for half a million, part of which he spent on a vacation in Hawaii where he had another big post-burn epiphany.

Against everyone's better judgment and over the fears of his friends, he walked out into the surf and swam. He refers to that moment as his rebirth, a second baptism: It was the moment at which he realized that there was nothing he could not do.

Soon he was in Colorado where he tackled snow-skiing; ski-poles lashed to his hands, he succeeded—and fell in love with Colorado. In the wilderness, he didn't have to explain to the deer and the eagles what had happened to him. And in the small town of Crested Butte, pretty soon everybody had learned the story behind his ravaged face and had gotten over it, allowing him to build deeper, more meaningful friendships than would have been possible in the shallower and more cynical city.

He had a nest-egg to invest as well. He bought a house and became part-owner of a commercial building called the company store. A bar on the premises went out of business and he bought it as well, and found he could tend bar better than most people with hands.

The big break, however, came when he invested in an invention—a new design for wood stoves that was, amazingly, 47 percent efficient and which turned out to be immensely profitable, selling well in all fifty states. Suddenly, W Mitchell was a millionaire. Life was good. Life was, in fact, better than it had been before the fire.

And then W Mitchell crashed his airplane when his wings iced up on takeoff.

Everybody except Mitchell walked away uninjured. Mitchell couldn't walk away, then or ever again. The X-rays would later reveal that the twelfth thoracic vertebrae in the base of his back was crushed.

After three days of tests at a Denver trauma center, his doctor told him: "Mitchell, it appears that you will never walk again. It appears you'll have to use a wheelchair for the rest of your life."

There is no good combination of words in the English language for describing how Mitchell felt upon hearing those words; completely, utterly devastated does not quite do it justice. He later recalled, "I had spent four years recovering from the most devastating injury a human being can incur and live. It had been the battle of a lifetime and I had won it. If anyone deserved smooth sailing for the rest of his life, I was the guy."

Shortly after he was hospitalized, a friend who was living at Mitchell's house overloaded the coal stove—and burned off the top floor of his house. Then one of his best friends suddenly died of a heart attack.

"It simply seemed to be too much for one person to bear. I lay in that bed and wondered if there was anything left of my life. Why me? No one had an answer for that."

But it turns out he'd made the right move when he went to Crested Butte, because most of Crested Butte now came to him, with literally hundreds of his friends making the five-hour drive to visit him, to tell him to hang in there, to tell him that they cared. That was very, very important.

Even more important was the call from a young woman in Crested Butte. "Mitchell," she said, "I don't even know if you remember this. But a year ago, when I was going through a really tough time, you said something to me that I will never forget. You told me 'It's not what happens to you, it's what you do about it.' Do you remember that?"

Recalled Mitchell, laughing, "Don't you *hate* when people do that?"

But it was the jump-start that he needed. Just as he had finally learned that there was no absolute relationship between being burned and being miserable, he also realized there was no linkage between being paralyzed and *doubly* miserable. Once again he realized that the experience would be exactly what he made of it.

So W Mitchell took charge, organizing honest-to-goodness happy hours for his fellow paraplegics and generally running that hospital to suit himself. No phone calls allowed after eight in the evening? Not over Mitchell's dead body—he had the phone company in the next day, rewiring the joint.

Then there was Annie Baker, a beginning nurse who was quite young and pretty and scared of dealing with a man who was first burned, then paralyzed, and further beset with disaster at every turn. A few years later, Mitchell would marry her. He returned to Crested Butte—releasing himself from the hospital over his doctors' objections.

Once home, he threw himself into an unembarrassedly hedonistic life-style, buying a swanky motorhome that he later recalled had been a "mobile home of debauchery" and the "scene of good times and general bacchanalia." And as usual, he got back on the "horse that had thrown him"; six months after the accident he was a passenger in a small plane again; and a few months later, he found himself at the controls of a glider.

But he acknowledges that it was basically a selfish life-style and that something was still missing. And when

Crested Butte Mayor Tom Glass came into Mitchell's bar for a beer, Mitchell found out what it was. Glass persuaded him to fill a vacancy on the town council.

It was an important time to be on that council because AMAX, Inc., the largest mining company in the world, was contemplating construction of a billion-dollar molybdenum mine. The more the council saw of AMAX, the less they liked the idea of this ugly raw hole in the side of the area's beloved "red lady," Mount Emmons. And Mitchell decided that, in spite of the fact that nobody had ever successfully blocked an AMAX mine, he'd be the first to try it.

He ran for mayor on an anti-AMAX ticket. He shook every hand in town several times over, spending fifty dollars on his campaign—about forty-nine dollars more than his predecessor. He won by twenty votes.

He then tackled the big boys, spending nearly $160,000 of his own money and playing the media like a Stradivarius. He did not hesitate to use his own unique situation to give the big publications a "hook" for the story; he waged his war in the pages of *Time, The New York Times, The San Francisco Examiner, The Washington Post,* and in appearances on the "Today Show" and "Good Morning America," as well.

Mitchell and his allies also waged their battle in courtrooms. Since the city of Crested Butte lacked jurisdictional authority, Mitchell and his advisors dug up a one-hundred-year-old state law giving cities the right to control its own watershed and promptly wrote restrictive clauses.

Some have described it as a David and Goliath confrontation, but as Mitchell recounted it, it became clear that the operating metaphor was that of Gulliver; the little people of the town managed to tie down a giant using "strings attached" and red tape.

They slowed down the giant company, and the recession of 1981 delivered the *coup de grâce.*

At the end of it, Mitchell was once again victorious, nationally famous, transported with happiness—and totally hooked on public life. He had also come to the same conclusion as had Charles DeGaulle: that politics is

102

too serious a matter to be left for politicians.

In addition to his increasingly heavy schedule on behalf of various environmental groups, Mitchell was still pushing his own limits, as usual—whitewater river rafting, skydiving. All the things that a paraplegic "shouldn't" or "couldn't do," Mitchell was of course doing.

But again, there was that creeping feeling that something was missing, and one day, digging through a pile of newspapers, he found out what it was. A notice appeared stating that Ray Kogovsek, Colorado's Third District congressman, was not going to run for a fourth term. Two Coloradans were vying for that seat; Mitchell decided to become the third.

Rather than describe the sixteen-hour days he spent in his airplane and on the stumps during the year-long campaign, I'm going to cut to the chase and tell you: He lost.

But he wasn't defeated.

"In retrospect, there were two main reasons I lost: I had made a noble but probably stupid pledge to take no political action committee money, and the Reagan coattail effect was brutal to all Democrats in 1984. But I tell people today that I didn't lose that race in 1984. I tell them that, yes, my opponent got a few more votes than I did and that hurt, but the wonderful lesson I learned is that the only losers are the ones who don't get in the race. I love to quote Theodore Roosevelt who said that the only losers in life are the people who end their lives 'having tasted neither victory or defeat.'

"Running for Congress was worth as much as three Ph.D.s. I honestly believe there is no such thing as defeat, that there is victory in trying, in learning what you can. I was able to convince 93,000 people that a burned-up, fingerless guy in a wheelchair could represent them better than an able-bodied chap with a nice complexion. To me, that's a victory."

Indomitable and undefeated, he embarked upon the public speaking career that occupies him now. The message in his speeches is the same as that of our "Unsung Heroes" programming: That the key for all of us who want to make a difference is to *act*—not to let who we are nor what we may not have stand in the way of doing good and of growing.

I preach this message.

W Mitchell lives it.

I said that, at the start of the interview, I was intimidated and awed by him.

Well, I still am.

Ryan White with his mom, Jeanne, at home in Indiana

RYAN'S SONG

RYAN WHITE

THERE IS ONLY ONE of our Unsung Heroes that I never met.

I never met Ryan White. By the time I got to his home in Cicero, Illinois, he had been dead four years. By happenstance, I interviewed his mother, Jeanne White, on what turned out to be the fourth anniversary of his death. In life, Ryan White was very much a "sung" hero.

I felt that he needed to be sung after his death as well. I don't know why I felt so strongly about this; perhaps I sensed there was another side to the young "public figure."

I feel that our "Unsung Heroes" viewers now know Ryan White very well—and that they are better for it. The world is too. And so am I.

For most of us, a tombstone marks the end of the story. For Ryan White, however, in a very special sense, death was only the beginning. The splash that he managed to make with his short life is still making big waves and small ripples. In fact, it will probably *never* be fully spent.

The world went just a little bit nuts over Ryan White in ways that were both good and bad—but even the bad led to something good, once it was publicized.

The AIDS that he contracted in 1984 as a result of contaminated blood products used to treat his hemophilia at first made him a pariah in his hometown of Kokomo, Indiana. Some people there went nuts in a bad way. It will forever be a black mark against that city that Ryan became the focus of a witch-hunt—of misinformation and innuendo.

When word first got out about his having the disease, his mother recalled, "I thought people were scared, but it really didn't become a real problem until we tried to get him in school, and then I really saw the hatred. I saw the people going to so many lengths."

Trash was dumped in the yard. Co-workers posted

pictures and newspaper articles about him all around the factory where she worked, as if it were so easily transmitted that they could catch it from working with her.

Someone slashed her tires. Some other brilliant someone fired a shot through their window.

"People were just so afraid of this disease, and they didn't believe that you couldn't get it by kissing, tears, sweat, and saliva. And Ryan used to laugh and say, 'They better hope that you can't get it that way, Mom, because I went to school with all their kids. If you can get it that easy, they'd all already have it.'"

There were letters to the editor of the local newspaper accusing him of biting people and spitting in food, and the local radio talk shows were filled with venomous speculation over his infectiousness.

Ryan fought back bravely in spite of his illness and was determined to fight all the way to the end. It was his exhausted mother who finally threw in the towel. And in retrospect, it was the right thing to do.

"Our house was known as the AIDS house. I was really criticized quite publicly for doing the TV movie. But with the up-front movie money, we could move. And it was one of the best things that could have ever happened to us."

The move from Kokomo to Cicero was more than a fresh start. Cicero was unafflicted with the hysteria that had gripped Kokomo over this still-strange disease—thanks not so much to Cicero's civic leadership, but to its children.

"We moved to Cicero, where we did not know the community would welcome us like they did. I can remember the first day."

People showed up to welcome her and her family and to allay any fears of more ill treatment. Also on that first day, five kids from the local school came to the house.

"I mean, we weren't used to that in Kokomo, because nobody came to our house. And all of these kids wanted to be his friends, so it was really, really such a change."

Ryan White never sought the limelight. He was passionate about three things late in his life:

Skateboarding. Automobiles. And, sadly, given his circumstances, girls.

AIDS awareness was not a passion: Ryan White saw it as a duty. He had it. He had to deal with it. He wanted the world to understand it, not so much for his sake, but on behalf of all who'd contracted this insidious disease.

"I think because young people listened to him... I think he helped put a face to this disease when very few people really wanted anything to do with the disease. And I think he made people think, Golly, what if that would happen to my kid? What if that would happen to somebody in my family?"

For himself, he wanted only to be seen for what he was: A normal teenaged boy.

That was never to be. The limelight came looking for him. And when it found him, it locked on tight.

The big national talk shows courted him like mad, especially after they became aware of his maturity, poise, and courage. You could not turn on the TV or open a magazine without finding out more about Ryan White, this "just another average" kid who'd transcended his own fears as well as the prejudice of others.

It is one thing to meet a celebrity like Elton John or Michael Jackson or Phil Donahue, and quite another to become an intimate friend. Jackson flew Ryan and his family out to California several times so that he could spend weekends with them. Elton John flew the Ryans to several of his concerts.

"How their friendship grew, though, was because Ryan became very ill after that and went into the hospital, and for two months, he coughed and vomited everything he ate. He was blind twice during that period, he had two diabetic seizures, he was down to fifty-four pounds, and we didn't think he was going to live.

"Elton would call every other day or so to find out how he was doing. He would send presents and say, 'Don't worry about it, buddy. You know, we'll... we'll go to another concert. We'll go to another concert.' And finally he called and said, 'Buddy, I'm going to end my concert in L.A. and fly you and your family out for five days. We'll have a good old time.' And that's what happened. I think he was just real impressed with Ryan."

He spent numerous weekends with swimmer Greg Louganis and was in close contact with actor Matt Frewer, then still enjoying "Max Headroom" fame.

"I mean, he had such grace and always had a smile on his face and never asking Why me, and I think he just kind of was so easygoing with... with the disease and with his life, and, you know, he wanted to be a normal kid. He didn't get caught up a lot in the celebrities and a lot of the things that happened to him. He didn't get overwhelmed by all of that."

"I asked Michael Jackson, 'You and Ryan were so close. Why Ryan?' And he said, 'You know, most people can't get over the awe of who I am, so nobody can ever act normal around me. Ryan knew how I wanted to be treated. You know, everybody always wants something from you. So it's really hard to get people that you can trust."

In fact, the shoe was on the other foot.

Recalled Mrs. White: "I think that he was famous because—I think the celebrities were always in awe of him, really, once they met him. I think they all felt sorry for him at first, you know, and that's why they were doing a lot of this, but once they met him, they didn't feel sorry for him any more."

And while Ryan of course enjoyed meeting celebrities, politicians, and world leaders, it always bothered him that his fame came not because of anything he'd done, but because of a disease. So in his new hometown of Cicero, he led what amounted to a double life. He kept quiet all his celebrity contacts, wishing only to be a normal high school kid.

But that was not to be. It was impossible for "normal" kids to view him as normal, because they knew him to be very brave—braver than "normal." Perhaps nobody can claim that, in the face of their own death, they feel no fear. But Ryan White didn't ever allow his own doom to terrorize him.

"My fondest memories of Ryan were of his funny nature, being able to find jokes in everything, being able to talk about anything."

Part of that was his deep but usually unspoken religious

faith. But another part was just pure character. He knew that if he started acting scared, the fear would infect his mother and his sister, Andrea, and all the many close friends he'd made in Cicero.

"The other kids wanted to be involved in his life. They wanted to do some of the things he was involved in. And he made a statement one time, he said, 'It's neat to know that you have other people fighting it with you. And it's nice to know that you've got friends there with you, helping you fight it.'"

Ryan didn't chase the celebrities; however, they chased him. And Ryan, while he liked them, was never awed. He was always looking for a means of advancing his cause—acceptance of people with the disease.

For instance, Ronald Reagan had never publicly acknowledged even the existence of the AIDS epidemic. Ryan decided to correct that, even though he knew that his own personal end was in sight.

There was to be an Oscars party, and the Reagans and Ryan White had been invited. Ryan was near the end and was actually probably too ill to attend.

He was failing fast, in fact.

His mother knew it when he said, "Mother, take me home. I want to see Dr. Kleiman." It was the first time he'd ever actually wanted to see a doctor. AIDS had finally taken a fatal toll on his lungs, liver, spleen, and other internal organs.

Dr. Martin Kleiman put him on a series of potent antibiotics and explained to him the gravity of his situation.

But Ryan said, "I really want to go, Mom. We can't even get Reagan to mention the word 'AIDS,' so I'm going to appear. I'm going to be there. He doesn't know it, but he's going to get his picture taken with somebody with AIDS."

So he went. And he got his picture taken with the former President in what would turn out to be Ryan's final public appearance.

Recalled Mrs. White, "We flew home that night. We took the red-eye back home, and they admitted him right to the hospital.

He lapsed into unconsciousness—thus was unaware of the last visits of Elton John, Michael Jackson, John Cougar Mellencamp, and Rev. Jesse Jackson.

While Ryan remained in critical condition and on a life-support system—unconscious and heavily sedated so that the life support equipment would work more efficiently—the "little people" and the noncelebrities showed their support as well: Thousands of messages of love and prayers poured in to the hospital's mailroom and switchboard.

Hospital switchboard operators said about one thousand calls a day came in from supporters expressing hope and concern for Ryan. Hospital spokeswoman Mary Maxwell said at the time that the incoming flood of calls "has been bedlam. We're getting calls from every small town in the United States."

A record of each call was passed along to the family.

And he'd finally gotten through to the movers and shakers.

Even as he lay dying, then-President George Bush, who was in Indianapolis for a political fund-raiser, planted a tree for Ryan at a ceremony one and a half miles from the hospital and told the national press, "He's been fighting a courageous battle against a deadly disease and also against ignorance and fear. Ryan has helped us understand the truth about AIDS, and he's shown all of us the strength and bravery of the human heart."

And he died at 7:11 a.m. on Palm Sunday, April 8, 1990.

Former President Ronald Reagan was moved to finally acknowledge the disease by remembering Ryan in one of his newspaper columns in *The Washington Post:* "Ryan accepted his situation with awe-inspiring courage and magnanimity. He did not run and hide."

Newspapers all across the country ran editorials praising him and his fight, such as this tribute in the *Dallas Morning News:*

> Although only eighteen when he died on Sunday, Ryan White made a difference with his life. The upbeat teenager, while waging his own brave battle against the deadly disease for five years, called upon

a nation to overcome the myths of AIDS and to show compassion for others living with the illness.

The prejudice that Ryan faced was no different from what many AIDS sufferers confronted. What made Ryan different was that the media focused in on his plight and, in so doing, put the face of a courageous child on a disease that many Americans thought had little meaning to their own lives.

Most of the other one hundred thousand Americans who have died of AIDS never became public figures like Ryan, but their deaths were no less devastating to those who knew and loved them. This young man's passing should remind us all of the terrible toll AIDS has taken and of the aggressive fight that still must be fought.

The funeral was of course huge and vastly overcovered by the media. Michael Jackson and Elton John were there. So was Barbara Bush, Phil Donahue, and a lengthy list of luminaries.

Elton John sang "Skyline Pigeon." And they buried him. And that might have been that.

Recalled his mom, "When Ryan died we got over sixty thousand letters. I mean, we had them everywhere. We had them at the bank, at the hospital, at the house, you know, they were just everywhere, all these boxes of mail that needed opening, and it was kind of unreal. We got so many flowers and cards and presents, too. And so it was pretty overwhelming to see how many people he had touched. I really didn't ever think we'd ever get them all opened.

"So, Phil Donahue, who is a very good friend of ours, and who loved Ryan a great deal, wanted this mail answered. And so he hired me a secretary to help answer them.

"And as we started opening these letters, we found out that they were all from young people, young people who had been impressed and touched by Ryan's life. That's who Ryan liked talking to, young people, so we thought what better group of people to reach, and there was nobody really addressing young people at the time."

As a result, the Ryan White Foundation was formed to

continue his work in AIDS awareness and education.

Ryan White was a hero, and he died a hero's death—that was his purpose. "I think his life had so many purposes," said his mom. "His battle with AIDS touched America's heart. His message moved us to action. He dared to speak out when others kept silent, and the whole world listened."

There are the big waves that Ryan left rolling around the world and throughout an entire generation, the largest of which is that almost all of us have had to rethink a disease that some of us once backwardly viewed as the Just Punishment of an Angry God.

That's his legacy. But there are smaller ripples rolling too—ripples whose results we can't foresee.

Jeanne remembers, "I've met a lot of celebrities. Celebrities may be heroes to a lot of people. But I don't think anybody taught me more than my son!"

While working on this story, I had the great pleasure to visit with many of Ryan's friends and former classmates. I was amazed to find so many of them entering the medical field and planning to become involved in AIDS research. Through these young people and the Ryan White Foundation, his legacy lives on.

Frances Richardson at her home with hospice worker

HOSPICE

FRANCES RICHARDSON

SOMETIMES THERE IS HEROISM simply in an attitude and a way of looking at life—and in proving that it's all in the way you look at things.

We got a letter from a woman named Frances Richardson who could not heap enough praise nor express enough gratitude for the hospice program that was caring for her. She just could not find enough kind words to say. She wanted the St. Joseph Hospice people to be Unsung Heroes.

So we looked into it. We checked with the hospice people. And in talking with them, we were soon convinced, as were they, that the real hero of any piece that was going to come out of this had to be:

Frances Richardson.

She's the real hero, and the real role model for every human being alive. Because one day we'll all be dead—as one day Frances Richardson will be.

Frances's doctors gave her two months to live because of her failing heart. She is eighty-five years old and has had a long life, measured chronologically. But she has learned, as all of us do sooner or later, that no matter how long we live, it won't be long enough.

Ever wonder how you'll feel, when the doctor gives you the news—the words that contain your death sentence?

Frances knows. And she'll tell you very straightforwardly that it is not a lot of fun. But life goes on.

She looks like everybody's grandma, except for the oxygen tube that allows her to keep on breathing well enough to continue puttering around her cute little house.

"When I was first diagnosed as terminal, I can't say that it was easy to accept, because it wasn't. To hear that you've got two or three months left to live, and that you need to get your affairs in order is bad news. No, I didn't like it. It wasn't easy to accept."

117

I don't know: If I were in the same boat, that fact
would be pretty much all I'd want to talk about. But
Frances usually quickly changes the subject. Not because
she's afraid of it, but because she doesn't want to bore
anyone.

Imagine.

Frances Richardson has taken one of the biggest
negatives life has to offer—the anti-life, in fact—and has
managed to look on the bright side of even that.

"I knew I had nice children, I knew that. I didn't
realize how fantastic children could be to a parent. That's
one of the biggest things that I'm thankful for. But I
didn't want to be a burden to them, and that's why I'm
so happy with the people at hospice. Having them has
allowed me an independence that everybody wants. All
of us want to stay in our own homes, among the things
we like.

"I'm thankful that I can stay in this little house. I'm
so thankful I can do that. I'm thankful that I can look
out the window and see the birds and see the children
riding their bicycles. I have so much more than so many
old people like me. I have so much to be thankful for.
We want to have our dignity, keep our dignity—and
hospice has allowed me to do that."

The word hospice once meant a way-station, a place
to rest on the journey. People at modern hospices are
there to ease the hardest journey of all, and Frances finds
a lot of comfort in that. They find a lot of comfort in
her, as well.

Working for hospice is rewarding, but in many ways
it is emotionally wrenching, employees say. They know
they are providing a priceless service. But many of their
clients aren't taking their situation as well.

Says her hospice counselor, "Frances wants to live and
laugh and enjoy life to its bitter end. She loves her family,
but she wants to be able to take care of her own needs.
We're here to help her, to provide comfort. In this
situation, comfort is the main thing, rather than cure. If
we put her in the hospital to die, she'd become just
another number. When people are allowed to live in
their own homes, they maintain a lot more control over

what they do, when they do it, how it's done to them, and who they see. It is, after all, the rest of *their* lives.

"And each one of them is special. There is something different about each of them. But with Frances, I know that I can walk into the house and she can lift my day in five seconds."

Frances, as usual, believes it is the hospice people who are doing the lifting. "These people don't come in here and think of me as an old sick woman. They think of me as someone very important, and that's nice. I wonder sometimes if I could have made it this far if it hadn't been for those wonderful hospice people. We laugh a lot together, and that makes for something very special.

"I've had a wonderful life, and it's still wonderful— though I have had to tone it down considerably. No, it's not easy to face death. There are times when I am laughing on the outside and crying on the inside. But I made a promise to my children to live every day to the fullest. And if I were younger and in a position to choose a career, I would want to be a hospice person. It can't help but feel good to be doing what they do. They are all my heroes."

We aired the show in November 1992 for our Thanksgiving special. At the time, Frances Richardson had been given only two months to live.

During the broadcast, we observed that "It's impossible to alter the direction of terminal illness, but hospice is making the journey a little easier. For that we can all be thankful."

And of course some of us cried for Frances. And we remembered her. She has stayed in our hearts the way all good people do.

In November 1993, our crew went out to her home to check on her. She was fine, it turned out.

And when we went to see her again in November 1994, same story, same happy ending so far—which is the best that even the happiest of us can say.

Senator Brooks Douglass

THE POWER TO
CHANGE

BROOKS DOUGLASS

I AM OBSESSED BY THE STORY of Brooks Douglass because of that central mystery: How does it feel to be him?

What will make him feel good again?

Such an awesome, painful saga.

On October 15, 1979, inside the home of the Reverend Richard Douglass, it was an almost too-perfect scene of quiet familial contentment and peace—the kind of scene young Brooks Douglass had come to take for granted.

Richard Douglass worked in his study on his sermon for the coming Sunday. A studious man, he spent much of his time there writing or reading.

In front of his three-thousand-member congregation, he was a powerful, forceful preacher with a commanding voice. But sometimes, during evenings like these, his family would gather around him on the floor to hear his sermons or listen to him reading Bible passages or practicing his sermons in a much quieter, much more personal way.

Tonight, they were going to gather around to hear the news that Richard Douglass had been keeping to himself all that day. Douglass hoped that they would take it as good news: The Baptist missionary board had approved his request, and the family was going back to Brazil.

He never got a chance to tell them. He apparently had planned to wait until after the evening meal.

The only unpleasantness marring the evening: Leslie bred Persian cats for sale, and one of Brooks's Dobermans had killed a kitten that had managed to get out of its pen in the garage.

Richard Douglass told Brooks: "Go out and bury the cat. And, Brooks," he added, "don't just take it and throw it over the fence. Bury it."

Brooks recalled, "I immediately walked downstairs, penned up the Dobermans, picked up the cat, and threw it over the fence. If I had buried the cat like he'd told me to do, I would have still been outside when they drove up. I might could have done something. I could have seen that there were two of them sneaking around. I could have gotten my guns out of the garage, or run across the road for help. So many things you think of that you could have done differently... "

But Brooks went to his room and went to work on the bookkeeping for his kennel operation and the car detailing business his father had helped him to build up.

The evening smell of smothered steak simmering on the stove filled the house as Marilyn Douglass set the table and arranged the fresh flowers she always insisted on having at her family's table.

Leslie was in the kitchen helping her mom when she heard one of the Dobermans bark. She looked out the front door and saw a balding, redheaded, bearded young man.

"Can I help you?" Leslie asked.

It was a man, a very bad man, named Glen Ake.

Glen Ake told Leslie that he was lost, that he'd been looking for the home of "the Mitchells," but couldn't find it, and that the directions he'd been given had brought him there instead.

She went to her father, who in turn told her to get Brooks, who knew most of the people in the neighborhood, and then he returned to his studies. On the way to the front door, Brooks grabbed a telephone book.

Standing outside in the darkness, Ake told Brooks he was trying to find "Mike Mitchell's" house. Brooks told him he wasn't familiar with the name, and, looking in the phone book, said it wasn't there, either.

"Did he give you a phone number?" Brooks asked, to which Ake replied, "Yes, that's what I was hoping to do—use the phone." Brooks let him into the house. Ake went to the phone, removed the receiver from its cradle, and said he'd left the phone number in his other pants, which were out in the car, and headed back out the front door.

Marilyn Douglass, standing by the stove, was the first to smell trouble and told Brooks to follow him out and get a look at the vehicle.

Brooks got a look at the old battered Malibu—but it was too dark for him to see Hatch sitting inside the car, or Ake giving sidekick Stephen Hatch his instructions and telling him, "This will be an easy one." Ake came back in the front door, and Brooks followed him back to the phone. As Ake lifted the receiver off the hook and dialed seven numbers at random, he clandestinely placed his thumb on the switch-hook, disconnecting.

Brooks heard the front door open and slam shut and looked up to see Hatch standing there with a double-barreled shotgun. He turned again to look at Ake, who had a pistol pointed at his face.

"Don't move," Ake said. "Be calm, or I will blow your head off." Brooks backed away and said, "Mom... " Leslie, who'd been sitting on the countertop, started crying. Mrs. Douglass came from behind the stove and said, "You can have anything you want, just don't hurt us." And Ake kept saying over and over: "You know what this is all about. You know what this is all about."

Ake forced them into the living room at gunpoint and told Hatch, "There is a man back over there in that bedroom. Get him out."

Brooks interjected, "Let me get him out. I don't want you to startle him." He walked over to the bedroom door, opened it, and said, "Dad, they have guns." Ake jumped through the door and crammed his pistol into Richard Douglass's stomach and forced him out the bedroom door and into the living room. His mother was holding Leslie in her lap in a chair, and Brooks was standing beside the fireplace.

Ake lied, telling them that he had just escaped from Fort Supply, the state hospital for the criminally insane. "I'm crazy. You better do what I say."

Ake told Mr. Douglass they wanted the money. Douglass replied, "My wallet is in my son's room." Brooks went to his room and returned with a handful of money.

Ake demanded, "Doesn't anybody else have any money?" Mrs. Douglass said she had some in her purse. Ake went with her to the bedroom to get the money while Hatch held his shotgun on the family.

Ake also ordered her to get a rope from a drawer on the back porch and told the family to get down on their stomachs in the living room.

He began questioning Leslie about money.

"I don't have any money," she told him.

"Well, are you sure?"

"No, I don't I'm only twelve years old. I don't have a job. I don't have any money."

Ake grabbed the rope and began hog-tying them, hands and feet behind their backs—first Brooks, then Richard, and then Marilyn.

Leslie he left free and told her, "You're going to take me around and show me where all of the telephones in the house are and where all the hiding places for money are."

She said, "We don't have any."

"Well, we're going to find some."

She led him around the house as he raged about, rummaging drawers and ripping telephones out of the walls.

And when they got to her room, he looked at her and said, "Take off your clothes."

"No—please don't hurt me."

"I said, take off your clothes!"

"No, no... "

"If you don't take off your clothes, I'll ram this gun up you and blow you up."

And so Ake raped her. When he was finished and after he left the room, Stephen Hatch came in and raped her. And then Ake came in and raped her again.

Brooks Douglass, Marilyn Douglass, and Richard Douglass lay there on the living room floor, helpless, listening to Leslie as she struggled and cried.

Mrs. Douglass wept. Brooks said to her, "Mom, we're going to be okay... please calm down. They're not going to hurt us." Hatch, standing guard, held the shotgun to the back of Brooks's head and said, "If I hear any more talking, I'm going to blow your heads off." Then he threw a shirt over Brooks's head, to keep him from watching him.

Ake finished and brought Leslie back into the living room, hog-tying her with the rest of them.

As Ake continued his ramblings around the house, the family could hear him ransacking the house and even the scrape of the cutlery and the clink of the pans as he ate their meal.

Passing back through the living room looking for more phones and hiding places, he would threaten them. "You sure you don't have any money? You know, there's nothing wrong with shooting people. I've been wanted for seven years and never been caught because I knew to always shoot the guy before he could talk."

And Hatch would interject his own tough-guy threats: "Gonna get a belly full of four-shot. Yep, a belly full," even though it would later turn out that the shotgun wasn't loaded.

And then Ake held out some hope for the family. "All right, I'll make you a deal," he said. "If you all won't call the police for four hours, then we won't shoot you."

"Okay, great," said Brooks.

Mrs. Douglass said, "It will take us at least four hours to get out of these ropes anyway, the way you've got us tied."

Then Ake asked them if they'd seen the car.

"No," the family said.

"Well, that's good. Because if anybody had seen the car, I would have to shoot you now." The two rummaged around some more.

Ake told Hatch: "Go outside, start the car, and get it turned around... and just listen for the sound." There were more whisperings between the men, but it was unclear what was being said.

From Ake's confession: "I told him to go out and turn the car around, and he told me not to do anything drastic, right, that we're already in bad enough. I told him to go turn around the car and don't worry about it, I wouldn't do nothin'.

"He hesitated for a few minutes, trying to calm me down because I was all spaced out. I was all messed up on this, I done a bunch of speed in the car before we got there. Drinking whiskey and speed, they don't mix. He was trying to calm me out of it, saying, come on, let's get out of here, come on. I said just go out and turn the car around and shut up... " And then the door slammed.

There was a long pause.

Then Brooks, blinded by the shirt, heard the voice of Ake behind him again: "Well, I'm in kind of a bad position; I don't want to shoot you, but... " BANG, and Brooks felt the bullet slam into his back. And then he heard another go off, and he heard his mother scream. Then, Brooks said, "there was kind of a long pause, and then I heard two shots go off."

Brooks saw his father's blood spatter the curtains. "And then a little bit of a pause, and then two more shots, and Leslie screaming." Then the sound of footsteps running out the door.

A long silence ensued. Brooks struggled to get the shirt off of his face, and he and Leslie began yelling. And their mother and father began moaning and gurgling.

Brooks struggled over to Leslie and, using his head, was able to lift her to her knees; he told her to try to go get to a knife. He then struggled over to his father and used his teeth to try to get him untied. Mr. Douglass had managed to roll over onto his back. Brooks worked on the bonds on his wrists with no luck, then raised up and saw the gag around his father's mouth. He was able to get it off his mouth, but it was tied so tight it popped back tightly around his neck.

"Go see about your mother," Richard Douglass gurgled.

Brooks writhed over to his mother, and as he gnawed at her bonds, his gag slipped back down over his face. Brooks was trying to get it out of his way when his father uttered his last words: "Don't worry about that thing, just get your mother untied." She was still breathing, Brooks recalled. "I could hear the blood gurgling and she was still struggling a little bit. I was able to get a good grip on the rope. I yanked it one time, and it all came loose.

"I moved down and looked at her. She was looking up at me. I said, 'Mom, you're loose. Try to get me untied.' At that moment, her hands fell down at her sides and her feet slammed back against the floor and she quit breathing.

"And I turned to my dad and I said, 'Dad, Mom's dead.' He was looking up at me and he didn't ever say anything else. He just—his breathing slowed down and the gurgling slowed down."

It was amazing that the two Douglass children were even alive, much less conscious and able to move. The point-blank .38-caliber bullet had entered Brooks's back and had gone through his chest cavity, abdominal cavity, right lung, and esophagus, and had nicked the pericardium of his heart. It exited through his left lung, his liver, and his spleen.

Leslie had been shot twice. The first bullet had entered her upper chest and had exited through her right breast. The second bullet went through her right forearm, right chest, and then her abdominal cavity, where it pierced her colon and large intestine.

Brooks had been intermittently calling for Leslie, trying to keep her from slipping into unconsciousness as she searched for a knife, but when she didn't answer, he decided that she was either asleep or dead, and so he wriggled his way to a coffee table.

And then he just very deliberately stopped. He recalled, "I remember thinking, I'm going to deal with this right here and now; I am going to face the fact that this has happened, deal with it, and make up my mind that I'm going to go on with my life. I stopped, turned around, and took a good hard look at both of them, just to burn into my mind that they were gone."

Leslie reappeared and was able to get them both untied, and she and Brooks ran to the car and drove as fast as possible to Okarche, four miles up the road. Brooks had the accelerator completely to the floor—and yet, as his lung was collapsing and filling with blood, he slipped in and out of consciousness, snapping back to alertness just in time to keep the car on the road; he was headed to the home of Dr. Jack Berry, a family friend.

"I remember Leslie sitting next to me and watching her bleed all over everything... " Brooks said, "Mom and Dad are dead."

"I know," Leslie replied.

Jeff Berry, Dr. Berry's son and a good friend of Brooks's

from high school, answered the door. Brooks, fighting increasing drowsiness, told him that he and Leslie had been shot and that his mother and dad were dead. Then he pushed his way through the door into the house and he and Leslie ran into the living room where Dr. and Mrs. Berry had been watching Monday night football and told Dr. and Mrs. Berry the same tale.

"They thought we were joking, but then Jeff came up behind us and saw the bullet hole in my back and the blood... "

This was a big deal in Okarche, Oklahoma, and for every concerned congregation member or well-wisher who tried sincerely to help the two surviving, recuperating Douglass children there was someone else trying to cash in on the publicity and notoriety suddenly surrounding them.

And there was another problem of course: The two killers remained at large—were, in fact, now fully embarked on a robbery and murder spree that carried them throughout the Southwest before authorities finally ran them to ground in Colorado and arrested them on capital murder charges.

Though Brooks had lost nearly forty pounds—dropping from 160 to 122—the prognosis was good for both him and Leslie, physically, at least.

Mentally, however, they were beginning to live out another story.

Leslie was, prior to October 15, just another popular twelve-year-old—except that she was well endowed for her age, and thanks to makeup skills learned in preparation for many beauty pageants, she had the mature good looks of a young woman five years older.

Now she had to lie in that hospital bed and wonder: Did my looks do this to me and to my family? Is that what got me raped? Perhaps as a subconscious means of avoidance, she began to develop a weight problem.

Then there were financial considerations. Brooks was trying to be not only brother, but father and mother to Leslie, and, almost from the moment he'd awakened in ICU, he had been working the phones selling off his own assets, particularly the Dobermans, since he didn't know when he'd be able to take care of them again.

Brooks was intent on remaining in the Okarche School District for his last year of high school and steadfastly refused to consider taking up life elsewhere with relatives before graduation.

At the time of his life when he should have been finding solidarity and sameness with his peers, getting ready for that leap into individuality, he was pushed away. Not out of meanness, but the obverse: Sympathy.

He was no longer Brooks Douglass, baseball player and good student, or Brooks Douglass, handsome and personable young man. He was the kid of those people who were murdered, the brother of the girl who was raped, the guy who got shot and nearly died.

For Leslie, of course, it was much worse: There was the same glare of publicity and the same discomfort at the sympathy of strangers—and the added stigma of the sex crimes. Whereas for most twelve-year-olds sex is still just a distant glimmer and a beginning of the sense of distant possibilities, for Leslie, it was the worst kind of reality, setting her further apart and making her even more "unusual." The product of this, in her case, was shame and withdrawal.

She was whisked away to live with her aunt and uncle in Lindsey, Oklahoma. Fundamentalists, they tried to change her from a beauty pageant participant into a much quieter and more "proper" kind of girl they could approve of—and here she began to have growing problems with interpersonal relationships:

"I sometimes got the reputation of being a snob, but I was just afraid to talk. I didn't know what to say. The feeling with me was, I already know you know what happened to me, so why should we have to talk about it?"

For Brooks, his experiences engendered a certain sullen willfulness, independence, determination, and aloofness— qualities which would both help and harm him in the years to come.

Brooks went to live with family friends in Oklahoma City, the Rudds, so that he could go on to finish high school there. Externally, he appeared to be a brave and strong young man who was "overcoming," but on the inside, there were problems.

The unbelievable physical and emotional trauma produced first a deep and inarticulate hurting, but this was soon replaced by a dark rage.

The once bright but serious young man now became simply morose and taciturn.

Each person felt the truly humane urge to express sympathy—but multiply that by dozens a day. The sympathy soon became oppressive and made the young man even more uncommunicative and irritable.

Brooks was becoming a fiercely private person. People who asked about his plans for the future were, at best, met with noncommittal shrugs and, at worst, told to go mind their own business.

Brooks now had an intensely intimate knowledge of a basic and inescapable truth—a truth that is best observed from a great distance, if one wants to live a carefree life.

That truth: No matter how hard you try, or how industriously you build up your life, or how devotedly and sincerely you love and hope and pray, it can all be ended in an instant, whether on the whim of a madman or the bursting of an aneurysm.

For Brooks, it was like a constant, dour chiming of the clock at Notre Dame, the one so cheerfully inscribed, "It is later than you think."

These feelings produced in him an almost obsessive drive for success and achievement that would pose personal problems for him for many years as well—yet which would ultimately bring him through.

The events of October 15, 1979, had been horrific; now the legal system further burdened the two surviving Douglasses with a seemingly unending reliving of it. The first two times they relived this nightmare—once in the trial of Ake, once for Hatch—they of course felt relieved, in a way. After all, they'd gotten those two monsters the death penalty.

What they didn't know is that, thanks to an appeals system that probably would have given Hitler a fair chance of acquittal, they'd have to testify again, and again, and again... until the recounting of it became almost as damaging as the events themselves.

They learned also that while the officers of the court went to great pains to keep Hatch and Ake advised, the surviving victims were kept in the dark, treated more as inanimate evidence than as the very hurting, damaged people the system was supposed to protect and uphold.

But worst of all was the growing knowledge that it was by no means certain that these men would not get out of prison to terrorize again.

Brooks was getting his first dose of how much the system was willing to do to help victims and survivors: Virtually nothing.

Every day was a trial.

As high school ended and the unending appeals process (with its equally unending publicity) became evident, Brooks was becoming increasingly alienated and distant. Ripped up by the roots, he was beginning to show signs that he would, like the proverbial tumbleweed, just go rolling away adrift.

He first went to Oklahoma Baptist University—but thanks to a growing listlessness and inattention, he lost his once excellent scholasticism and lasted only eight weeks, dropping out before they kicked him out.

He got a job in the trust department of the First National Bank in Oklahoma City. At first, it was a tolerable enough atmosphere—but then the publicity once again reared its head. A headline on the front page of the OKC paper screamed, "Douglass Estate Settles for $166,000."

Brooks recalled, "First of all, that wasn't true. The reporter got it wrong; it was for half that amount, only $80,000 from the insurance company, and that was to be split between Leslie and me. But I went back to work the next day, and there were all these people staring at me. All these people thinking that I've suddenly come into a fortune. Everyone was whispering around behind my back. And I took a lot of harassment from the Rudds; they thought that I'd done an interview with the reporter. But by then, I'd had it. The next day, a Friday, I got off work, drew all my money out of the bank, took all my stuff out of the Rudds' house, and just took off for Denver."

He became what he called a "road scholar," working at odd jobs a week or two before moving aimlessly on to the next town, Denver, Dallas, New Orleans, Houston, across the Gulf States to Florida, no clear goal in mind—increasingly numb, increasingly adrift, and ever more and more like those people who so fascinated him during his last year in high school.

One day, passing aimlessly through Alabama, it hit him: If Richard Douglass were alive, what would he think of his son?

Time to face facts, he realized. Time to compromise. Time to figure out just exactly who Brooks Douglass was going to be.

He didn't have the answer. But having the question, at least, was the first glimmer of possibility he'd seen since those dark days of October 1979.

Seeing his life through his father's eyes pulled him out of a spin that could have carried Brooks into obscurity. But for years to come, living life for his father left him no life of his own.

He headed north because he had grandparents up in the town of Pell City, Alabama.

Nobody had heard from the young wanderer in more than six weeks, and the family had been beside themselves with worry. His grandparents were overjoyed to see him—but while he was washing up, they telephoned Chattanooga, Tennessee, to tell Brooks's uncle, Lloyd Lacey, that he was there.

Then they took Brooks to church.

When they returned, Uncle Lloyd was waiting on him. Lacey was not only Brooks's legal guardian and the administrator of the Douglass estate, he was also the only person left who Brooks viewed as any sort of parental figure.

He told Brooks straightforwardly: "The way I see it, you've got three choices: Work, school, or the military."

Brooks opted for school.

In spite of the fact that these should have been perhaps the best times of Brooks's life, they still contained that inescapable sadness and apartness. That feeling of being different from his contemporaries and somehow incomplete as a person shadowed his life. At Christmas, for example, the campus at Baylor University in Waco, Texas, would be empty and the students would go home; Brooks, by now estranged from his sister, would have no home to go to. At these times, he would just sit in his apartment, alone.

His relationship with Dana McClendon, who he'd dated off and on since high school, was deteriorating, as were the continuing problems resulting from the trauma of the murders.

A positive note is that these problems actually were the beginnings of his recovery from the numbness that had plagued him since 1979. Dana and a female friend of hers were visiting him in Waco, staying in his apartment. Brooks and Dana hadn't been getting along, even though he'd always been crazy about her. He was walking around outside his apartment; the two girls were inside, and when he passed by the window, he overheard them talking.

The girl said, "Do you think you and Brooks are gonna keep dating?" And Dana replied, "No, I don't think so. I really don't see it."

Brooks recalled, "It felt like a kick in the gut. It just hurt. But what was so strange about it was that at the same time I felt upset, I was also happy, because I remember consciously saying to myself, Man! I feel something! I haven't felt anything in years! That was nearly three years after the shootings."

It is not uncommon for a survivor to memorialize the dead by trying to let them live their lives through him. In the case of a young man of Brooks's intelligence, drive, and energy, such an obsession can have impressive, if not spectacular, results.

But it is, after all, a sacrifice, a giving up of one's own life and desires. So the next period of Brooks Douglass's life was highly productive and successful—but still quite sad.

While still a student at Baylor in Waco, he was commuting back and forth to OKC, building houses with a partner there. He was also building up an importing business, and generally running himself to death.

And through it all—Ake and Hatch, Ake and Hatch.

He was in his apartment in Waco studying for winter midterms. The phone rang. A reporter was on the other end.

"The Supreme Court has just overturned *Oklahoma v. Ake*. Do you have any comment?" There were no words for what he was feeling. All the bitterness, all the rage washed over him again. He knew Ake had appealed on grounds that he had not received proper psychiatric evaluation and counsel, but Brooks had resisted thinking about it. Now, the receiver felt like the gun Ake had pressed to his head.

"Mr. Douglass? Are you there? What do you think about Ake getting a new trial?"

"No... no comment," he said, and hung up the phone. He put on a jacket and stepped out the door into the chill air. He began to walk aimlessly around the campus area, passing a restaurant.

Two men, eating in that restaurant... and suddenly he could almost smell that smothered steak, could hear Ake scraping the fork across the bottom of his mother's pans... *I don't want to have to shoot you but... BANG,* and could hear the blood bubbling under his shirt, his father's last gurglings, and the sound his mother's feet had made when they lifelessly hit the floor.

He went back to the apartment, picked up the phone, and called the Canadian County District Attorney, Kathy Stocker.

"Kathy, do we really have to do it all over again?"

"The state didn't appoint a psychiatrist to substantiate Ake's insanity defense," she said sympathetically, "so we have to start all over."

This trial was the worst one from an emotional standpoint, and from a legal standpoint, the prosecution, in spite of good intentions, left holes in this one that you could drive a Mack truck through. Thanks only to an equally incompetent defense attorney, instead of getting a not guilty verdict by reason of insanity, Ake was again found guilty.

The 1986 trial would have a great impact on Brooks personally: The psychological stress and simple logistics of being constantly available to testify brought back the world he thought he'd left behind; all the old memories came crashing back down on him and plunged him into the worst bout of the bitter, sullen depressions that Dana, now his wife, had been dealing with since high school— depressions that were putting more cracks in an already-shaky marriage.

Brooks's rage translated itself to the courtroom as well. One afternoon, after leaving the stand, he glanced at Ake as he passed by. Ake gave him a slow, malicious little smile.

When the jury finished deliberating the sentence, Brooks, who'd been there throughout the trial, went into the courtroom.

The twelve jurors came in. The foreman stood.

The death penalty was history. Ake got life imprisonment instead.

It took Brooks's breath away. And suddenly he had to get out of that courtroom. He stood, struggled through the crowd, and staggered down the corridor. *How could they have let him live?* And turning a corner, there beneath the fluorescent lights, stood Ake. He was manacled. And Brooks was no longer a terrified teenager. And this time, Ake didn't have a gun.

A gun! A jailer stood next to Brooks, and the gun in his holster was inches away. It would be easy! Reach for that gun, grab it, aim, fire. One bullet would stop the anger and the hurt and the rage, the memories, and the questions, and the loss; why were his father's last words wasted on such evil men? And then, one more memory comes floating across the years from that lost life, those good old days.

Brooks is sitting cross-legged on the floor of that study in his home (where a stranger now lives), and his father is reading from Psalms.

Richard Douglass is talking about how hatred poisons faith: "Cease from anger, and forsake wrath: fret not thyself in any wise to do evil." Suddenly, there in that corridor, staring at that gun, it hit him. Over the past seven years, he'd become so hate-filled and angry that he'd even cut himself off from God.

135

"Lord," Brooks prayed, "please. Please, free me from my wrath."

It was as if a strong and gentle hand grabbed him by the shoulder, turned him around, and led him toward the light shining through the doors at the end of the corridor.

Cameras flashed as Ake was escorted past.

But this time, finally, Brooks could look away. And it was from this point on that Brooks truly began to recover.

Brooks realized that he came very close to destroying his own life as well as Ake's in that courtroom corridor.

Increasingly, he was beginning to see that the law could be his gun instead. After graduating from Baylor with a degree in business in 1985, Brooks enrolled in Oklahoma City University.

While at OCU, he worked as an intern in the criminal division of the attorney general's office and as a clerk for Oklahoma Supreme Court Justice Ralph B. Hodges.

It was in these two jobs that Brooks began to perceive that the only way he could change the system would be with political power.

Brooks received a law degree in December of 1990. That same year he started two businesses. And he decided to run for the state senate and won.

The workaholism and the desire to memorialize his parents with his own life continued unabated. In addition to the heavy public-appearance demands of his political career, he was also running two full-time businesses.

His marriage finally fell completely apart. The bottom line is that she left him because of his unending case of the have-to's.

Had to work hard at three jobs. Had to be successful. Had to run for senate. Had to go to all the parties, make all the speeches. And, about the time he both got elected and bought them the house they "had to" have, she left him.

And so at about the time of his inauguration, he moved into the empty, unfurnished house that he'd known he would "have to" really fix up, because of all the structural and plumbing problems.

"And now here I was, the new state senator sleeping on a mattress on the floor and living out of a cardboard box. Yep, here I was. I'd had the businesses and gotten elected to public office. I was supposed to be successful. I appeared successful. But I just kept on making myself miserable, pushing harder... " He'd pushed his wife out the door and almost pushed himself to a nervous breakdown.

But some things about Brooks Douglass were about to change...

In the Capitol, Brooks soon came to be regarded as a bright and rising star—a serious, softspoken young man with ambition to higher office.

Toward the end of the first year, the *Tulsa Tribune* did a splashy front page story recounting his personal travails and triumphs, and soon his mail was flooded with desperate letters from other survivors and victims of crimes.

So by the interim between the session's end in June and the beginning of the next one in December, Brooks "had seen so many cases in which the victim or the family had been shut out of the process, and the survivors were all saying, Isn't there anything you can do?"

Brooks had to do something. The time had come to avenge the murder of his parents—in a positive, constructive way. "I couldn't stand by and let victims be further victimized by the system."

Brooks realized that the issue of victims' rights was not simply his own personal axe to grind, but a widespread and painful problem for the people of Oklahoma and the whole United States.

So Brooks and his staff painstakingly drafted the bill that was to become SB 816, the Oklahoma Victim's Rights Bill, and they soon followed it up with SB 451, which enumerated further rights.

The sweeping victim's rights bill contains provisions protecting victims' and survivors' privacy rights and rights to property used as evidence, and contains a requirement that prosecutors keep victims and survivors fully informed of the progress of cases and of the status of defendants or convicts.

But the most important provision is the one that allows victims or survivors to testify against convicts during the sentencing phase of the trial.

This may be a moment that Brooks will never have for himself. Ake is safely out of danger of ever facing the death penalty. And though Hatch's death penalty remains on appeal, there will probably be no further hearings in the case; appellate judges will make their decisions based on existing transcripts of testimony and judicial record rather than on new testimony.

But Brooks had a moment of exultation nevertheless—one every bit as satisfying; he was at Oklahoma Governor David Walters's elbow when he signed Douglass's bill into law.

"It was one of the most rewarding moments of my life. I remember that when the governor and I sat down and were talking about it, I started thinking about all the things that had happened to me over the past thirteen years and all of the man-hours of work that had gone into writing that bill and then fine-tuning it so that everyone's rights would be respected and there would be no chance of reversible error—all the things we'd gone through to make it possible.

"And it was just amazing to sit there and watch the governor sign it and know that at that moment it became the law of the land; at that moment, victims had rights."

I found Brooks Douglass to be pretty amazing. He has survived. And he has conquered.

John and Mona Parthun

In From the Storm

Mona Parthun

I DO BELIEVE THAT MONA PARTHUN was genuinely surprised and maybe even mildly shocked the day her bosses summoned her to the employee break area—and the surprise party her co-workers and the crew of "Unsung Heroes" were hosting in her honor that day.

I've looked back at the videotape several times: Yes, she was most definitely surprised, mainly because she does not see herself as being anyone unusual. Most of our heroes are that way: They think they are just "doing what they do."

One of our viewers, as often happens, had been moved to write us. She wished to draw our attention to a co-worker she considered a true hero—this Mona Parthun.

What impressed the viewer most is that her friend Mona Parthun is always smiling.That impressed us, too, when we learned more about her.

Mona Parthun *is* always smiling—and to look at her standing there and to walk with her around the streets of Wichita Falls, you wouldn't even suspect: She doesn't have any legs. None at all.

They're artificial. All the way up, and then some. While it's true that there are many double amputees across America, three things make Mona Parthun's case uniquely interesting and inspiring.

First is, how she got that way. This was no auto accident, nor was it a radical cancer cure.

Mona Parthun was hit neither by automobile nor a disease, but a tornado—one of the biggest and most dramatic in American history, in fact: The mile-wide roaring funnel that on April 10, 1979, came down out of a cold spring sky and almost leveled the town of Wichita Falls.

It was one of history's strangest storms. This was not your traditional tornado—the sinuous ribbon of cloud snaking down out of the sky, or the thicker but still recognizable funnel-shaped tornado from the picture books and TV footage.

No, this was a one-of-a-kind meteorological monster. At its base it was a mile wide; it was like being in a cloud, according to Mona, only it was a cloud that was whirling in excess of two hundred miles an hour, destroying almost everything in its mile-wide path of destruction. It destroyed one thousand homes. It killed forty-five people and injured seventeen hundred more. Of the ones who lived, Mona was among those who sustained the worst injuries.

There was no particular reason for this cloud to have singled out Wichita Falls, which is basically considered, as Texas towns go, either a large town or a small city; it has a modest population of three hundred thousand.

Its importance lies in the fact that it's the biggest trading center for many hundreds of miles in any direction. It presides alone over the North Texas plains—and is smack in the middle of Tornado Alley.

Mona Parthun was, at the time, as unremarkable as Wichita Falls. She was a pretty, bright, former high school cheerleader who had just gotten off her job as a secretary at 5:00 p.m.

She was then Mona Brake, married to an oil field supply clerk of that name. She stopped off to pick up her then-husband, Ronald, at the oil field supply firm. She scooted over to let him drive her to her cake decorating class at a Wichita Falls mall.

"It was one of those things you always think happens to other people, not to yourself. As we were going to the mall, the radio said we were under a tornado warning, that one had been sighted on the ground. We looked around; it had just turned a greenish black color all around us."

Two blocks from the mall, they heard the warning sirens. Mona looked out the window and screamed. She saw that gigantic mass of cold, whorling clouds of rain and black debris filling the entire sky to the southwest, already leveling the housing development known as Faith Village and claiming the first of its many victims.

Ron swung the car around and tried to escape, but others were hastily abandoning their cars, and his path was blocked by their emptied vehicles.

They both jumped out and ran the thirty feet to a small tree in front of a church. As they ran, something strange was happening: Their Toyota was running along beside them. And sometimes, it was actually flying ahead of them.

After that, a blank, until Mona and Ron Brake awoke on the curb, leaning against each other, with no idea how they'd gotten there. Wichita Falls was bedlam. Panicked motorists passed them by, presuming the muddy, bloody couple was already dead—until one man noticed Mona moving feebly in his rearview mirror. The man who took her to the hospital saved her life.

Meanwhile, her family, like most families in Wichita Falls that day, was in a complete panic: They knew that Mona had been headed for her cake class that day, and they knew that her path and that of the tornado had intersected.

"It was like a war zone," her mother recalled. "All the phone lines were down, and there were no longer any landmarks. We could hardly find our way to her house."

For the next twenty-four hours, Mona's frantic mother and father searched the hospitals and morgues, and like thousands of others begged for help from the overwhelmed bureaucracy.

Finally, her father ran across a policeman he knew, and the officer told him that he'd seen the name "Mona Rakey" on a list at General Hospital. That was close enough. He and Mona's mother hurried there.

"They were bringing people in so fast you couldn't find beds for them," Mona's mother said. "They were lying in the halls, in triage, and the staff was taking only the worst possible cases into surgery."

Mona had been placed in the recovery room—not because she was recovering, but because that was the only space available for her. Staff members said she stood out from the rest, because they couldn't stop the bleeding, and couldn't schedule her for surgery because of the huge overload of patients.

When her parents finally found her, they were in for a shock. There was the blood—and her haggard, black circled eyes. "She hardly moved," her mother recalled.

143

"She looked up and said, 'What took you so long to find me, Daddy?'"

During the height of the nightmarish storm, while clinging semiconsciously to that tree, she had been shotgunned by the debris borne on those two-hundred-plus–mile-an-hour winds; glass, pebbles, dirt, and splinters had been blasted into her legs, and once inside, soon began to poisonously fester.

By the time the exhausted physicians finally got around to treating her, they counted at least thirteen different strains of bacteria completely infecting the tissue of her legs, many of which had no known antibodies.

"They put some of the finest young doctors on my case. They were always there, hour after hour, night after night. And my parents never left my side."

"That's because," her mother said, "nobody expected her to live. Nobody. But I simply could not give her up. I've always heard that God doesn't give you anything you can't handle—so I told God every day that He couldn't take her, because I simply could not handle it. We couldn't give her up. We simply couldn't. I told him I guess I would have to handle her without legs, because she still had a good brain and a good heart."

After a valiant effort to save her legs, the medicos finally reached the conclusion that they would have to be amputated, along with much of the tissue from her lower torso as well; it was her only hope.

After a week or two, she was officially out of danger, but she was far from "out of the woods." And it was during the long and arduous process of physical therapy that Mona revealed the stuff of which she was made: She had to learn to walk again, only without any legs. Her recovery was almost miraculous because of her determination to return to a normal, productive life.

The physicians had predicted she would remain wheelchair-bound for at least six months, but she'd put aside the wheelchair after only two weeks and was getting around on crutches, rapidly learning to use what remained of her hips to move and position her artificial legs. The doctors again underestimated her. Whereas it takes most patients several months of grueling physical therapy before they can set aside those crutches, in Mona's case, her mother says, it was a matter of days before "we looked up one morning and saw the crutches leaning against the wall, and it finally dawned on us that they'd been there for quite a while."

And soon, even the cane was set aside.

The daunting physical challenges she faced were of course not her only problems. Her husband could not face the rest of his life with a legless woman; their marriage was another casualty of the tornado.

And not long afterwards, she lost another vital source of support. She'd always been a "daddy's girl," and her father died.

Photographs of Mona during that period show a woman who was, as her friends are always quick to note, always smiling. But there was a lot of hurt on the inside.

"Ronald had made her feel so ugly and unwanted. And then her father died. I told her, 'Mona, you can feel sorry for yourself and stay down and everyone will understand. Just stay down, and everybody will baby you and do whatever you want done. But you won't have a good life. Or you can get up and live your life. Nobody will feel sorry for you anymore. They'll admire you. You have a good mind and a good heart. Who needs legs?"

Said her physician, "A lot of people, despite the fact that they'd gotten through the physical rehab, would have given up at that point. Mona is not that way at all. She wanted to get back to work, and maybe find someone to spend her life with."

Mona was in fact back at work by November 1979. "I wasn't dating. I was living on my own for about a year, but I had family and friends, and I felt like that was all I needed."

At work, she and her co-workers would listen to a local radio station, KTRN. And there was a voice on that station she came to admire, that of John Parthun.

And a co-worker dared her to call him. As usual, Mona rose to the challenge, and three nights later, she had her first date since the tornado had blown away her life.

John recalls coming to her apartment to pick her up.

She came to the door, then walked over to the couch and sat down. "I asked her about her limp. I had noticed it and thought maybe she'd hurt herself skiing. When she told me she had two artificial legs, I thought she was joking."

He saw the true beauty of Mona and realized that a woman with enough spirit to overcome so massive a loss was worth far, far more than lost legs. Legs are, after all, only tissue; Mona was more than the sum, so to speak, of her parts.

Two years later they married. And not long afterward, Mona's lifelong dream came true. It was something of a miracle, because the doctors had been forced to undertake heroic measures not only in taking her legs, but in reconstructing, through skin grafts and other means, her reproductive organs. It was very touch and go, and none of the physicians dreamed she could ever have children.

Said her husband: "They had literally put her back together again. They took parts from other parts and just prayed it would work. All of this was purely flying-by-the-seat-of-the-pants–type surgery. Well, it worked."

Because sure enough, the rabbit died. Actually, she could probably have figuratively extinguished *two* rabbits: She was pregnant with twins.

Said her doctor, "I had very mixed emotions about it. I knew it could be extremely difficult, and we were afraid that some of our surgical procedures might be undone by the delivery. But Mona came through like she always does."

Of course, everybody has a hero. But John considers himself lucky to be in a lifetime partnership with his.

"To do what she's done, to go through all those physical and emotional upheavals, and then add the two kids; to have all the things that come flying at her every day… There are a lot of things she isn't able to do, because of those artificial legs. And it's hard for me to watch her in the kind of pain walking on them causes her. But instead of growing apart, we've both grown much stronger together."

Her minister most succinctly described the kind of quiet heroism embodied by Mona Parthun: "Mona

Parthun helps us all to see what we can become. If I could just become a little more like Mona, I'd be a much better person every day of my life. And so would we all."

Mona Parthun's sunny disposition and constant smile left a lasting imprint on my heart.

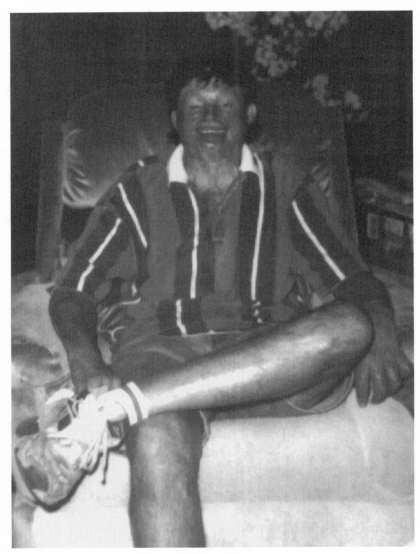

James Sullivan

ONE GOOD TURN DESERVES ANOTHER

JAMES SULLIVAN

WHEN I FIRST MET James Sullivan, I flinched. On the way back to the car to grab an extra video tape, I told the crew that this was one interview I didn't think I could pull off. How in the world could I look at this man and not "stare" at him. It didn't take long, however, before I saw past the scars—to his inner beauty.

His eyes peer out of a face that is almost inhuman—literally a melted face, a mottled and ravaged melange of tissue, that, the first time you see him, even if you've been warned, causes that sudden involuntary lurch of shock.

This is a face from hell, because, quite literally, for a few moments back in 1985, that was where this face went.

There is nothing but ragged flesh around the eyes and a forever-grinning, gaping mouth. All other recognizable features have been blasted away, leaving only the charred and tortured flesh.

You may at first find it darkly humorous to hear what this young man does for a living:

He sells used cars.

Would you buy a used car from this man?

You would indeed, if you knew what was behind that face, what its owner had lived through, overcome, and then surpassed.

James Sullivan took us on a tour of the woods near his Longview, Texas, home, where his ordeal of overcoming so casually began on an overnight camp out.

He knew the instant he did it that he'd made a mistake, that it was a dumb thing to have done—but he was just a kid then, that night back in November of 1985, when childhood suddenly ended.

He and some friends had been camping out in those woods, as young East Texas boys are very much inclined to do. These woods are thick and luscious and filled with

149

the smells of the woods and the sounds and the stirrings of wildlife. The boys had built a fire and then had talked on into the wee hours. One by one they fell silent. Those woodland sounds accompanied Sullivan to sleep.

When he was the first to awaken in the morning that fateful November 22, 1985, the fire had died down. James Sullivan was cold. Shivering, he put on his jacket and crawled out of his sleeping bag to try to rekindle the fire.

It seemed like the easiest way to get it restarted, so he threw gasoline on it.

It didn't ignite.

He threw on more—and then it did, with the sudden whoosh of an exploding fireball that seared those silent woods and mushroomed up into his face.

The next thing to ignite was his jacket, made of a synthetic fiber that was highly flammable. And so did his hair and the rest of his clothes. He ran through the woods, clothes still blazing, screaming, setting still more of the woods on fire while his terrified friends tried to catch him and put him out.

His mother was looking out the window when she saw her young son coming up the road, his arms held away from his body out to his sides. "It looked like melted wax was hanging off of them, but it was skin. And what at first I thought was some kind of fright wig was his hair, all burned up."

James took our crew through those woods, where you can still see, after many years, the burned places among the trees.

Over time, those trees and woods will heal. But James is as good as he'll ever get. He'll never again be the remarkably handsome young man who stares out of a photograph taken shortly before the accident. He is remarkable now for how he looks on the outside. The inside is pretty remarkable too.

He was first taken to a hospital in Longview, where they tried to stabilize him but knew that his injuries were beyond their scope. He had burns over 69 percent of his body, especially on his face, arms, and torso.

Said James, standing by the old campsite: "At first, I couldn't face coming back to this spot, but it doesn't bother me now. I vaguely remember the ambulance ride to the hospital, and then I woke up—two months later."

There is some slight consolation, very slight, in looking at still more of those photographs, this time taken of him as he lay comatose in the world-renowned burns unit of Parkland Memorial Hospital: He looks terrible now. But he looked much worse then, back before the six months in the hospital and the forty operations to graft what was left of the good skin onto his charred flesh.

His mother stayed at his side constantly, from the time he arrived in the wee hours of November 23, only sleeping two or three hours in the waiting room each night, until one month later, when doctors decided that he would probably survive after all.

When he first got a look at the extent of the damage to his face, he told his mother simply: "*Damn*, I'm ugly."

His mother did not try to tell him otherwise. She said instead, "It's not what's on the outside that counts. It's what's on the inside that really matters—how you feel on the inside. You could be beautiful on the outside and still be ugly on the inside. You're beautiful on the inside, and you'll make it."

After that, with James still confined to Parkland, she moved into the nearby Ronald McDonald House. It provides a service like no other. For parents, Ronald McDonald House provides a home away from home while their children—often dreadfully or even terminally injured or ill—are treated in the nearby hospital until they are either well enough to come home or... not all the endings are happy.

And for people like James Sullivan—well enough to leave the hospital but still requiring daily treatment in a facility a long way from home—it is equally a godsend. They may stay as long as they need to, free of charge.

He spent six months there.

And while there, at first, he paid a lot of attention to his own undeniably horrible predicament: not yet a man, yet disfigured for life. But slowly, he started to pay attention to some of the other people around him as well.

Kids ravaged by chemo that in some cases only

forestalled the inevitable. Kids waiting for liver transplants. Kids... dying.

"I'd be riding down the road years later and I'd think back on this one particular kid. Every time I saw him, he'd have this big smile on his face. He had a smile on his face right up to the day he died.

"I got to looking at some of those kids and realized that maybe I didn't have it so bad. At least I was free to come and go from the place pretty much as I pleased; a lot of them were restricted, couldn't go anywhere, for medical reasons. At least I knew I was going to live."

After about six months, James Sullivan was finally deemed fit enough to return to his Longview home. He'd sustained what doctors say is the most painful physical injury that a person can have. Now it was time to go home and face another kind of pain—the emotional kind, from insensitive people who looked only at the outside instead of seeing the person inside. He endured the stares. He even sometimes found cause for amusement, out with his friends and encountering those shocked stares.

Said his father, "The main thing was, it was the worst shock to see him change so much almost before your eyes. After the accident, he didn't look like my son. We had to accept it, though, from that moment on. It probably was the roughest time."

Said his mother: "I lost something out there that day. I lost my son. But yet, I gained a son. I got another one in his place."

Echoed his father: "That day out there, he lost his childhood."

Life went on. People who spent any time with James Sullivan soon forgot about the disfigurement, instead getting to know the person inside. And the ones who didn't, well, James Sullivan doesn't spend too much time thinking about them.

He continued through high school and, in the evenings, tinkered with cars. Bought a few here and there, refurbished them, and sold them.

And then in spite of it being the last job in the world for a man with a face as shocking as his, he decided he would open a car lot and sell used cars. People bought the cars because they knew him well enough to know that he was a man they could trust, and that his looks had nothing to do with it.

One of the people who got to know him over the years was Barbara Collins, the director at the Ronald McDonald House. She still remembers James Sullivan and the six months he spent there. Staffers at Ronald McDonald cannot help but bond with their charges, and vice versa.

She was there to witness the remarkable thing that happened to him: While he was healing on the outside, he was growing on the inside as well.

Said Barbara Collins, "He has had an experience that would change anyone's life. Nobody could go through what he's been through and not be affected. Not everybody takes a healthy child home. There's not always a happy ending, and James saw a lot of that."

Says Sullivan: "I saw a lot of disfigurement, a lot of terminally ill children, and some miracles happening. It was amazing. You get to thinking how bad off you are, and then you see someone waiting for a liver transplant... "

Even now, these years later, James Sullivan and his parents are struggling to pay off those leftover medical bills, which were staggering.

And James is not exactly doing a land office business down at the car lot: A man can have only so many friends, and they can buy only so many cars.

But he's selling a few here and there. He's getting by. New customers who do buy from him come back to him.

A car here, a car there—but here's what's special, what makes James Sullivan beautiful:

Every time he sells a car, whether he earns a lot on it or only a little, he takes fifty dollars and puts it in a special bank account. Then, when he feels like there's enough there, he transfers it back over to his checking account.

Then he writes a check to Ronald McDonald House for several thousand dollars, gets into one of his cars, and follows that same route back to Dallas that the ambulance followed years ago. He goes to Ronald

McDonald House, and gives that check to Barbara Collins.

They didn't charge him anything for staying there. Everything he got was free of charge. But beyond the care and the lodging, he got a lot more besides: He was given hope.

"People have come up to me, crying," says James Sullivan. "They tell me that before they met me they thought their problems were insurmountable, but that seeing me cope with much worse gave them hope. I think I give people hope. That's what I'm trying to give back to the Ronald McDonald House: hope. It took me a long time to get my car business going, but I did. The more business I can do, the more I can help other people."

Said his mother during our visit: "He survived all of this, and is still willing to give back."

And his dad: "There are a lot of heroes out there. Heroes that people don't even know exist. There are a whole lot of heroes in this world. My son is one of them."

Our feeling at "Unsung Heroes" is that the more people know about these heroes, the better a place the world seems to be.

So thanks, James. From you I have learned what true beauty really is.

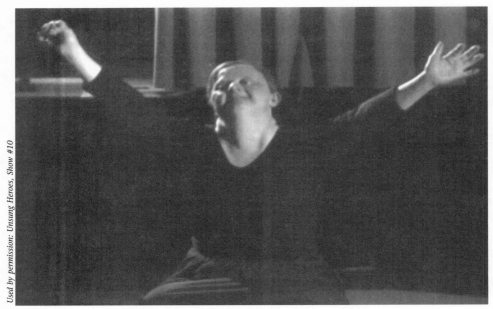

Images in Motion dancer Judy Johnson at a
performance in Denver, Colorado.

Patricia Fulton,
founder, director, and
choreographer of the
Images in Motion
Dancers

Tripping The Lights

The Images In Motion Dancers

HEROES COME IN ALL FLAVORS—all shapes and sizes, sexes and races, and all levels of ability.

The Images in Motion Dancers, for example.

These people made me really look at them and see them for who they really are. They made me see through how they look, by making me see what they really do.

And what is that?

Well, since they are dancers, they dance.

They flow and swoop and twirl, expressing their inner essence, moving their limbs in time with a song that comes, not so much from musicians, as from their very souls.

But once upon a time, the most modest achievement that even the most average of people in the course of an average day would have been the high point of these dancers' lives.

And self-expression? Once upon a time, almost an impossibility. Of course they have feelings, but lack the words to express them.

Because these people are profoundly, undeniably, and severely mentally retarded. In a less enlightened time, they might have been referred to as "basket cases."

The very basic activities of life are sometimes almost impossibly difficult for these graceful dancers to retain and repeat. Even playing some kinds of especially rhythmic music for them, rock music in particular, may cause them to withdraw, to uncontrollably turn inward, to move repetitively to the rhythm, lost in a bleak internal landscape.

For much of their lives, this darkness, this emptiness has been the normal course of affairs. Not that their families didn't try to love them, try to reach them— though, sad to say, almost *naturally* some have been casualties of an understandable form of parental frustration and subsequent benign neglect.

These were human islands lost in banks of leaden fog, floating alone, unknown, until the dancing came along.

Why are they dancing?

Because they can. And once you look beyond the obvious—the severe Down's syndrome in some cases, or in others, that sadly blighted lack of facial expression—you see something much more important: You see the souls inside.

With IQs as low as thirty in some of these cases, it's courageous to even attempt to teach such "specially challenged" people very much of anything at all—unless you learn *their* language—their true language.

Someone discovered their language and taught them how to better speak it.

That person was Patricia Fulton.

And the language: Dance. Dance—a matter not of knowing the right word, but feeling the right motion.

The interesting thing here is that she's learned from them almost as much as she's taught.

So have audiences—once they get beyond the limitation of mere appearances.

Patricia tells us, "I think audience members are inspired to look inside themselves and perhaps see what they hadn't discovered about themselves before. They tend to look past any limitations or outward signs of limitation and see the beauty in other people. Many of them have told us that these people have just inspired them so much."

The strongest testimonial is the change her program has wrought in these people's lives—in their self-confidence, their ability to communicate in other realms, and most of all, their view of themselves.

In 1986, when Patricia first began encouraging the dancing, the participants were considered hopelessly damaged and dependent—were, in fact, institutionalized in a residential facility in Boulder, Colorado.

At first, it wasn't easy.

"We wanted to dance, but performing was not a part of our original conception. It was the dancers themselves who wanted to perform. I personally found this amazing for people who have been institutionalized for much of their lives. How incredible for them to even think of it."

Not long after they started dancing, one of the dancers, Donald Meskimen, now forty-eight, told her that they didn't just want to dance, they wanted to perform.

Fulton was of course skeptical at first. She felt that their skills were so basic that it would never work, and parents expressed the fear that people would make fun of them. But the dancers—and their families and friends— were willing to take a chance; the chance that the public would see not the problems but the people inside.

"In the fall of 1986 we decided to become a performing company, and we've been going ever since. Each year I always think, well, maybe this will be the last year, but we keep going."

At first it was very scary, both for the dancers and for Fulton.

"We had no idea what anybody would do when we got out on the stage," Fulton recalled. "In the beginning the dancers didn't know how to improvise, so if something went wrong they just stopped, and I'm out there trying to dance around them. Over the years they've become much more professional, and very beautiful dancers. Many things go wrong at times on stages but the audience never knows that because the dancers are so professional now that they just keep right on going."

Going indeed: The dancing—and getting paid for it— were so beneficial to their self-esteem that ultimately they were able to move out of the residential facility and into independent living on their own.

"We've begun performing nationally, and we would like to continue doing that, to go to different states around the country. I think these dancers are wonderful goodwill ambassadors and they're inspiring to a lot of people."

But the real changes have been on the inside.

"I think they can express much more clearly what's inside. They're more adventuresome and want to try new things more readily, and they're actually very creative."

"If I had brought in a piece of artwork and showed it to them at the very beginning when we first started dancing, they wouldn't have known what to do with it, because they didn't have a vocabulary. They had no way of relating to it, no way of translating visual art into movement. But having gotten a foundation and a movement-vocabulary and performance experience, now when they looked at these pieces of visual art, they take right off. They know how to express themselves. Through dance."

Breaking down the barriers of darkness on the inside has brought these people together emotionally as well, in ways that otherwise wouldn't have been possible.

"Onstage, when we become one, and even in the studio, we love dancing together, improvising for two hours at a time without taking a break, and collaborating with professional musicians or other dancers. Times like those, when we can come together collectively and work together without speaking in an improvisational way, are a great joy."

Sometimes, with people like these, it is difficult not to wonder:

How much light shines into these minds? How much of what is good in life gets through these damaged circuits to shine onto these souls?

Unknowable, perhaps.

Perhaps the better question lies in a different direction: How much light shines out? In this regard, the Images in Motion Dancers burn so very, very bright.

As we left, I went to say goodbye to my new friends. Each one reached past my outstretched arm to me—to give me a hug... those are hugs I needed, and won't soon forget.

Charlie and Lucy Wedemeyer

WINNING THE GAME

CHARLIE WEDEMEYER

I WAS ON MY WAY to another of those amazing "lights" of human nature—only you couldn't tell it by me.

It was one of those days in which everybody and everything in the world seemed deliberately engaged in a conspiracy to make me mad, get under my skin, drive me nuts; it was like being pecked to death by ducks while drowning in a deluge of little boring details.

We'd had to make a mad and panting dash through the airport, both luggage and heavy camera gear in tow, and had almost missed our plane.

Before the flight was over we would almost wish we had. The plane was hot and crowded and full of jostling elbows and passengers every bit as irritable, hassled, and surly as we were. Making matters worse for us, we'd been traveling for days already and working sixteen- and seventeen-hour shifts trying to get the next "Unsung Heroes" edition in the can. I had a bad knee (still do), and it hurt. Because of the start-up, on-a-shoestring nature of "Unsung Heroes" at the time, I couldn't afford insurance and therefore couldn't have the knee fixed, and I was mad about that, too.

Tempers were short and nerves were frayed. We were tired and tired of each other. We hit the San Jose airport mad at the world and each other and everyone else in it, which only seemed to fray us further.

And then we met Charlie Wedemeyer and his wife, Lucy, and all of that went away.

True, it's not uncommon to be going along feeling just awfully sorry for yourself over life's little hassles— and then come 'round the corner and suddenly spot someone horribly afflicted and forever confined to a wheelchair.

Then there's that moment of shame over such self-absorption and self-pity in the face of what is in your own case really only fleeting unpleasantness. But that feeling is more a kind of guilty thankfulness, the old

163

"there but for the grace of God go I" realization.

In spite of the fact that he is indeed forever confined to a wheelchair and is indeed horribly afflicted with Lou Gehrig's disease, that's not the feeling Charlie Wedemeyer engenders in those who meet him. Not a feeling of pity and "there but for the grace," but more a feeling of awe. Of, "Gee, you're neat."

You can't help but notice, of course, that he can't move a single muscle other than those in his eyes and his lips, and that he is only able to breathe thanks to a respirator plugged into the tracheotomy hole in his throat.

His paralysis is total. Beyond total: This disease, which usually only tortures its victims for a couple of years or so before it mercifully kills them, (usually, because even their autonomic nervous system fails) has been raging unabated in Charlie for nearly twenty years.

It's safe to say that Lou Gehrig's disease has taken Charlie Wedemeyer where no man has gone before and has kept him there for longer.

Charlie can't even speak; by reading his lips and repeating his statements to interviewers—of which, over the past seventeen years, there have been many—his wife, Lucy, and son Kale serve as interpreters.

It was about Lucy that we'd been thinking, when we weren't bickering back and forth or feeling sorry for ourselves, back on that long, hot, crowded flight over Texas, New Mexico, Nevada, and then on to California. Our gloomy thoughts about the upcoming subject matter only added to our sense of misery, because we were just sure that what she probably felt was dull and unending misery; that she was going to be another of the Brave Little Soldier types we'd met in the course of other shows—brave, silent, stoic sufferers; good examples for people under duress, but not a lot of fun to be around. They'll stand there and smile grimly for the press, and then, I suspect, go home and cry their eyes out.

And I'd been thinking about her in particular from a woman's standpoint. In the pictures we'd seen, she was always smiling, smiling, smiling. But what kind of marriage must this be? What kind of companion could he be—unable to move, unable to even go to the bathroom by himself, unable to dress himself, even undress himself, unable to feed himself, unable to... an endless, deeply personal list.

Unable to be intimate in the positive physical sense, yet deeply dependent in all the negative senses of intimacy; it sounded to me like the makings of a nightmare.

What must it be like to be married to a man who is miserable? Someone so passive, impotent, dependent, and humiliated. And what must it be like for him? Unable to stand up before his children. Unable to take a place in his community—unable to get from the bed to the bathroom and back; unable even to help his family when they help him. Unable to protect, or even resist; his family having to carry him, literally. A sack of immobile, inert, living, suffering flesh.

The smiles in the photographs all looked to me too good to be true. Because the Wedemeyers had lived what should have been a hell on earth.

Making their sad saga even worse, it seemed to me, was that their lives had started out so, well, pretty, so storybook, with all the makings of Happily Ever After.

He'd been a hotshot football player back in high school in Hawaii, and she'd been his high school sweetheart. Ironic, that Charlie Wedemeyer had always been such a highly physical man.

Athletic achievement—motion, exertion, impact, pure physical power—was what he lived for. In fact, he'd been selected Prep Player of the Decade in Hawaii, then received a football scholarship to Michigan State where he made the college all-star team.

Charlie married his high school sweetheart. After college he and Lucy moved to San Jose, where he landed a dream of a job, teacher and head coach at Los Gatos High School.

The two of them soon settled into what was a dream of a life, a personal heaven. They had it all. And then along came one more thing than they'd bargained for: the runner stumbled. Literally. He could no longer trust those feet that had carried him so fast and so far across the football fields of high school and college and into a coaching career.

While standing at the blackboard of a classroom in 1976, Charlie could never have imagined that his fairytale life with Lucy was about to begin a tumultuous tumble downward as a single piece of chalk dropped from his hand. He would later learn that this was a sign of what was to come.

At first, he thought he was just getting clumsy, but it got steadily worse. And then he was diagnosed with Lou Gehrig's disease, which, before it's all over, eats away nearly every tissue in the neuromuscular system. It gobbles away the myelin sheath that surrounds each nerve. With the insulation gone, the nerves can no longer function. Yet enough sensory feedback travels up those lines that Charlie could *feel* his body as it slowly atrophied away; feel the itches he couldn't scratch and the spasms of eroding tissue; it's like being buried alive.

They gave Charlie a year to live.

Lucy said, "I remember the morning after Charlie told me. I remember looking outside and the sky was gorgeous; it was a sunny day. The flowers were blooming, and everybody was acting normal. How could they be normal when my world had just been shattered? That was the hardest thing, because you can't walk around and say to people, 'Excuse me, but my husband has just been diagnosed with a terminal disease. My husband's going to die—that's why I'm acting weird.' And there's no way to process that—that you're going to die—because it's the biggest fear that any of us have."

That was seventeen years ago. Some of those years, especially the first ones, were long, hurtful, and hard. Every bit as bad in fact as, on the plane, I imagined them to be. No man and wife in their right minds would get news like that and just say oh, well, la-de-da, honey, what's for supper?

And they didn't. They went through hell.

Bitter, increasingly paralyzed with both the disease and the fear of dying, Charlie prayed to God to save him, heal him of the insidious and always fatal disease.

Lucy prayed for that, too.

God apparently chose to ignore that request, or certainly at most to put it on the back burner.

For a while, it looked to them like maybe God had indeed sent them straight to hell. Charlie, feeling that all he could offer his family was a huge burden and a life of misery, frequently told them they'd be better off if he just died.

As Lucy said, "My frustration in the early years of Charlie's disease was that I'd thought that if I loved him enough, then that's all it would take. But gradually he got worse. I had sort of made a pact with myself: I wasn't going to cry. I wouldn't let him see me down, I was always going to be positive."

This was the phase of noble, self-sacrificing stoicism I mentioned earlier.

It was the faith of a child, their son Kale, who brought some sense and direction back into their lives. His faith ultimately became theirs. Charlie remembers, "We were in the midst of our adversity. Kale was the rock in our family. He gave encouragement to each and every one of us. He has bestowed so much love and compassion on us. He was always there when we needed him."

But staying stoically cheerful and positive and self-sacrificial (all the things we think we are supposed to be able to do under adverse circumstances and at which we are always doomed to failure) got harder and harder as the disease progressed. In the final stages of this insidious disease, even the muscles and nerves required for breathing stop functioning.

And in 1985, Charlie indeed stopped breathing. Doctors had to perform an emergency tracheotomy, ending Charlie's ability to speak even if he *could* breathe. And they had to put him on a breathing machine. They figured it was probably a matter of weeks.

Yet he lived. Weeks. Months. And then years. Then decades.

Lucy had long since quit praying for a miracle cure. Instead, she prayed for strength. And she got it.

The family was deeply in debt from astronomical medical bills and the loss of Charlie's income. One afternoon, struggling to get Charlie's limp and useless body loaded into a borrowed van, Lucy finally lost it. Lost it, in fact, completely and forever.

"I felt this huge lump coming up in my throat, even though I didn't want to cry. I got out of the van and went around to the back of it, and in the middle of this parking lot with all these cars, I just yelled out— cried out—to God, 'I NEED SOME HELP! I CAN'T DO THIS BY MYSELF ANYMORE, YOU KNOW!' It was... I think it was the first time that I've ever done that. And all of a sudden, I was filled with the most amazing strength. I... I can't explain it. It's like, like you have a—this void in your inner being, that was all of a sudden filled."

Then Charlie changed his prayer as well: If you won't heal me, then, God, please *use* me.

Apparently, that was something God was willing to do.

God seems to have used him as an example, not of a miserable human being dying of an endlessly wretched disease, but of a man who accepts life's slings and arrows and tries to enjoy every waking—every *living*—moment in this life and on this planet to the very fullest extent possible.

Charlie Wedemeyer became, almost overnight, a man who accepts that everything there is to have is right here, right now, whether his life lasts another day, week, year, or decade.

He decided to make the most of every moment, and his life turned around 180 degrees.

In spite of his illness, by the fall of 1984, Charlie's high school football team had compiled an incredible record, and Charlie had been named coach of the year for the third time in his short career. When Charlie's speech became difficult to comprehend (a common side effect of ALS), Lucy joined Charlie on the sidelines, reading his lips and relaying the plays to his assistant coaches.

Charlie lead the Los Gatos Wildcats to the championship and said this to his team in his post-game speech, "You have accomplished something that no other Los Gatos team has ever done, and you're going to remember it for the rest of your lives."

Local sports broadcaster Robert Braunstein has closely followed Charlie's successes from the sidelines. "I think a lot of times kids in high school think they know it all, that no one can teach them anything. Then they see Charlie and realize that this is something they've never experienced, something they know nothing about."

Former student Mike Scialabba remembers playing for Coach Wedermeyer. "You have to admire this guy just because he gets up every morning and survives day to day. For us to complain about getting up for school or about homework—it just makes our problems so minimal compared to his just surviving every day."

Charlie Wedemeyer can't move a muscle, yet still he coaches a football team. More important is his second career as a public speaker.

He can't even speak aloud—yet every year, through his lectures, his books, and his example, his message reaches hundreds of thousands of people.

It was of the utmost importance to Charlie that, despite his horrible physical condition, he could achieve true happiness in order to be a good example.

And all that is really required to get to that point, for anyone, anywhere, in any circumstance, is a realization like the one that Charlie had.

"At some time in each of our lives, if it hasn't happened already, we will all be faced with some adversity that may seem too difficult to live with. When that time comes, you have to remember that God has given us the power of choice, and we can choose to feel sorry for ourselves, to be bitter and angry and cause everyone around us to be bitter and angry and miserable, or we can choose to go through that circumstance, knowing that we'll become a better and stronger person for it. Pain and suffering are inevitable. We will all go through it. But misery is optional. We make that choice."

Charlie pauses to rest and Lucy chimes in: "You know, we go through life ninety miles an hour and don't stop and look at the things that we take for granted around us. Too many people deal in the negatives. We really have seen, and God has shown us, the miracles of life— just life. Just the fact that a baby's born, you know, that a flower blooms. All those things have become so brilliant to us, whereas unless you face a tragedy or unless you live through a trauma or difficult time, you really lose perspective. You're so busy achieving, you're so busy looking for success and looking for happiness, when it's right there. That's our miracle."

Initially, Charlie relied on his own strength and determination, then he came to realize that he had to lean on Lucy. Charlie explains, "I wouldn't be here today if it weren't for Lucy. I am so gratetful that God put us together since high school. Researchers have said that 72 percent of marriages break up when a spouse is diagnosed with a terminal illness. But God knew, ahead of time, that Lucy would be the one who would help me and love me unconditionally."

The Wedermeyers have experienced numerous miracles. One of the greatest is that Charlie and Lucy are now sharing their seventeenth year together since learning that Charlie had ALS.

There will be an unfamiliar sight on the sidelines this football season. Kale, a recent college graduate, will be joining his father as a coach for the Los Gatos Wildcats.

Charlie said, "I have really enjoyed working with Kale because he is so knowledgeable about the game, and to have my son out there with me is special."

Kale responded, "Of course we have different philosophies and different opinions about football sometimes, so when my dad calls a certain play, sometimes I second-guess him. It will be interesting to see how it goes this year." When I asked who will have the final word, Kale said, "Actually I have the final word because I can read anything off his lips that I want." Then both father and son began laughing.

For the "Unsung Heroes" crew, the flight back to DFW is a lot different this time. The thing we can't get over is how—in a person whose physical life is so nearly the embodiment of a living death—Charlie's eyes shine with so much life, twinkling with humor and an endless interest out of that almost-dead, muscleless face.

There is a lively soul in there. And in spite of all that he's been through, that soul still has those eyes, those windows on a world that he knows to be good.

170

And of course on the plane we take up the philosophical question—whether Charlie and Lucy's genuine happiness is a bona fide minor miracle from God, or just two very strong people who used their strength and positive outlook to save themselves.

There are indeed elements of something bordering on miraculous here in this unmoving mass of God-made flesh: Here is powerlessness that empowers, immobility creating movement and change. Here is helplessness that helps others, paralysis that reaches out to others around the world, and an inability to speak that comes out so wonderfully loud and clear.

So to the question of whether the miracle is man-made or a gift from a Supreme Being, the answer is that it's probably both. When you think about it, who's to say where the miracle leaves off and the personal strength begins?

And then we all realized what had so impressed us:

Charlie is completely and urgently alive; in spite of every problem and every difficulty and the death sentence that's loomed over him for seventeen years, he gets more out of every moment than anyone I ever met. I think sometimes about those eyes of his, so bright, animated, happy, and alive.

Given that all we ever really get, after all, is moments, Charlie has a pretty good deal.

And Charlie knows it.

Charlie's "got it."

Sometimes when I think about the Wedemeyers, I want to cry—not for them, but for all the rest of us: the ones who don't have it nearly so good. The ones who haven't "got it."

I pray someday that we all get it—from whatever source "it" comes from.

Kale concluded, "It is ironic how a disease that is terminal, that is life-threatening, that would normally destroy a family has really brought us close together. We just thank God that it happened that way. We have so much love now that it's really hard to say I wish it hadn't happened, because who knows where we'd be today?"

Lucy adds, "It's been an all-consuming love that's

engulfed our family. We are so blessed. The excitement of today is that we live every day as if it's a miracle, a gift. And we have been blessed with the responsibility to help everyone learn that lesson."

Linda Jones, founder and director of On Our Own

A WAY OUT

LINDA JONES

SHORTLY BEFORE THE TIME I met Linda Jones, I went through a painful divorce.

While my husband never threatened me physically—and, in hindsight, comported himself decently, considering how emotionally trying such circumstances can be—it's still true that any woman going through such a time is fearful of violence.

So yes, I was very ready to relate to Linda Jones when we went to Chicago to interview her and find out more about her program, which amounts to an "underground railroad" for battered wives and girlfriends who are trying to get out of destructive relationships.

Most of our Heroes are "about" making good things happen for others; Linda Jones is about keeping *bad* things from happening to women and children. Given the fact that she has an unrelated full-time job, she is quite a crusader.

She is fighting a deadly enemy: More than 70 percent of female homicide victims are killed by their spouses or ex-lovers, and more than half of these murders occur after the woman has left her abuser and has already survived several stalking incidents. And for every one of these unfortunate victims, there are thousands more women who remain in dangerous relationships simply because they believe that there is no safe way out.

Or they stay "for the good of the children"—when the truth of the matter is that children in such violently dysfunctional families stand a far greater chance of growing up to become drug dependent, criminals, or stalkers themselves.

High unemployment, increased gang membership, and youth crime all stem from family abuse. It's a societal problem as well: yours and mine.

Linda came to these concerns the hard way: She herself was being stalked, but got no help from authorities.

"I would get off work at 7:00 a.m., and he'd be waiting

for me in my garage. Then for a while he was hanging around my workplace. Or he'd be in front of the house, or on the terrace, or even at my parents' house. If I was able to get there without him seeing me leaving, he'd let the air out of my tires or steal my battery—things to make me have to come to him and talk to him.

"The distress in such a situation is equal to physical injuries. By the time my case came to trial, he had eight violations of the protective order. But the Stalking Bill had not yet been passed. He finally got jail time—but only for the property crimes, not the stalking. At that point, I didn't care; they could have jailed him for jaywalking as far as I was concerned, as long as he was jailed."

Later she thought about it and became amazed that it was property and not human life that the authorities were most concerned with.

"I didn't know anything about stalking, or even domestic violence before that. Before that, I was like the rest of society: it's something that happens to other folks. But I was spending a lot of time in the courtroom myself. I'd be sitting there waiting, and someone would lean over and ask what they should be doing in their own cases."

While not highly educated, Linda is a savvy and street-smart woman; while she was in court, gradually other women began coming to her for advice and assistance in getting away from their own abusive relationships, and before long, she had taken in eight women—three staying with her and five at her mother's house. Understandably, her mother finally said, "We need to talk."

It was then that Linda realized that her calling was bridging that huge gap that she and women like her faced.

"There is no place to go. Even at a battered women's shelter, they don't have any way to actually hide you; the volunteers don't have the resources to get you out completely. And most of these women have got to be hidden to have the breathing space."

Linda is more like a one-woman "witness protection agency," going so far as to arrange new identification and to make sure that other records are withheld from prying husbands and ex-husbands.

In the severest, most threatening cases, she arranges bodyguards and security, and furthermore, she takes it upon herself to help these women get back "on track" in life.

Most of them are so beaten down they don't think they know how to do anything on their own. She teaches them the skills and abilities denied them by controlling, grasping husbands: how to raise their children, how to take care of a checking account, how to find a job. Once you take responsibility for someone in such a case, the list of needs can become rather long. To meet their needs as well of those of her child, Linda Jones works at her regular job every night, then goes home in the morning to see to her kid, and then heads for the courthouse and her office to make herself available to her "clients."

She knows the ropes. She knows the first thing you do is get a restraining order or peace bond so that the minute either is violated, the husband or boyfriend has broken the law.

Any divorce has the potential to turn unpleasant, and Linda Jones learned early on just how bad it can get. Learned it, in fact, on her first and worst case.

This woman was afraid her husband would kill her when she went to get her things from their house, and so she asked the police to go along with her.

Police went to the door, where the estranged husband was all smiles as they talked to him. "Oh, man, what are all you guys doing here?"

Officer replied, "Well, your wife here thinks there may be some problems with moving her stuff."

"Officers, there's just not going to be a problem," he said. "She can come in and get whatever she needs. We don't need the police."

Several sisters and brothers accompanied her into the apartment to help unload furniture and to protect her.

As the brothers were carrying a sofa out to the van, the husband pulled a Tech 9 (much like an Uzi) and shot her thirty times. Emptied the clip into her. Then pulled out another pistol and shot her point blank in the head, then he shot himself.

Police were hiding behind their cars. "One of them tore his pants trying to hide under his car."

Jones's point is not that the police were cowardly, but that if the police are afraid of domestic violence, how do you think the women feel (and, for that matter, stalked or threatened men, as well; women can shoot, too.)

That is the kind of danger Linda Jones herself faces every day; in the case of every woman she helps, she's in danger as well, because she's the one providing the protection. And a lot more besides.

Her organization, On Our Own—Hear Our Cries, was formed in the winter of 1992 as a response both to the rise in fatalities and to the sometimes inappropriate handling of domestic abuse cases by law enforcement officers.

From the time abuse victims first contact Linda and her volunteers agency until the time they can be considered permanently safe from the abuser, the people at On Our Own literally walk each client through each step of the sometimes confusing and disheartening process of ending an abusive relationship.

At first, the woman who leaves an abusive spouse will be practically immobilized with fear—the fear that he's going to look for her and find her, and that this time will be the very worst.

The effects of having lived through long periods of abuse leaves emotional and psychological scars long after the victim has been removed from the abusive environment.

She will be numb with fear and inert with confusion. Because of her passive role in the abuser/victim relationship, she may have great difficulty taking charge of her life.

Once a woman leaves an abusive relationship, she is more at risk of being killed—and she is furthermore instantly homeless.

In high-risk situations, On Our Own provides emergency housing for its clients and their children for up to three years—or permanently, if necessary. And On Our Own goes to great lengths to hide the victim's location from the victimizer. They are adept at hiding the "paper trail" by having mail rerouted and access to computer records strictly controlled by banks and credit firms.

And On Our Own holds the hands of these confused women as they face the legal system. The five full-time staffers and four part-time volunteers get involved in every aspect of the mediation process, with an eye toward getting jail time for serious offenders. They work closely with the detectives and prosecutors to collect and present information that will strengthen their demands for actual jail time.

Getting women free of their relationships is sometimes only half the battle. Many victims of abuse return to similar relationships. Through counseling and group therapy, On Our Own helps repeat victims to understand and break the cycle and helps them develop coping skills that will enable them to handle the stresses of everyday living.

On Our Own counselors are available seven days a week, twenty-four hours a day.

The children of abuse victims are victims as well, and On Our Own addresses their needs through youth programs focusing on stress and peer-pressure management, leadership development, and educational development.

Equally important to On Our Own's staff is getting out the message: Domestic violence has to stop. The nonprofit agency's aggressive style of getting media exposure for the situation has brought the facts into living rooms across the country.

There are signs that On Our Own is starting to win its battles legally as well: The agency was the first to force a domestic-violence offender to have to wear an electronic monitoring bracelet as part of the terms of his wife's protective order.

And staffers were involved in the first Chicago case in which a Chicago police officer who had been accused of abuse was ordered by the court to surrender all his weapons until the outcome of the case.

Prior to 1994, in Illinois the most severe punishment handed a perpetrator of domestic violence was a combination of probation and counseling. In the past eighteen months, the efforts of On Our Own have landed ten of these offenders in jail.

It is definitely true that many women owe Linda Jones their very lives. The ones she has not quite literally saved, she has helped to begin new, better ones.

I left Chicago with nothing but admiration for Linda. Not only does she face her own problems but those of others as well.

She's every inch a hero, especially to the women she's sheltered. As one of them, Shana, (last name withheld to protect her identity) told our crew:

"Six months ago, I couldn't imagine that I could be where I am now. And it's only getting better. They are helping me to get myself back together. Six months from now, who knows how far along I'll be? It's helping me to strengthen myself and to be a better person.

"I feel safe. I feel content. And I love coming home."

When I returned home from this trip and reunited with my precious daughter, Bethany, I saw in her face the innocent children I met on this story—children who are every bit as frightened and abused as their mothers. It was then that I fully realized the magnitude and depth of Linda Jones's efforts for the women *and* the children.

Mike Tufariello, a former United States sailor who
blew the whistle on Navy corruption

WOUNDED EAGLE

MIKE TUFARIELLO

MY FATHER WAS A WHISTLEBLOWER. It cost him dearly to report the wrongdoings he witnessed, but I know if he had it to do over, he would make the same choices.

From personal experience I know what courage it takes to be a whistleblower—the kind of courage Mike Tufariello possesses.

When the national anthem is played, few stand as straight and proud as Mike Tufariello. He served in the Navy for over twenty years, first as a gung-ho nineteen-year-old who volunteered for combat in Vietnam. Few foot soldiers saw more action than Tufariello. He signed up for tour after tour of duty, working toward spending his entire adult life in a uniform. His collection of medals and outstanding service records are testimony to his intense love for the military. During his career he was even named the Navy's Sailor of the Year—their Top Gun.

Almost overnight a source of pride turned to shame for Mike. An act of bravery changed this decorated soldier into a disgraced and broken man. After two tours in Vietnam and several years of shore duty back in the U.S., Mike earned the rank of chief petty officer and was transferred to the payroll department of a naval air station in Texas. All seemed well until he discovered blatant examples of financial irregularities. The proper thing, he felt, was to report the payroll problems. Once he opened his mouth, his life became a nightmare.

Mike Tufariello has been twice a hero—once in service to his country and again in the service of those his country has deeply wronged.

This weight-lifting and iron-armed former soldier's nickname says it all: "Chief Tuff"—a good guy until you mess with him.

Tuff as nails.

But he was more than just tough. He was efficient. He

was intelligent. And most of all, he was dedicated, honest, and brave.

It was that dedication, that honesty, and that bravery that would both effectively end his distinguished military career—and lead him to his second cause in life: fighting to right the injustices of the military against its own whistleblowers.

He was assigned to the Dallas Naval Air Station. There, in 1983, during the course of his duties in the payroll section, he discovered that officers were routinely authorizing training pay for reservists who were actually not even showing up for "training days"—in effect, just giving away the government's money in exchange for nothing.

He also found that officers were deliberately doctoring the paperwork to show some of those weekend warriors "present" and on-base when they were home watching television or mowing the lawn.

Our tax money, taking a nap.

And Tufariello notified the inspector general of his findings. The navy took action—against Tufariello. And it was the kind of logic and action more often associated with the old communist regime in Russia: if they don't like the government, they must be crazy. And if they're crazy, they need hospitalizing.

Which was exactly what happened to Tufariello. His attempt to follow the rules and regulations landed him in a bureaucratic nightmare.

First, the officers at the Dallas Naval Air Station set him up. As he was at home awaiting a meeting with the inspector general to whom he would document and detail his allegations of fraud by the military against the taxpayers, the phone rang in the garage. Tufariello, frustrated by the foot-dragging of his superiors, was working out. When the phone rang, he was pounding hell out of a punching bag.

It was one of his "colleagues" at the Naval Air Station.

"How's it going, Chief Tuff? Do you know where your meeting with the inspector general is going to take place?"

"No," said Tuff, honestly.

"Well, how do you feel?"

"Frustrated and nervous. Waiting for that phone call to come, I'm goin' outta my mind; I feel like jumping off the Brooklyn Bridge."

Tuff's immediate supervisor was standing by, listening in on the call. And when Tufariello said that, the supervisor knew they'd gotten him where they wanted him.

The supervisor went to the executive officer and said, "We've nailed him now. He's threatened to commit suicide," regardless of the fact that Tuff was far from suicidal; in fact, this was the biggest day of his life. And the Brooklyn Bridge was a long way away. He only chose that analogy because, after all—as his accent readily attests—he's a native New Yorker.

The supervisor called Tufariello a few minutes later and said, "The meeting is set. Put on your dress uniform and come on down to the base."

And Tufariello did. But awaiting him in the master chief's office: Not the inspector general's staff, but the very people he'd turned in.

"I start talking and nobody is talking back to me. They're just nodding their heads and then—boom. These two Marine guards just grabbed me by the arms and said, 'Let's go.'"

The guards loaded Tuff into a staff car and drove north and northwest for nearly three hours in total silence, the flat North Texas landscape scudding by; Tuff, at times, thought that he was about to become the victim of a military "hit," that he was being "taken for a ride."

"I remember at one point we stopped for coffee; I honestly thought maybe I'd be saving my life if I made a break for it. But where would I go? There was nowhere."

The truth was almost as shocking. He was well inside the big building at Sheppard AFB when he finally realized where he was. As he was escorted off the elevator, his knees buckled. It was the psychiatric ward. The loony bin. The nut-hatch.

"Have you ever seen *One Flew Over the Cuckoo's Nest*? I stood there looking at the exact picture. The nurses in the glass encasement. The steel doors, the wire mesh windows. The dazed-looking men wandering around in the halls."

Tuff himself was both dazed and amazed as the Navy

checked its "lunatic" into the laughing academy.

He recalls that at one point, after they'd taken away his clothes and given him a hospital robe: "I looked down at my feet and I saw the slippers. They had 'happy faces' on them. The year before, the Navy had given me a plaque for being Sailor of the Year—and now I'm being rewarded with slippers with happy faces on them. I had gone from one end of the navy's elite to being a fool madman."

It was not until his wife finally tracked him down and hurried to him that he finally broke. She took one look at him, wearing his robe, his jammies, and his smiley-faces feet, and both of them burst into tears.

Of course, Mike was not crazy (except to the extent that his co-workers and superior officers were driving him nuts), and the doctors of course soon clearly knew it, but would not state otherwise.

They released him after a couple of days' evaluation, saying he was "clinically stable" and "the prognosis for military life is excellent."

But the Navy didn't really need him to be diagnosed; simply by sending him there and then spreading the rumor on base that Tuff had "gone nuts," they had done enough damage to effectively destroy both his reputation and his credibility.

But Tuff wasn't going to take it lying down. If crazy was what they wanted people to think he was, a little dose of "crazy" was what he would give them.

When he returned to the base, he went to the master chief's office—who was rather surprised to see this physically imposing muscle-man "back so soon."

The officer began, "You'll be glad to know there'll be no formal charges... " and Tufariello closed the door, grabbed him by the collar, slammed him against the wall, and said, "You son of a bitch! You were supposed to be helping me out and instead you helped them set me up!"

Unofficially known now as "a crazy man," Tufariello was stripped of most of his important duties at the Dallas Naval Air Station. He may not have been crazy, but he sure was mad. Fighting mad; determined to bring justice to the base if it was the last thing he ever did.

All those years spent typing routine reports were paying off: One thing about Tuff is, for a brawny, physical sort of fellow, he sure can type.

And he set to it with a vengeance, wallpapering his superiors with anonymous letters, attempting to get someone, anyone, to pay attention to the problem.

Finally, on October 11, 1984, the force master chief, the senior ranking enlisted man in Tuff's division, summoned Tuff to his office.

He said, "We've been getting these anonymous letters, and we're pretty sure that it's been you writing them."

Tuff replied, "That's right."

"Tell me what happened," said the master chief, and so Tuff did, chapter and verse.

And the chief said, "Looks like we're gonna have to do an investigation." And they did.

But twenty-four hours later, they brought Tuff back into that office. "They couldn't look me in the eye. They stood right there in front of me and said, 'Chief, you were right. It was fraud, and a cover-up of fraud. But there are too many people in the upper echelon of this thing, so it has to be swept under the carpet.'"

"You've got to be kidding," was Tuff's amazed and honest response.

"Nope. We gotta bury it."

But Tufariello knew that until the payroll scandal was corrected, his reputation would forever remain tarnished. He'd always be the "crazy chief petty officer" who paranoically imagined scandals and conspiracies and bogeymen hiding under his bunk.

His personal life had begun to erode from the moment his wife saw him with his "smiley feet." She stood behind him—and does to this day—but the rage and bitterness his treatment inflamed in him was enough to make her wonder if, well, maybe he wasn't just a little bit crazy. He had always been intense; now, feeling wronged on such a monumental scale by the men and the uniform he'd served all his life, he became obsessive.

Even his own children were inclined to believe the rumors about his insanity. After all—hadn't the Navy said Dad was suicidal?

His wife knew better, but other trials awaited her.

Because tirelessly, almost to the point of self-destruction, in fact, an increasingly embittered Tufariello spent every spare moment trying to get someone to pay attention to the problem—the fraud, the waste of taxpayers' money.

In fact, Tuff was determined to do what he'd sworn himself to do twenty years ago: He was obligated to serve and to protect the citizens, even if it was from the abuses of his own branch of the military.

All night long, night after night, year after year, he'd sit at the typewriter, cranking out yet another letter to yet another congressman, or general, or bureaucrat, or the President. And for his efforts—for his bravery and patriotism, he received the usual reward of letter-writers everywhere: standard form letters. Thank you for your concern. My staff is looking into the matter. Yours, regards, and the signature of a machine.

Ronald Reagan—form letter.

George Bush—form letter.

Tip O'Neill—form letter.

Phil Gramm—form letter.

And the list of rejections went on and on.

During this period, Tuff's personal life really began to decline. Because while he'd write and write, he'd also drink and drink. And drink.

And increasingly, since no one seemed to want to believe him no matter how hard he tried to tell them, Tuff did indeed begin to behave as a paranoid. Gloomy and suspicious, drunk and suspicious, hung over and suspicious.

Thanks to some media coverage of his case, other whistleblowers in the military began to see him as their leader and inspiration and came to him with their own horror stories. Tuff was not alone, at least; in fact, psychiatric "evaluation" seemed to be the standard operating procedure for countering those whistleblowers:

Many were like Tuff—clapped into mental hospitals after they blow the whistle. Tuff also began to hear from and counsel with military personnel with horror stories to tell of rape, sexual harassment, dishonorable discharge— the full gamut of tools the government can use to retaliate against its noisier soldiers.

Tuff felt that more needed to be done, both about the problem and for its victims. So he banded together with these emotionally injured and traumatized soldiers and sailors to form a support group, the Wounded Eagles, which offered legal advice and shoulders to cry on.

Still his typewriter churned out the mail. Do something, do something, do something is the best summary of their content.

And finally, in 1988—nearly five long years after he'd discovered the payroll fraud—the right letter landed in the right mailbox: that of Congresswoman Barbara Boxer.

She was interested.

She contacted him.

And before she knew it, she was also in contact with Tuff's whistleblower network. Slowly, government interest and media support was building in favor of Tuff and the other whistleblowers. This was back in 1988 and 1989. People were finally beginning to listen.

Barbara Boxer's name is perhaps as appropriate as Tuff's. Because the more she looked into the problem, the more "fighting mad" she became.

In a television appearance, she raged: "They are being intimidated, they are being harassed, they are being isolated, they are being frightened. I mean, when I first heard the stories it sounded like this was not America. It sounded like this was the Soviet Union at it's worst, when people are sent for psychological harassment, to break them. Essentially, I've asked the military to come up with some regulations to prohibit this, but what they have come up with is nothing; they just like having this ability, it seems to me, to intimidate their people, and I just don't think that's American."

One by one, through the efforts of Tuff, Barbara Boxer, and the increasingly interested news media, the horror stories were coming out.

In some ways, the experiences of others were more damaging than Tuff's. A frequent means of countering female soldiers' complaints was to accuse them of lesbianism, grounds for discharge.

For instance, Army Reserve Lt. Victoria Hudson, an MP during the Persian Gulf War, claimed that she was the victim of constant sexual propositions from her boss, who begged her to write him dirty letters. She complained—and suddenly found herself under investigation.

That also happened to Tanya Domi, a former Army captain. While on a tour of duty in Hawaii, she brought charges against a captain who she said had made a "lewd sexual remark" to her in front of another officer—and within the month, she was under investigation on charges of being a lesbian. The charge against her was eventually dropped—but so was her complaint against the captain.

In the decade from 1980 to 1990, the military discharged 16,750 enlisted personnel and 169 officers for being gay, lesbian, or bisexual and acknowledged that women were discharged for homosexuality at rates consistently three times as high as their per capita in the military.

In fact, investigators have found that there is a pervasive fear among female personnel that any accusations of sexual impropriety against male officers leads almost de facto to countercharges of lesbianism—the old high school "failure" excuse having become grimly all too real.

Boxer, Rep. Pat Schroeder, a democrat from Colorado who joined in pursuing these claims, Tufariello, and others of his Wounded Eagles gave testimony before two Congressional hearings—with the result that Congress passed the Military Whistleblower Protection Act in 1989. Under the act, such harassment of whistleblowers is punishable... but it's also very difficult to prove and difficult to enforce.

Tuff and the Wounded Eagles, to this very day, are fighting for more restrictions on the military's handling of those who would dare to come forward and tell the truth.

Some of Tuff's pain has been replaced by a renewed pride in knowing that he had the guts to come forward and tell his story, and in the fact that his Wounded Eagles organization is giving other soldiers that kind of courage as well.

Tuff believes the fight will never be over and that it may not be winnable because of the very nature of the military: Obey your superiors, period. Speak when spoken to, and otherwise, shut up and CYA. But he continues in it for the same reason he first joined the navy:

He loves his country. And if not him, who?

Tuff retired from the military and went to work, rather ignominiously after such a distinguished military career, for Jiffy Lube in 1990.

And, with the public pressure and the spotlight focused on him, the navy finally had to make some response to his charges.

The Secretary of the Navy sent him an official letter of commendation both thanking Tuff for his vigilance and apologizing for his mistreatment at the hands of the navy—but without ever actually acknowledging those cases of fraud in the early 1980s.

Nor did the navy ever actually prosecute nor even officially reprimand a single officer accused in the fraud case.

In fact, that letter commending him actually makes Tuff mad. Particularly since it came two weeks after this man, who only wanted to serve his country, had to finally leave the military, finally drummed out and rendered ineffectual and unbelievable by the rumors and the insanity perceptions.

That letter makes him particularly mad when he's sitting there in a uniform that says... Jiffy Lube.

It wasn't the one he wanted to wear.

But in spite of Mike Tufariello's personal pain and suffering, he continues to fight for other "wounded eagles"— people who had given up. Mike continues to give something back. His medals of war rank second only to his badge of courage. He continues to receive hundreds of calls and letters from people seeking his assistance. His bravery is providing others with the strength to fight back.

PART III

THE HEALERS

IN THIS SEGMENT we will turn our focus to healers and helpers: those selfless people who sacrifice time, money, or, in some cases, an entire career just to help their fellow human beings live better lives.

The one thread common to all is that, whether the healing or the helping is a matter of medicine or money, it comes out of the goodness of their hearts—and creates more goodness wherever it is given.

Thomas Henderson, former football star
of the Dallas Cowboys

Hooray
For Hollywood

Thomas "Hollywood"
Henderson

WHEN PEOPLE HAVE HAD ENOUGH of the O.J. Simpson trial to make them choke, we leaven the loaf with Hollywood Henderson, the former and famous Dallas Cowboy who descended into a hell of sex, drugs, alcohol, and, finally, a prison sentence. Then by pure courage and commitment, he pulled himself out of his nightmarish spiral. Henderson, truly free of all his demons, is now helping thousands of others in prisons and recovery programs all around the country—and he's become a positive role model for some high-risk teens. An O.J. story—in reverse.

"I came from a real poor background. I was physically abused by my mother growing up. So I didn't feel real good about who I was."

Thomas grew up in a neighborhood in the shadows of the state capitol of Texas, where most dreams of a better life are distant—and where a child named Thomas grew up to be one of the most successful, and disgraced, athletes in professional sports.

Thomas Henderson has been politely described as a flamboyant, renegade football star during the glory days of the Dallas Cowboys, a defensive hero whose career and personal life hit a brick wall at a hundred miles an hour. A brick wall called alcohol and drug addiction.

Thomas Henderson speaks candidly about his painful past and his plan to single-handedly save the lives of others. "Hey, I've been to hell and back.

"I thought drinking and drugging and sex were what was happening. And when you look at somebody like Bob Bruenig, Roger Staubach, and Tom Landry, just to name a few, I didn't think they got the message. I thought they were square and crazy. And so in retrospect, I wanted everything Tom Landry had. And I resented him for having it and me not having it. So if he had it and I

195

didn't, maybe it was fake, phony, and fraud.

"I created my own world, if you will. Because after all of my troubles—of going to the penitentiary, and in spite of playing in three Super Bowls with the Cowboys—and all of my early success, I was a drug-addicted alcoholic and ended up locked up in jail. And I knew that the reason I went to prison was not because of what I was charged with, but because I was an alcoholic and addict.

"I have embarked upon probably my finest work. I am executive producer of a film called *Staying Sober and Staying Free*. You know, if people had told me in, say, 1977 when I was on top of my game as a Dallas Cowboy that I'd be producing a film for convitcts, I'd go, 'you're crazy.' And that's exactly what I'm doing. And I'm a real happy man today. I'm a nice man. That's what recovery and change have done to me. I've become the man I've always wanted to be. I resented Tom Landry when I played for him because I saw a nice man. I saw a Christian man. I saw a man with a family and respect, and I resented him because I didn't have that. I didn't have that inside, outside, or anywhere else. But today I understand it, and I got it."

We often think of people who have fame and fortune as having it all. But living life in the fast lane can be a very high price. And Thomas Henderson knows that all too well. However, he's convinced that others can learn from his mistakes.

"I want them to know that—in spite of their mistakes, in spite of their convictions, in spite of whatever wrongs they have committed—if alcohol and drugs had anyting to do with it, I want them to know that they don't have to live like that anymore. I want them to know that *they* are not their mistakes. *They* are not their disease. What they are is who they're going to become. You know, that's who Thomas Henderson is. I'm who I've become, I'm not who I was.

"I'm screaming out to the world that alcoholism is the number-one killer in the world. And I think God spared my life. You see, I got high with people like John Belushi and Marvin Gay. I got high with these men. And I got high like them. I used that kind of quantity. I did a lot of dope! And so I don't undersatnd why I'm alive."

Thomas is taking the message out of the prisons and onto the streets. The same streets where he began his own downward spiral years ago.

"See, I'm a drug addict. I'm a dope addict, period.

"I'm not concerned about who accepts me or rejects me. What's important is how I feel about me. See, what you feel about me or what you think about me is none of my business, because I am who I've become. I don't look back and get depressed and angry and sad. I look forward. I look ahead. And what I'm looking to do now is make a difference in convincts' lives. I'm out to let them know that Thomas Henderson has changed, and you can too. And the longer I'm sober, the more people are believing that boy, that man has really changed.

"I've played in three Super Bowls with the Dallas Cowboys, but you know what I'm in every day? The Sober Bowl. Every day. And I'm a winner every day. Every man and woman, boy and girl in America who is stuggling to say sober, or who is staying sober—those are my heroes. I've got a lot of them. A lot of people out there you know are staying sober a day at a time. And they don't live like that anymore. Those are my heroes, yeah."

I recently went to an important event for Thomas. It was a dinner and roast to celebrate his ten years of sobriety. All of the money raised was earmarked for his non-profit organization, whose mission is to serve the youth in the community who want to participate in educational and athletic-related activities. His first project is to restore Yellow Jacket stadium and track at old Anderson High School where he started his own career many years ago. And he decided to raise funds for his organization by hosting a fund-raiser celebrating his ten years of sobriety.

He invited many former football stars, including many former Dallas Cowboys. Thomas was worried that they wouldn't show. But they did: Tony Dorsett, Drew Pearson, Too-Tall Jones, Roger Staubach, Tom Landry, and many, many more. They were all there for Thomas Henderson.

"The only feasible way to think of this is to think that they might come to my funeral, and if they didn't come to my funeral, they may send condolences and sympathy. But for them to come here to celebrate ten years of a guy who really had a rough time, to come share my recovery with me, it's almost like—what else can happen, it doesn't get any better than this?" During the roast, many people from Thomas's past got the chance to remember him in their own ways.

Tom Landry: "I remember when Thomas and I had a few talks in the office, and I just didn't know what to do, to help him out, and I guess we ended up saying that we needed to get rid of him because we had no way to take care of him."

Roger Staubach: "I didn't know back then that his problems were chemically driven. Thomas has got the balance today because he's sober. And I'm proud to be part of his life."

Drew Pearson: "Thomas, I salute you, I applaud you, I respect you, and I'm proud of you. Remember... one day at a time."

It was an evening Thomas won't soon forget. The man had come full circle from the Super Bowl to the sober bowl. A man who, today, likes himself. And he'll gladly tell you that he's proudest of, not his glory days as a Cowboy, but his glory days as a sober man who is making a difference.

Thomas ended the evening with his own final thoughts, "And I say this prayer on a daily basis. It's dear to my heart, it's what I really mean, and it's my prayer to God—God, thank you for letting me laugh and smile again. But please, God, don't ever let me forget that I cried."

When I speak at schools and ask kids who their heroes are, I hear the names of sports stars and celebrities who are heralded by these young people for their wealth and status, as opposed to their accomplishments. I follow up with the story of my friend, Thomas Henderson—a real hero.

Melissa Poe, founder of
Kids for a Clean Environment

NATURE'S CHILD

MELISSA POE

EVER MEET SOMEONE WHO WAS A HERO—and you just knew that one day in the future, he or she would do something extraordinary again?

I'd bet the farm that one day down the road we'll be hearing about Melissa Poe again. And considering that she's only fourteen, we've heard a lot already.

Because Melissa is out to save the world, literally, and is doing a pretty good job of it already.

And in retrospect, I think that when our crews arrived at the Poe home, she was readier for us than we were for her.

She's a remarkably bright child—yet unlike so many "child prodigies," she is well rounded. Unimpressed with herself, but not overly impressed with anyone else, either.

Her attitude seemed to be, "Hmm... Gonna be on national TV. Well, if it will help the cause, that's fine. I've got a minute."

You also need to understand that her parents, while very nice and making a comfortable living, cannot account for that bright insightfulness that is so far beyond this young teenager's chronological years. Her thinking was very "adult." Not that she acted like an adult; I have seen many such children, and even with the best of them, it's role-playing and showing off, and it usually gives itself away as trying to act "serious."

Melissa didn't act at all serious—although she's up against some very serious problems that she takes very seriously.

You need to know that she started the whole shebang six years ago, when she was only nine. She decided to save the world.

It was a dark vision of the future that put Melissa Poe on her trek to get America to change, an episode of the late Michael Landon's "Highway to Heaven" series presenting a stark portrayal of the future consequences of global pollution: people forced by a dying atmosphere to wear gas masks. Water selling for $100 a gallon. People fighting and killing each other over the most basic necessities.

Nine-year-old Melissa Poe, of Nashville, Tennessee, watched that program.

"I was watching it while we were folding clothes. In the show, it said that unless people start paying attention, the environment may not be a place where our children can live."

Melissa explains it all matter-of-factly, but her mother says she was actually deeply upset and crying by the end of the show. She had wondered, Could it really happen? And she decided she didn't want to risk it. It hit her where she lived—or would live, someday, in that possible future thirty years up mankind's road.

Said her mom: "I think it was having felt the ugly realities of something like that that really terrified her, because she just really felt that might be what her future would be like."

Melissa interjects, "People who care will do something. And that's what made me get involved and made me want to help."

One frightened little girl, glimpsing a possible future and fearing for herself. A lot of little girls saw that program—but Melissa Poe decided to do something about it, to turn that fear into something positive. First, she wrote a letter to then-President George Bush.

> Dear Mr. President, please, will you do something about pollution? I want to keep on living until I am one hundred years old. I'm nine years old right now. Please, Mr. President, please, will you do something about pollution?

But that was only the beginning. Because Melissa Poe is not the kind of person who takes no for an answer— not even from the President. In fact, if Melissa Poe ever writes you a letter, you'd better write her back—or face the music. Just ask George Bush.

"I felt the President wouldn't listen to me because I was just a kid. So I decided to maybe go put up my own signs, with my letter to the President on it, so maybe he'd be able to see it anyway."

Things snowballed—no, avalanched—from that point. First of all, Melissa's mother was not particularly interested in staying up all night hand-lettering sign after sign after sign. As a matter of fact, Mrs. Poe realized that she'd be better off, time and trouble-wise, if she just paid for Melissa to rent a billboard for a few days. She figured that it would blow over.

Mom didn't have to pay for it, though. Because once Melissa called them and outlined her program, the Nashville sign company, Lamar Advertising, rather astutely realized that they had the makings of a barn-burner of a public relations campaign.

Up went the sign.

But then Melissa got to thinking some more.

"I was thinking, you know, the President doesn't actually go to Nashville all the time. So I thought it would be easier, maybe, if I put one up in Washington, D.C., too. So I asked Lamar Advertising and they gave me the name and phone number of someone in Washington. And I got a billboard up there, too."

And she got to thinking some more. If she could get one billboard for free, and then two... "So I called Outdoor Advertising Association of America."

Before you could say "spotted owl," the association had put up 250 signs all across America—and George Bush had missed a bet.

By then, she'd gotten the attention of the entire country—and the kids at her school.

"So that's when I decided that I wanted to start my club. So I started the club with six members, and we started doing things, planting trees, doing like smog detectors, just simple things that we all could do that would help. And maybe it was a few weeks later, I got my letter from the President. It was addressed to 'Dear Young Citizen,' and in the letter he was talking about drugs and how I shouldn't use them."

Which is of course true—but hardly germane to the point when it was a form reply to a girl who had managed to snowball an idea into a national campaign.

And snowball it most certainly did. Her club, Kids F.A.C.E. (Kids For A Clean Environment)—has grown from six members to an international organization 200,000 children strong, with a newsletter that goes to nearly two million people. And she's running the whole shebang out of some extra space in her father's office at home.

The world has recognized her, if Bush has not: She was only one of six children in the world to be invited to the Earth Summit.

"I was never trying to make it a big thing; I just stuck with it. I say, stick with whatever you are doing and you can make it big."

Melissa Poe is the kind of person you want on your team, not pulling against you. The world may still turn out the way it was depicted back then on "Highway to Heaven." But Melissa Poe can say she's done all she could to prevent it.

Melissa has learned—and by her example, teaches— that age is no barrier to action.

Melissa Poe proves something very important: There is nothing so big that you're too small to do something about it.

When a really good idea comes along, there's almost no stopping it. People want to help, and they will; in fact, whole corporations will get behind a really good one.

Oh, and George: Read my lips. Next time you're considering ignoring Melissa Poe, remember that it wouldn't be prudent.

Janet interviews Larry Jones, founder of
Feed the Children, with photographer Duane Conder.

PUTTING
MONEY WHERE
THEIR MOUTHS ARE

LARRY JONES

IT HAS GOTTEN TO A POINT where I don't even like for my nine-year-old daughter to watch the news. I've raised her to believe that most people are "good" in this world. And yet she sees the unrelentingly horrific sides of the Bosnias and Rwandas of the planet, true stories that are darkening an already too dark world. I want to show her another view—a prettier view. A good start might be a trip to meet Larry Jones, the man whose Feed the Children organization has fed those same starving people in Bosnia, and hundreds of thousands more all around the world.

Both his face and his ministry are all over the airwaves—Larry Jones and Feed the Children.

One unfortunate side effect of that kind of fund-raising is that some viewers associate him with the dark side of televangelism. And it's true that in televised appeals he has raised millions upon millions of dollars.

But all over America and the rest of the world, literally millions of impoverished people and disaster victims know the real truth about Larry Jones: He puts that money where their mouths are.

Jones was the first to realize something very, very important. He realized that while people might be intellectually aware of the fact that, yeah, there's hunger in the world, they wouldn't care enough until somebody put a face on that hunger—a child's face.

It all began with a nickel and a little boy. Jones was at a rally in Haiti, one of the world's poorest nations, when he was approached by a half-starved but friendly little boy who walked up to him and asked for a nickel.

At that point in time, Jones's home state of Oklahoma had more than 35,000,000 metric tons of wheat stored in its elevators as *surplus*.

Recalled Jones, "I thought, This is wrong. We've got all this wheat, and here's a child who doesn't even have a roll to eat, and he goes hungry all day, an hour and a half by air from the U.S."

Jones came back to the U.S. obsessed with telling that story to Americans. He told people in private. He told it from the pulpit. And he told it on his Oklahoma television show. Yes, it is depressing and sad, and it is also the truth. Jones was bent on showing America what he knew up close and personal—that millions are hungry, and hunger in the face of a world full of food was just plain wrong.

He wanted them to know that in this world, every day, 40,000 people (14,000,000 a year) die of hunger and malnutrition. That's twenty-eight a minute—and of those twenty-eight, twenty of them are children.

In the Third World the daily reality of hunger is a child going blind and eventually dying due to vitamin deficiency, or a child dying of diarrhea because he or she is so weakened by malnourishment. Depending on which year you choose, from anywhere between 12,000,000 and 26,000,000 Africans are actually at risk of dying of hunger and its resulting diseases.

And sadly, the description "Third World" is now applicable to many parts of the U.S.

America is by no means immune to the problem of hunger. Hungry faces of children peer out at us from the hollows of Appalachia, the sun-baked barrios and colonias of Texas, and the homeless shelters of our downtown cities. Hunger or undernourishment, defined as the lack of nutrition necessary to growth and health, affects nine percent of the U.S. population—20,000,000 Americans, 12,000,000 of them children. And in the South, where it affects them most, more than one fourth of the children in some states don't get enough nourishment.

Larry Jones wanted people not only to *know* about those people, but to see the children's faces.

And America has responded.

"Our phones went off the wall. Farmers called and gave me wheat, and the next thing you know, a trucker called and said, I'll truck it to Miami... since that time, we've not been able to keep up with it."

That was in 1979. Since then, Larry Jones and his Feed the Children organization have learned many things, but perhaps the most important thing is this: "I think one of the unique things about Feed the Children is we don't know a wrong way to feed a hungry child. We've discovered that so many people have ideas about how we can better help hungry children in our world."

Larry Jones is quick to say that while Feed the Children may have started with Larry Jones and a little boy on a Haitian street corner, the American public is the real hero.

"One of the things we've discovered about Americans is that they want to be a part of something. We discovered that when there's a disaster, that most people want to be a part of it. They say, 'Would you send a truck our way? Because we'll fill it up.'"

Nobody is more amazed at the success of Feed the Children than Jones himself.

"I didn't go to college to do this. I didn't have a mentor; we just jumped in and started. And I guess you might say we're still in the school of hard knocks and we're still learning. I guess that's the other thing. We're not ashamed to say that there's probably a better way to do this than we're actually doing it.

"But the thing that brings me back to earth is at any moment the phone can ring and somebody can call with the biggest project that we've ever witnessed, and we're not afraid to tackle that project."

While Jones will say again and again that if there's one absolute right way to feed children, nobody's told him about it, one thing people soon learn about him is that, right or wrong, Jones is rigorously and thoroughly honest.

The amount of money passing through the hands of Feed the Children is impressive—nearly $100,000,000 in 1993. But the amount of scrutiny Jones not only allows but invites is equally impressive.

"With the scandals that've gone on in the charitable world, so many people really wonder what happens to the product as well as the money. So, we'd like for you to walk with us, and we'll let you walk as much as you want to. In fact, we'll let you roll up your sleeves and be part of the actual process of putting things on the truck."

Less than four percent of that $100,000,000 is used to fund administrative costs, with the huge remainder going for child care and feeding, medical care, relief, and development.

Barely six percent goes to fund-raising. The reason that that portion of Feed the Children's overhead is so low is pretty simple. Jones gets by with a little help from his friends—and some are pretty well known. Jones has shown a strong inclination to involve showbiz types in his crusade, and they in turn warm to the idea of using their fame to help others.

He's collaborated with Garth Brooks, the Oak Ridge Boys, John Conlee, Randy Travis, Ricky Van Shelton, and others to raise both money and food for the hungry.

One of the biggest of these came when Waylon Jennings, Johnny Cash, and Kris Kristofferson got together to perform in Texas as The Highwaymen—and instructed their fans to bring canned goods. Jones and his volunteers filled two semitrailer trucks.

It was the same story with Garth Brooks at the biggest concert in Texas history. Garth Brooks sold out for three straight nights, 65,000 people per night: Every night, Jones and his volunteers were sacking up the goodies.

The famous want to do more than merely be famous during their lifetimes. They want to cast shadows that last longer than their lifetimes, and Jones provides them with that opportunity.

"The Oak Ridge Boys said they wanted to do a concert for us. They did it in Nice, France, and gave us $40,000. And they said, you do with the money whatever you want. So we started four water wells in Kenya, and we named a well after each one of them. So I said to them, 'Now, when you wonder what happened to your $10,000, you can go to Kenya and, out there in the middle of the desert, there's going to be a water well with your name on it.

"One of the things that I say to people who want to work with Feed the Children is we're willing to do it any way that you want to do it. We were down in Baton Rouge, Louisiana, and I had Randy Travis and Ricky Van Shelton, who are two top country stars, and I mean it was hot, it was humid, and there we were in a warehouse taking food off a truck. Many people were astounded that these two guys were actually out there, and they were working."

But the true heroes of the Feed the Children story aren't the celebrities, but the people who respond—not always with the big checks and the huge donations, but with whatever they have. Because whatever you have, it can be used. Whatever it is, someone needs it.

As Jones put it, "There is so much product in America that is not being used, and I tell people all the time, whether it's a corporation or a small business, please don't throw anything away. We've got so many people who are hurting. We've got so many families where the husband and wife are both working, making the minimum wage, with no benefits, and when you put a pencil to that, it's hard to pay the rent and feed the children. And if they hit any what I call bumps in the road, anything that happens all of a sudden, they're sinking, and they're sinking fast.

"And so what we try to tell people is, whatever you have, Feed the Children will put it to use, whether it's bottled water for a flood or it's Starter jackets for kids who don't have coats, or Nike and Reebok shoes for children who don't have tennis shoes, we'll take those seconds, or we'll take your overruns, we'll take your surplus, and we'll get it to people who really need it."

Jones and his Feed the Children teams respond to natural disasters. And they respond to depressed economic conditions both at home and abroad. But perhaps where they count the most are in those places where it is man's inhumanity to his fellow man that has gotten out of balance. It's in places like these that Jones has put even more than your money where their mouths are; he has, a time or two, been willing to lay his life on the line, in places like Bosnia.

"I've been afraid on more than one occasion. I've gone in behind the war zones many times. I guess my greatest fear is going into countries where I know that people really do not like Americans, and sometimes they want to take Americans hostage. I think that the thing probably that touched me the most is when I recently went to Bosnia."

People were reading at the time about all the food and supply convoys that were getting turned back—but Jones, a veteran of such situations, is an expert at getting through. The food *does* get where it is supposed to go in most cases.

"I knew ours were getting through, because we were sending small trucks, two and three at a time. We've sent in over ten million pounds since the war began. But there's only one way to *know* it's getting through, and that's to put on a helmet, a bulletproof vest, and go right in the middle of a war. That was the first time that I went right into the middle of a war. I mean, we took mortar fire, we took machine gun fire, we took sniper fire. We were under the auspices of the British troops, who were actually UN troops, and we went right in. Shells were actually popping, you know, less than a hundred yards from where we were, plus we were within three blocks of machine gun fire.

"For people to get food, they had to come out of their houses, and one place we delivered, the day before, a man was shot. I visited in the hospital with a fourteen-year-old girl who caught a bullet in the collarbone, and it was still in her.

"We were standing out there knowing that at any moment a shell, machine gun fire, or a sniper's bullet could take us out, handing this food to those people. We're saying to Americans, We're not going to give you any fluff. Yes, a bullet may hit me and I could be killed right here, but I want you to know something. We are serious about feeding the children, because, number one, they didn't ask to be born; number two, they didn't ask to be in a war-torn area; and number three, if they're born in poverty in America, they didn't ask for that either. And so I think it's our responsibility to help the next generation."

Jones pauses here, a little amazed even himself at the

depth and the strength of his commitment to feeding the hungry.

"I will die in the ditch, and that's where I want to die. I want to die with my hands being dirty with the problems of people who are trying to crawl out of that ditch. I want to help people out of that ditch."

It's a very *big* ditch. It circles the world, from Haiti to Somali, from Bosnia to Rwanda to Ethiopia.

And even when personal danger is not a factor, Jones and his staff and volunteers must still face the heartbreak of human tragedy on a monstrous scale.

"Probably my worst days were four days in a row when I went to the Ethiopian famine. The first day there was Thanksgiving Day 1984, and sixty-seven people died. The next day seventy-four died. This is a little village that set out to be 3,000 people, and it ended up being 27,000 people. The next day, something like eighty-seven died. The last day I was there of four days, ninety-one died. I had never seen anything like that. That was hunger at its worst. I've held the dying child, and then I've held the mother whose child it was. And so when I do get emotional—and I try not to—it is because I know what hunger does. And so I just say to people, if you walk the road that I walk, if you'll come with me, together we may not feed the whole world, but right now we're going to feed that child right over there. And over there... "

Jones is not only a hero. He's a man who offers the rest of us a chance to be heroes as well.

As Congressman Mickey Leland said a few weeks before he died in a plane crash during a fact-finding mission to Ethiopia:

"This pluralistic nation has a common moral vision, a covenant with God, if you will. It calls us to a universal challenge—feeding the hungry of the world.

"The struggle is in our history and our hearts. We can no longer allow petty selfishness and fear to confine the immensity of our compassion. We are at our best when we no longer endure injustice, when we take the moral high road, when we see the world as one family."

That is what Larry Jones and Feed the Children is really all about.

The success of the organization in meeting its goals—feeding hungry people and meeting other basic human needs in war-torn areas, following disasters, and in other tragic circumstances—has been phenomenal. Jones, a quietly friendly and unostentatious man, is perhaps the nation's premier expert on the problems and logistics of hunger.

He can tell us, after all, how easy it is for them to be helped and how little is required of each of us.

Before I left Oklahoma, Larry reminded me that he is not the "hero" of this story—that the true heroes are the people who respond to those in need—not always with the big checks and the huge donations, but with whatever they have.

The Orbis plane that travels the world
giving sight to the blind

A PLANE FULL
OF MIRACLES

PROJECT ORBIS

IN TELEVISION WORK you soon learn to see and think visually—less in words and more in pictures.

Words and ideas are of course indispensable in carrying a story and must be included, but for the story to really be powerful, the images at its core have to be powerful as well.

There were powerful images in our segment on Orbis: images of a big jumbo jet cutting through clouds and blue sky as it circles the earth, almost ceaselessly.

Images of the world's teeming millions in India, China, Latin America; images of grinding Third World poverty.

Images of doctors, of surgeries, of children.

But the central irony of Orbis and our images can only be expressed in words: Until that plane came, most of the people in the countries it visited could not see any image at all, our telecast nor any other, for they were blind.

With a little creative thinking, we can imagine some of what it must be like to be blind.

Imagine knowing that the sun has set only because the air is cooler.

Imagine that "green" is only the way the world smells after it rains.

Imagine that you have never laid eyes on a child, or a tree, or a sunset, or a rainbow.

Imagine that you know storms only by their thunder and your loved ones only by their voices and the way they feel.

The sad and shocking truth is that forty-two million people in this world don't need to imagine it at all, because they are blind.

Even more shocking is the fact that two-thirds of the world's blindness is unnecessary: Nearly thirty million more people could see again if only they could be treated with modern technology.

What we cannot readily imagine is what it is like to be blind in the underdeveloped, impoverished nations.

The blind there live lives of unending darkness, either as beggars or throwing themselves upon the kindness of already hard-pressed families; families who may not have much kindness left to give. Blindness is a death sentence in many of these countries.

The Orbis jet is not just any airplane; this plane is special. People around the world are praying for miracles, and this American plane brings them, all around the world, on an almost daily basis.

It quite literally brings sight to the blind, and the number of people who cannot see is growing smaller every day, thanks to this DC-10 and the caring men and women aboard it.

The name, Project Orbis, is an appropriate one. In Latin, *orbis* means "of the eye"; in Greek, it means "around the world." Orbis, a nonprofit organization based in New York, is bringing sight to eyes around the world. In fact, this American plane seldom ever comes home.

Eye by eye, person by person, Afghanistan to Zimbabwe, Angola to Zaire, Orbis is restoring vision everywhere it lands.

It first began roaming the globe in 1982, and during its first ten years it restored sight to nearly twelve thousand people eye by eye, patient by patient, country by country.

But perhaps as important as the surgeries are the people who are observing the operations as they are performed—the doctors and nurses of the impoverished nations Orbis serves.

Because while Orbis does restore sight in its operating rooms, its premier function is educational, and, over time, that is the function that will have the more far-reaching effects.

As the surgeons perform the surgeries, other doctors monitor the operations' progress—and learn the techniques—by watching a closed circuit television in the cabin of the plane. They can also ask the doctors questions as they operate, via a two-way intercom.

The ophthalmologists, doctors, and nurses aboard

Orbis are all unpaid volunteers, taking vacation time to serve Orbis.

The pilots are also volunteers, who are either retired or taking time off from their airline jobs, as are many of the other members of the fifty-person crew which travels with the plane.

It's hard work; the minute the plane touches down, the staff hits the ground running. They must convert the plane from a more or less traditional flying configuration into what amounts to an instant hospital, complete with operating rooms, examination areas, recovery areas, and an observation lounge for the country's visiting doctors.

One sad aspect of working for Orbis: The volunteers know that while many patients are called, few are chosen. During an Orbis visit, the country witnesses what could be considered a pilgrimage of the blind. Blind people converge from all across the country, sometimes traveling hundreds of miles under arduous circumstances in hopes of being among the blessed ones. Orbis workers sometimes find themselves overwhelmed, with as many as five hundred people—often with their doctors in tow—coming to be treated by Orbis.

One of these, when Orbis traveled to Managua, Nicaragua, was Alejandra, a thirteen-year-old girl who had been blinded by an untreated corneal infection in one of Nicaragua's remoter villages. The infection, plus a poor diet, combined to produce opaque scars on Alejandra's cornea—perhaps the commonest cause of blindness in the Third World.

She had been abandoned by her mother and left in the care of her elderly grandmother. That's not unusual in the poorer countries, where life is an unending struggle to survive.

Alejandra was lucky because she had someone who would take care of her. She once told her grandmother as her sight declined that she dreaded going blind because it meant she would never see her grandmother again. And every day thereafter, Alejandra's grandmother prayed for a miracle.

The miracle came when Orbis came to Managua. Alejandra's physician, Dr. Delgado, had heard of the program and thought the Orbis doctors might accept her as a teaching case.

She and her grandmother made the long journey to Managua and joined the other patients in their tense vigil, waiting to learn who would be among the lucky ones. Finally, her name was called.

Orbis doctors determined that one eye could not be saved, but there was hope for the other one—but only if they performed a corneal transplant. And that required a donor. Finally a suitable donor was found through the eye bank—the cornea of a crack addict who died in New York.

As doctors watched on the closed-screen TV—and Alejandra's grandmother watched on another screen in the rear of the plane—Alejandra got her cornea.

And a few days later, her sight.

Alejandra was very lucky, however—as is every patient actually treated by Orbis. Because Orbis takes only those cases that will be instructive to the local doctors, which Orbis hopes will continue the sight-saving work. So during an average visit to a country, only thirty or so of the hundreds trying will get through Orbis's screening to actually receive sight-restoring treatment.

The Orbis volunteers are saddened that they cannot possibly reach all of any one country's blind—much less the world's.

But they take consolation in the fact that perhaps now the country's own doctors will be able to restore vision to these poor people.

And there are other rewards.

In spite of the heat, the long hours, the often-uncomfortable lodgings, and the time away from their families, one smile makes it all worthwhile.

There is no gratitude like that of a man who can work once again to feed his family because his eyesight has been restored, or a woman who can once again care for her children.

There is nothing to compare with the look of wonder in the eyes of a child who is seeing for the first time—or who was afraid that she'd never see again. And in the face of a grandmother, whose prayers were answered.

Orbis is bringing vision and hope to the world with a plane full of miracles. Eye by eye, person by person, Orbis is restoring vision. Because of their educational sight-saving skills, more than six million people have been touched by this program. They carry with them the gift of sight and a dream with no boundaries.

There is a way for you to help, of course, to be a hero as well. No, you don't have to give vast sums of money, or any money at all to Orbis. And no, you don't have to fly with them on these grueling but rewarding journeys around the world.

You don't have to do a single thing until the day you die, other than sign the back of your driver's license on the line authorizing use of your corneal tissue. There are thirty million other people who can use it when you are through.

Grandma Sadie hot air ballooning in
Phoenix, Arizona, after a day with residents
at the Valley of the Sun School

ACCEPTING THE CHALLENGED

GRANDMA SADIE

PEOPLE WHO WORK IN TELEVISION all have something in common: they are prone to succumbing to arrogance and believing their own press releases. All of us fight it most of the time, and all of us lose some of the time.

Such was the case with the woman everybody calls Grandma Sadie. We had rented equipment, hired a crew, and advanced expense money so that "Unsung Heroes" could go to Phoenix and follow her as she made her appointed rounds through the course of a typical day in her volunteer work at Valley of the Sun School.

At the start of the day, she was merely indifferent. She stomped past us with barely a word as she rushed to greet the new arrivals as they got off the school's bus.

The cameraman, the sound man, and I continued to follow her about the school. She barely said three words to us the whole time, answering our questions with only the most terse yes or no. By midmorning, she was downright irritated. Well before noon, she was downright hostile. The eighty-five-year-old Romanian lady looks small, until she gets angry, and then she looms remarkably large. Hoping to defuse the tension, I finally persuaded her to take a break and asked her what was the problem.

She summoned what little restraint yet remained to her and said:

"You... are... getting... in... my... WAY! What I do here is IMPORTANT! This television business is NOT, and it is preventing me from doing what I do. Which IS important."

Oh. Apparently Grandma Sadie didn't know who we think we are.

She was right. We were wrong. We backed way, way off. We got out of her way. We gave her plenty of room to move and thereafter tried as hard as possible to be just large-ish "flies on the wall."

Because what Sadie Tomy does *is* important. Very important.

Grandma Sadie loves people. She's been doing it day in, day out, missing not even one day in her fourteen years as an unpaid volunteer at the Valley of the Sun School and Habilitation Center. The reason she won't miss a single day is simple: These people need her love almost desperately. Many don't get it anywhere else.

And to these damaged and underdeveloped minds, there is no real sense of time. So a day and a moment is a now and forever. Come hell or high water, Grandma Sadie is determined to be there for them. She spends eight to ten hours a day reading, singing, talking to, and caring for the most severely disabled of the school's "students."

There's Ricky, an Apache man. He loves her, and shows it the only way he can—by looking at her, smiling, and saying "Aaaah, aaaah." These are the only words he's said to anyone in his life. That sound, Sadie knows, is only for her—and so she takes him in her arms and rocks him until he dozes off.

Then there is Diane, a profoundly retarded woman in her early forties. Diane doesn't talk either—until Sadie enters the room. Then she begins to smile, and Diane begins excitedly calling out to Grandma Sadie.

Grandma Sadie had had a long and fulfilling working life, serving as cashier in the snazzy Blackstone Hotel in Chicago. If that sounds boring, keep in mind that she met Presidents Truman, Nixon, and Kennedy in that capacity, which may explain why she wasn't nearly as impressed with us as we were.

She'd raised a child and now has two grandchildren and a great grandchild, but after retiring, felt unfulfilled—and even more so after her husband died in 1972.

That was when she decided she still had something to offer the world—and she soon found out the world had something more to offer her as well. Keeping this schedule and level of activity has kept her younger than her years. "I don't have time to get bored or sick," she said. "What would these people do?"

The hard part for us, in fact, wasn't in giving her distance. It was in keeping up with her.

The school itself is the result of a dream of Mrs. Bernie Kussell, a hero in her own right. She had worked in the Arizona State Hospital but decided that more needed to be done for the afflicted and handicapped children.

Hard to say what motivates one to go the extra mile. It may have been moments like the one Mrs. Kussell later wrote about, probably pertaining to one of the children in the state hospital.

"'Mommy, did you born me?' I looked down at little Sue as she leaned heavily on her crutches. Her eyes were pleading with me to tell her that she was my own little girl. Several of the other children were crowding around, waiting for my answer.

"I knelt down and drew the little crippled child close to me. 'Darling, I am the only mommy you have ever known, but I didn't "born" you.'"

Bernice Kussell fell in love with the children, and observing that there were no truly appropriate facilities for mentally challenged children, began taking a few home with her. Before long, she was realizing that the large family for which she had often prayed was coming together in a strange and wonderful way.

In 1947, with nothing more than hope, faith, and a belief in a better life for the retarded, her "family" kept growing until, in 1951, she founded the nonprofit Valley of the Sun School and, a few years later, the Bernice Kussell Group home in Phoenix.

She was also something of a poet, and this poem of hers describes her philosophy and the efforts of the school—to take the handicapped and help them to help themselves become self-sufficient:

Put him away, the people said,
He will never earn his daily bread.
He doesn't know the way to go,
His mind is dull, his speech is slow.
There's no place for such as he,
Put him away, and let him be.
But from the crowd a Master came,

Who took his hand and called his name.
Then day by day with patient care,
He taught him how to work and share.
Back to the crowd he came one day
To his place and to them did say:
"Give me work that my hands might do;
I can mow your grass or fix your shoe.
A thousand jobs I do today,
Thanks to the Master's patient way.
Oh let it never again be said
That I cannot earn my daily bread."

The work of Mrs. Kussell lives on in Grandma Sadie and the efforts of the staff and other volunteers at Valley of the Sun, which got a major shot in the arm in 1990 when yet another hero was added to the piece.

Valley of the Sun was in serious trouble when George Elliott took over as executive director in 1990. He had only been there a month, and the school was facing having to ask for bankruptcy protection from its creditors and to protect its fleet of leased vans.

If it weren't for Elliott, neither the center nor Grandma Sadie would be there: It was Elliott who initiated belt-tightening measures that saved it—including cutting annual employee expenses by half a million dollars, a move that made volunteers like Grandma Sadie all the more crucial to its success.

Says Elliott: "Grandma Sadie was here when I got here, out there helping unload clients every morning, pushing them up the wheelchair ramps, talking to them one on one, socializing with them. The students here become her family, and she settles for nothing less than a daily routine of making their dreams come true."

"She knows how important it is to be here on a day to day basis. She knows these people are important, and she knows that she has to be able to keep on taking care of them. She loves the people she works with. They are, in her eyes, her kids. They'd be at a loss without their daily time with Grandma. Everyone looks for her to be here. She means so much to the Valley of the Sun."

While the majority of Valley of the Sun's two hundred

clients can be habilitated and, with training, can find a productive life either independently in the community or in one of Valley of the Sun's sheltered workshop operations, Sadie gets the worst cases to oversee. Some are vegetative; about all she can do is turn them every fifteen minutes and hope that some beam of her love and concern gets through the mangled cables to the captured souls inside.

But for the others, the ones who are slightly better off, she gives love and gets it in return. She is their friend, their parent, their teacher, and their protector.

As Sadie put it: "They need me, and I need them. If it weren't for Valley of the Sun, these people would be hidden away so nobody could see them, put in the attic and maybe fed a little bit. Being here helping them makes me feel good. It keeps me young. Well... not young, but able."

On one of our reels of "Unsung Heroes" videotape, there's a shot of Grandma Sadie. With her, as she walks about the campus, is one of her charges, a young man who is ambulatory but profoundly retarded; he has to hold on to her the whole time.

His daily walk with Grandma Sadie is not only the high point of his day, but the focus of his life. It is why she is fiercely determined to be there, day in, day out.

It is sort of a dramatic, emotional-looking shot. There they are, in the middle distance, content to be privately isolated in a world of their own.

I wish that it had been my idea—but the sequence was not intentionally shot that way.

It merely reflected Grandma Sadie's stern admonition that we had better stay out of her way and keep our distance.

As a mother, I guess I should have known... Woe betide the person who tries to come between a mother and her children.

Bobby Dotson and Cassie

THE POWER
OF LOVE

BOBBY DOTSON

IN 1991 I HEARD ABOUT A MAN who cared for a little child who was not only handicapped, but also HIV positive. As a mother, I was particularly touched by his story in a way I cannot fully explain. I was in the process of putting together my new television show about people who make a difference—people who make our world a better place to live in. I knew Bobby would be the perfect subject for my first show.

I contacted Bobby. He was nice to me on the phone, but not particularly receptive to having a story done about him. He said that he didn't consider himself a hero. I asked if I could meet him and Cassie the next time he came to Dallas, and he said okay. So my daughter Bethany and I went to meet Bobby and Cassie that weekend.

I watched Bobby with Cassie. There is a magic that happens when the two of them are together. I can honestly say that I've never seen a person more dedicated to a child. He spends hour after hour with her, totally immersed in her. That day Bobby did not spend much of his time or attention on us. He was not at all interested in publicity. He was there to visit Cassie. We were along for the ride. And what a ride it was.

Here's Bobby's story: Ten-year-old Cassie has seen a lot of doctors in her life, and many of those doctors never imagined that the little girl would still be around. She's not only still around, she's thriving, learning, and growing—largely because of Bobby Dotson. He is no relation whatsoever to Cassie. Just a man who has spent the last several years fighting for a little girl it seemed that nobody loved.

Dotson, a former policeman who now works on offshore oil rigs, had heard about Cassie from a secretary at his credit union. She'd told him the sad story of a little girl who was living in the hospital who seldom had visitors.

"This thing started when I overheard a conversation about a little girl who had lost her will to live. That's what caught my attention. And it seemed this little girl, Cassie, was in the hospital. No one ever came to see her, and she had just given up. And it just touched me in a way that I decided that I would go see the child," said Bobby.

Cassie was born almost without a fighting chance. Her mother, an unwed sixteen-year-old, couldn't possibly care for a child as sick as Cassie. She was born prematurely with enormous physical problems and needed constant medical attention just to survive.

Deaf, mute, almost totally blind, with life-threatening heart and lung difficulties and diagnosed HIV positive after a blood transfusion, she's been called an AIDS orphan. While just an infant, her home, her entire existence became a bed at a Galveston hospital. Bobby Dotson became Cassie's only regular visitor. He came once, and kept coming. "I would come there every night and stay with her. She began to grow and pick up weight."

Divorced and the father of two grown children, himself an orphan who had been given up for adoption, Bobby felt an intense concern for this lonely and unwanted little girl.

He decided that it was no more than his duty as a human being to make sure the little girl knew she had a friend, and he called the hospital to tell them that he would be visiting her. He knew the second he entered the room that they were bonded for life—however short that little life might be.

A nurse in the room when Bobby first met Cassie said to him at the time, "I knew you were coming. I knew God was sending someone to take care of this child. I've been waiting for you." Dotson didn't let God or the nurse down. And he'd die before he'd let Cassie go unloved.

He started dropping by the hospital after work every evening in spite of his long hours as an offshore oil rig worker. And during the next two years, he never missed a night, bringing her a gift of toys or clothes and always a hug and a kiss, and then, weather permitting, taking her out of the hospital for a stroll in her carriage. He often stayed with her in her room until midnight. Suddenly, poignantly, there was somebody there for Cassie.

Dotson kept almost religiously to his routine, loving a child of whom most people were now only deathly afraid because of the virus she carried. He wore rubber gloves when he changed her, but he refused the surgical gown and mask because it would have placed a barrier between him and Cassie. Cassie needed a friend. Cassie needed what any child needs: Kisses and hugs and soft talk. And anyway, Bobby Dotson, a big tough-looking hombre of a man, is not very much afraid of *anything*, which led to the next round of troubles.

Bobby Dotson doesn't merely love Cassie. He's also her champion and advocate.

Some hospital workers and state personnel say he's done too good a job of it. Others are more blunt. They say he's a pain in the butt.

If he felt that Cassie wasn't getting her diapers changed often enough while at the hospital, he'd make that very clear to staffers. Startlingly clear, some say. He demanded that she not be kept in isolation. In fact, Bobby just wanted to make sure Cassie received the best of care.

Cassie and Bobby's bond continued to strenghten until the day they moved Cassie to a facility in Dallas, more than 200 miles away, and Bobby's world came crashing down.

"When they decided to take her to Dallas, I'm sure they intended to move me out of the picture altogether and break the bond. In fact, they talked about breaking the bond between Cassie and me."

Perhaps some of the experts in charge of Cassie's well-being found it hard to understand the unusual bond that had developed between Bobby, the complete stranger, and Cassie, the little girl with so many problems. Desperate to keep Cassie in Galveston, Bobby hired a lawyer, and the fight for what was best for Cassie became a court battle.

His first legal battle began when he filed suit to stop the state from sending her to a foster home in Dallas called Bryan's House and tried to force the hospital to accept responsibility for Cassie's care permanently. Dotson was adamant. His take was that the hospital in Galveston was her home; she didn't know anything else. He felt that since UTMB-Galveston had given her AIDS, she should be able to stay there.

Attorney Tim Beeton agreed to take Bobby Dotson's case but refused to accept one penny in payment. Tim explained, "Here's a fellow who's given up so much of himself. He's given up mountains of his own time, given of himself so freely, and he is being shut out of the decision-making process about this child. He needed legal help.

"He doesn't qualify under any of the normal legal headings. He's not an adoptive parent, he's not a natural parent, he's not a grandparent."

Bobby and Tim soon found out that their struggle wouldn't be easy. Family codes and state laws weren't written for children in Cassie's shoes. Tim Beeton spent hundreds of hours pouring through past cases, and time after time he and Bobby were defeated in the courtrooms. "I lost every hearing, including the one in the court of appeals. From a technical, legal standpoint, I lost them all," said Tim.

Bobby added, "I would have adopted Cassie and taken her home then if I could have been certain that I would have been able to have somebody with her when I couldn't be there. I was often working sixteen hours a day." Bobby also had concerns about her health care, because his medical benefits would never cover her many needs.

Every attempt to keep Cassie in Galveston failed. Bobby lost the suit, and CPS moved Cassie to Bryan's House in Dallas.

The suit had angered Child Protective Service officials. It had been, perhaps, a tactical error, but Bobby's heart had been in the right place. Said Dotson: "They wouldn't allow me to see her the last day, not even to say goodbye. I wanted to bring her to Dallas on the plane, but they wouldn't let me."

In Dallas, at Bryan's House, a special home for children with AIDS, worse trouble awaited. They'd already heard about Bobby Dotson and his determined advocacy for

Cassie, and they were determined to prevent a repeat of his pain-in-the-butt behavior. They restricted his visits to one a month, and to further snarl him, since he was a working man, they decreed that it had to be on a weekday.

Dotson raised such a stink that the case was referred to a mediator, and thanks to a preliminary injunction pending the state's final ruling, Dotson received a bit more access to Cassie for a while. His desperate struggle seemed to finally be opening the eyes of the court system. In the intervening three months that he was not allowed to see her, Dotson says, "Cassie never forgot me."

But the officials in charge of her custody at Bryan's House haven't forgotten Bobby Dotson, either, and probably never will.

"She knows that every weekend I'm coming to see her. There will be no doubt that I will be there. She waits for me to be there."

Tim added, "It'll give you religion, if you don't have any, to meet people like Bobby and see the way he relates to that child."

Cassie, the little girl born with everything against her. The little girl it seemed nobody wanted. Her survival alone is astonishing. Family codes and state laws, it seems, were written without considering the Bobby Dotsons of this world. He's just a man struggling to make a living, but more important, struggling to help a young friend named Cassie keep living.

"I want Cassie to be all that she can be. I want her to experience all the nice things in life that she can. I just wish so much that she could have a normal life and grow up to be healthy and happy. That would be my greatest wish in this world. I won't realize it, I'm sure; it can't happen. But that's what I would wish for," said Bobby.

Cassie, now ten, has full-blown AIDS. And she spends her days waiting to catch a blurred glimpse of a familiar bearlike shape. Waiting, in fact, for just about the only good thing she has going for her in her young, blind, deaf, and dark life: Bobby Dotson, Cassie's best friend. The good news is, she couldn't ask for a better one.

In the last five years, the sixty-year-old former policeman has spent nearly $40,000 on airfare and hotel rooms, flying back and forth from Houston to Dallas every weekend to be at Cassie's side.

The bad news is, the state of Texas and others have tried over and over again to stop him. Dotson has fought a valiant and expensive battle to remain at the side of this terribly unfortunate little girl, to give her, in her lonely and perhaps terrifying little life, a hand to hold, a shoulder to cry on, and someone who will hug her.

At Bryan's House, Cassie's life took a sharp turn for the worse, and so did Dotson's war with the bureaucracy.

Stephanie Held was the woman who built Bryan's House. And she brought more than professionalism to the kids; she, like Dotson, brought them love. Every morning she would not begin her official work until she had picked up and hugged every child in the establishment at least once.

And though she had had some initial clashes with Bobby Dotson, she soon realized that whatever it was he was doing for Cassie and however much it might irritate the staff, it couldn't be denied that it was working. Her initial resentment of him slowly turned to admiration, if for nothing more than his incredible consistency and determination to see that Cassie got the very best care humanly possible and for his willingness to stake everything he had to see that she got it.

Stephanie Held herself had the children's best interests at heart. That seems to have been her undoing. The Bryan's House AIDS children got all their medical treatment at a local children's hospital where they were reportedly often forced to wait with other, non-AIDS children for the one doctor the hospital had assigned to them, a doctor with a large pre-existing caseload of his own. She objected and complained to members of the board at the children's hospital, but they refused to make changes. She went next to Parkland Hospital, where the director gave her everything she wanted. But when she severed ties with the children's hospital, costing it tens of thousands of dollars in federal aid, it also cost her a federal pediatrics demonstration grant for Bryan's House.

Held had weighed the pros and cons and had decided that they were better off without the money if it meant a better standard of health care for the kids. But her own board apparently didn't agree. Reportedly, under pressure from the children's hospital, the Bryan's House board asked for Stephanie's resignation.

In came the new management philosophy and a lot of "new ideas." Here, Dotson says, entered a new director—and the exact opposite of the woman who founded it, Stephanie Held.

"They loved me at first," Dotson said, "until I started asking questions. Now they fear me worse than death. They don't want anyone to know what's going on there."

Soon after the new staff came on board, Dotson came to the conclusion that Bryan's Place was pushing Cassie too hard to be independent. Nurses insisted she change her own diapers, though she is uncoordinated and would cry helplessly when her bottom was wet.

Especially troubling to Dotson was the fact that they took away all of Cassie's "comfort objects," the many soft dolls, blankets, and other items Dotson had been bringing her steadily over the years. They refused to let her have them except at bedtime, saying it was to "encourage interaction with other children"; never mind that Cassie is deaf and blind.

Dotson says the harder they pushed, the more distressed she became. He says one night he found her curled up on the floor of a closet, terrified and crying in the dark.

The situation came to a boil in the summer of 1993 when Dotson formally accused Bryan's House of abuse after a handful of workers there told him that nurses at Bryan's House had instructed them to hurt Cassie. Dotson was not alone in alleging serious problems at Bryan's House. Several former workers sent letters to a former Dallas city councilman who was chairing a committee that controls federal AIDS funds in Dallas County, a substantial sum of which supports Bryan's House.

Of the four witnesses who Dotson supplied to CPS to support his allegations, only one was interviewed by a caseworker and only after Dotson, in frustration, brought the witness to CPS offices in Dallas and insisted that an investigator talk to her. It seems the state was dying to look the other way when it came to Cassie and Bryan's House.

CPS visited Bryan's House and "determined" that Dotson's allegations were inconclusive. But they did take action—against Dotson. Dotson was forbidden to set foot in Bryan's House, or even on the land on which it sits. On his visits to Dallas, he had to hire an intermediary to pick Cassie up to meet him on neutral territory.

Officials there were very tired of talking about the trouble Dotson and the others had caused them. The new management dismissed Dotson as a disruptive and meddlesome force at the facility and said the concerns of others were largely motivated by "nostalgia for the way Bryan's House used to be." Amen: "It used to be pretty nice. There used to be a lot of love there. Sad, how good ideas turn into good projects—and then sometimes decay into bureaucracies."

In predictable official jargon, the new administration told the press: "...It changed from a medical model to a child-development model. A medical model is where a child is sick and a person tries to normalize the child's life in the middle of medical management. We found that the medical model didn't work as well. In a child development model, whether a child is sick or well, the kids are getting the kinds of things they need to develop socially, intellectually, and physically."

Well, I got to witness both models personally. I met both directors and some board members—and I have to say that I saw a big difference in the care given to the children. I wouldn't allow my child to stay at the latter model. And I know that I was not popular there, either, because I decided to stand up for Bobby Dotson. When Bobby came to me for help, I put him in contact with state officials who cared, with media contacts who could help him get his message out. I even wrote a letter to a judge about allowing him visitation. Bobby Dotson taught me the importance of sticking out our necks to do the right thing.

Bobby Dotson and others allege that Cassie and the other children were being warehoused, apparently by people who just plain didn't care: One health-care worker at Bryan's House reported that one night last year she heard Cassie screaming, went to her room, turned on the light, and found the little girl covered with red ants, biting her all over her body. This health-care worker said she tried to wake the woman who was night nurse at the time; she didn't budge. The worker then said she bathed Cassie to ease the sting, then put her in another bed to keep the ants away. The night nurse finally roused long enough to tell the worker it was "nothing"—and then the next day wrote this caring health-care worker up for *exaggerating*.

This same nurse, according to the health-care worker, fed Cassie too quickly—using a plunger in the child's stomach tube to do in five minutes what properly takes a half-hour.

Another time, when Cassie had been up with a fever most of the night and it came time to get her up for school, the health-care worker couldn't wake her. "Send her to school," the night nurse said. "If she wants to stay up all night and play, that's her problem."

We have to recognize that we cannot *know* how Cassie really feels, because she cannot tell us. We can only imagine—and imagine that it must be a most horrific world for this damaged and terrified little soul.

There's no way to explain to her that she is being stuck with needles and tubes for her own good, or being forced to learn toilet training because it will make her a better person; all she knows is much pain and one pleasure: The big burly blur of the man who loves her and holds her and gives her the soft things that were now being taken away—the man whom the state tried also to deny her.

This is the story of a sick little girl lost in the bowels of bureaucracy, and the story of the Quixotian white knight who still fights as her advocate—though the deck is stacked against him, since "official" word is law and backed by the state.

A lot of folks hear the Bobby Dotson story and say, I don't get it. Why'd he care so much? There are a lot of reasons. One is that he'd been an orphan himself and had to respond to a little girl he saw going through the same tough problems. He was also a father and a grandfather. He had been a police officer for fourteen years and had developed an even softer spot for abused and injured children during his career as a cop. In fact, though he had loved police work, he had had to quit because, after working a case that involved a father who was abusing his crippled child, he realized that there was a very real danger that, if he ran into such a situation again, he might lose complete control of his better judgment.

In truth, however, the finger will always point back toward us. The question is not why does he love her— but why are we so *surprised*? Why don't we love as much and as well when we find someone who needs it so badly?

Once, while he and Cassie were taking their nightly walk, a doctor asked Dotson: "Why do you do this when you know she doesn't even know who you are?"

Dotson paused before replying, "How do you keep an idiot in suspense?"

The doctor replied, "I don't know. How?"

Replied Dotson: "I'll tell you tomorrow."

His battles have followed the same course, mostly. Administrators in nearly all the facilities in which Cassie has been placed over the years would initially view him as a contentious and bothersome meddler, a busybody telling them how to do their jobs. In most cases, over time, however, as with Stephanie Held, they would, after a while, have to notice his determination and his steadfast refusal to back away from Cassie. Finally, after long periods of time in many cases, his efforts would break the barriers of "professionalism" and "objectivity" and "conventional wisdom" to touch the truly caring humanity inside each of them; in other words, they would realize that this "outside meddler" was himself a caring human, and that their "patient" was, after all, just a little girl.

They realized that this man loved this little girl, and at last, they would relent and get out of his way. About the time a suitable arrangement for all would be reached, Cassie would be moved yet again, and Bobby Dotson would have to begin the whole process anew with the bureaucrats at the next institution.

Not long ago, Bobby got what he thought was more bad news. A decision was made to move Cassie again. Bobby Dotson will always maintain that she was moved because Bryan's House became convinced that she was dying, and the powers that be didn't want her to die there. Another alternative theory, of course, is that they were tired of having to wage war with Bobby Dotson and just decided to send their "problem" on up the road, to a MHMR facility in Richmond, Texas. Bobby says when he heard that news, he was so shocked he almost had a heart attack. He then resigned himself once again to slogging through the whole process, bitter with the knowledge that if he were blood kin to the child, nobody would dare question his motives or feelings for her.

Though most religions and philosophies agree that we are all each other's brothers, sisters, mothers, and fathers, it seems like that philosophy is seldom followed when it really counts.

Whatever the reason, Cassie was transferred. Bobby reported that she was not in very good shape when she arrived in Richmond. He said that she was running a high fever, and, since she had never been able to understand why that uncomfortable feeding tube was in her stomach in the first place, she had caused herself considerable damage by tearing at it. With surgery and medicine, doctors at a children's hospital in Houston were able to repair the damage. To let them accomplish their lifesaving work, Dotson stayed out of their way.

Once she had fully recovered, however, Bobby once again prepared to do battle. He marshaled his arguments. He steeled his resolve. He put on the armor of his resolve and went to the officials at Cassie's new home. Officials there listened to him only briefly before raising their hand to silence him. Look, they said, you'll find we treat people a little differently here.

I wish that you could see Bobby Dotson and Cassie today. If you visited them, you would most likely find them running, or flying a kite, or sitting on a bench together. It wouldn't matter what day or time you chose to visit, because now Bobby Dotson can visit Cassie just about anytime he pleases. You can bet he's there for her.

The results of having someone to love her have been spectacular for Cassie, the little girl who wasn't expected to live more than eighteen months. Her health has stabilized. The tube has been taken from her throat, and she has learned to breathe on her own. She has learned to communicate with sign language. She has learned to walk, and then to run, and to laugh, and to play. Slowly, she is learning to be a little girl.

She may not have a long life, but in what remains of it, at least she will have had a childhood.

Today, when I see Bobby, I no longer just see a hero and the victim he is fighting to save. What I see, in every sense but the one which counts least, the legal one, I see a father and his daughter.

(Note: I have learned that Bryan's House is now under new management and dedicated to the mission of caring for children who are HIV positive or have AIDS.)

Mark Miller of the
American Association for Lost Children

Has Anyone Seen This Child?

Mark Miller

ONCE UPON A TIME, Mark Miller had it made.

He was a successful stockbroker. He drove a fancy car. He had a closet full of clothes, he owned his own home, and his wallet was fat with credit cards.

Mark Miller had done lots of things. He'd worked for a computer dating service. He'd played the stock market. Recently, he'd added to his business interests by buying a Houston convenience store. He had good looks and a gift of gab.

Life in the fast lane was good, except that it wasn't. Something was missing from his life. In the back of his mind, there floated that free-form kind of dissatisfaction that most Americans suffer sooner or later in this materialistic culture.

It was, in fact, the same question I used to ask myself.

It's the question: "Is this all there is?"

Like everybody else in America, Mark Miller had seen children's pictures on milk cartons and on the fliers: "Have you seen me?"

But then one day, *the* flier arrived in his mailbox.

This time, instead of tossing it, he actually looked at it. There on the page: A picture of a big-eyed, skinny-legged little girl.

Those big sad eyes pierced his heart.

And they also answered his question, is this all there is? No. Not by a long shot.

Suddenly, Mark Miller had a lot of other questions as well. He called the number on the "Have you seen me?" flier and asked the people who'd printed it, "Do you actually *look* for these kids?"

Well... no.

He started calling other child-find groups all around the country and asking them the same thing. Invariably, the answer was no.

No, we are sitting behind a desk.

No, but we sure do *hope* that child gets found.

Mark Miller said, to heck with that. And he also said to heck with his life as he knew it, as well. Goodbye, house, goodbye credit cards, goodbye flashy car, for there is more to life than this.

That was 1987. Since that time, lost children have had no better friend, nor their abductors no more implacable foe.

As of this writing, more than sixty-five children have been found.

Please take another look at that statistic and understand exactly what it represents: sixty-five parent and child reunions.

Each of them is priceless by itself. It's an end to the stark, gibbering ball of fear in the stomach that only a parent can know.

Like any other private investigator, Miller does some of the work from his office, using a computer and a telephone. The gruntwork involved in these public record and utility company trackings can take months or even years as Miller tracks down every clue.

Whatever it takes is what he'll do—shadowing relatives, pretending to be a mourner at a funeral, posing as a pizza delivery man, Miller is determined to get abductor and his child. With virtually no surveillance equipment or law enforcement experience, Mark Miller and a small band of volunteers conduct intense, all-night, undercover investigations. They are protected only by prayers.

Miller is usually actively working fifteen or so cases at any given time, and another sixty or so await his attention in his desk drawer at the little Houston house that is his headquarters.

The children he reclaims amount to only the tiniest of drops in a huge bucket, he acknowledges, because the statistics are truly scary.

Many of the children Mark finds are taken by a parent without custody of the child. Each year, more than 300,000 American children are taken in violation of custody agreements or kept at least overnight past the end of the agreed-upon visitation problem. The real problem, though, is that of those, roughly half—

163,000—are still missing after one month. While the kids are far, far safer than if they'd been abducted by a stranger or sex criminal, it is still a bad situation.

Such a relationship is in itself abusive; add to the general ongoing trauma the gritty specifics of life on the run, moving from town to town, missing school for months at a time. There's no way that anything good could come from the situation. Miller says more than 90 percent of the children he has found have been physically or sexually abused.

Miller, more than any other single operative in the country, brings many such crimes to an end.

He is not a natural-born sleuth. He has read many books to learn detective techniques and has spent many hours talking to private investigators and police detectives to learn the ropes.

Part of his high rate of success is that he takes a practical approach, only taking those cases in which the parent has legal custody of the child, the abductor is known, and a felony warrant has been issued for his arrest. The reason for this is clear and simple; it keeps him on the right side of the law. If he took a child away from a parent who was not accused of abduction, he'd be a kidnapper as well.

Since there is a warrant, he can let the police do the dirtier, dangerous work for which he does not kid himself that he's equipped. The police, for the most part, appreciate his efforts. Frequently these fugitives are wanted for other crimes as well. Police will readily tell you they are too overwhelmed with tracking the more violent crimes to take time to look for children who are the center of domestic disputes; Miller handing them these cases virtually for free gets their case loads down and their solution rates up.

Miller's only reward is happy endings—or, sometimes in the wake of so-so endings, the tenuous hope of a good beginning. Not all the cases are so joyous. As often as not, they are bittersweet.

Even the happy endings have some downsides because of the nature of the situation. The longer it persists, the greater the problems will be.

There's the case of a Dallas-area mother named Jackie Gatewood whose daughters he traced to Texarkana, Texas. Emily and Anna, then two and four, had been abducted by their father eighteen months before.

For Mark, it was the culmination of a five-month investigation, but he had to have airtight proof of the girls' whereabouts. These were not just Jackie's children, but they were her very *young* children at the time of the abduction. Would they still remember her? Would they know that she had not deserted them, but that they had been stolen?

Finally, Mark found proof and took it to police.

The police walk up to the door of a trailer that has no stairs—just a door about three feet off the ground. Almost before you can tell what's happening, they have yanked a man out and spread him on the ground to cuff him while a little girl, Emily, stands scared and confused in the doorway.

Jackie, watching as well, was crying. She was crying even more after officers described to us the scene inside.

Cans of food, open, rotting on the counters. Filthy.

Bugs crawling around. It was wintertime, and the trailer was unheated.

The youngest girl had what appeared to be burn marks on her legs.

The children were therefore very glad to see their mother, and their crying, hugging reunion served as a reminder that yes, there is some good in a very imperfect world.

Mark was joyous but exhausted; he'd been going nonstop for days. "A lot of people don't realize what we go through—the days and days of stakeouts. We've put in a lot of hours in these situations, and we don't get much sleep. In the last eight days I've been averaging maybe four hours."

Then he looks at Jackie Gatewood reunited with her little ones and says, "But at times like this, it's worth it."

Mark Miller performs these services for free, because there are many parents like Jackie Gatewood who cannot pay a high fee to a professional investigator to find a missing child.

His motivation is obvious. Nothing warms his heart like one of those mother-and-child reunions.

Whatever the cause, it's results that count.

There is no one else who can match Mark Miller's success record of bringing parents and their abducted children back together. With no professional training and no law enforcement experience, Mark Miller somehow continues to baffle legal experts and private investigators all over the country with all that he has accomplished with just stubborn determination.

Carol Gray with Gary and Albert Gray with Sylvester at
The Children's Center, Bethany, Oklahoma

Used by permission: The Children's Center

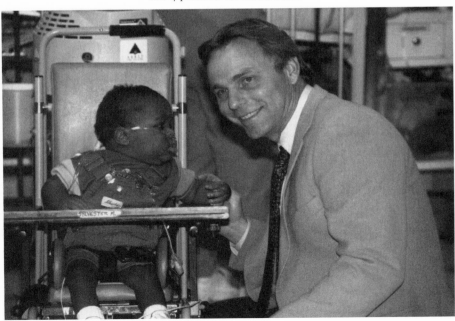

FOR THE LEAST
AMONG US

ALBERT AND CAROL GRAY

ONE OF THE POINTS we like to make with our program is that being an unsung hero is not always a matter of self-sacrifice and voluntarism; in fact, we are often at our best showing heroes at their jobs—heroes who are making a living by the continuing practice of altruism.

That is the case at the Children's Center in Bethany, Oklahoma, where we met a staff and administrators who are providing a miracle a minute to some children that desperately need them.

The Children's Center is for Oklahoma's chronically and terminally ill cases, with most of them profoundly retarded and physically impaired by their vast array of birth defects and other problems. Carol Gray calls these children her "little angels."

"I really do believe they are little angels," says Gray, a pleasant-looking woman who has made the center her life's work. "They do have a mission in life. All of us have a mission. I think theirs is to slow us down a little, to make us care for them and love them."

Dr. Eric Meader has an interesting take on these kids and their problems. "Almost all of them have psychomotor retardation—but then, we all do; it's just a matter of degree. Some have more, some have less, but we all have it. These kids just have more of it than most. We all have psychomotor retardation or we'd all be Michael Jordan or Einstein."

It is a cheerful place full of bright lights, pastel colors, toys, mobiles, and loving volunteers who come daily to rock the children, to hold them and love them, and to try to stimulate them to be more aware of their environment.

Under less enlightened direction, this place could easily

have become a human warehouse, because these are the type of people who were once readily warehoused. Some are vegetative; others have IQs in the low double-digits. It is easy to assume that in these sad cases "they don't know what's happening to them, or what's going on around them" and just warehouse them: Stack them up in darkened wards, see that they stay alive, and ignore them. After all, they seem to be ignoring the world around them.

But that is not the case at the Children's Center, not even for the most damaged cases. One reason is that Carol Gray and her brother, Albert, who run the center, are determined that each child should be treated as precious because, in their view, they are.

And even if they were not, there are still the parents to consider.

"This isn't a place where children are just dumped. We want to serve the child and the family, as well, and try to help keep it intact."

There is no more tragic occurrence in the lives of a new young couple than the birth of a profoundly impaired child.

Families often find themselves immersed in a sudden hell of shock, guilt, blame, expense—and, too often, a lack of what they perceive as humane alternatives, as is reflected in the term "put away."

Parents are grateful in the extreme for the alternative offered by Children's Center.

Nancy Gray's child, for example, was born with crippling respiratory trouble and other problems as well. In the first year, not counting maternity time, the child spent sixty-five days in the hospital. "We were finally at our wits' end. We sat down and said, 'We can't do this any more.' Luckily, we found Children's. I am so grateful for the people who work here, the constant giving. Some of these children can't even acknowledge what's being done for them, yet the staff never loses patience."

Carol Gray first came to Children's in the 1970s as the volunteer services coordinator. She was only getting paid for twenty hours a week, and two dollars an hour at that, "but I knew my heart would never be the same."

The center back then was losing about $10,000 a month, and the board of directors felt it was only a matter of time before the facility had to be closed. In fact, they originally brought in Carol's brother, Albert, to liquidate the assets of the school and shut it down.

Albert realized, after spending some time around the staff and children, that he too had found his life's work, and took measures to turn the center's finances around. He succeeded.

But both Albert and Carol maintain that the real heroes of this place are the paid staff and the volunteers.

"One of the things the parents always want to know: Where do we get the heroes—the employees, who make all these wonderful things happen day to day? I tell them it's got to be a 'heart thing.' You cannot do this without the heart."

Sharece Smith is one such hired hero. She is paid slightly more than minimum wage to care for a roomful of some of the center's most profoundly damaged children, some of whom are never conscious.

Sharece Smith thinks she's quite rich, however.

With tears in her eyes, she tells us, "God has given me a wonderful job. There are six children in this room, and for eight hours a day, they are mine. I go to the closet and pick out the best outfits I can find and hairbows to match. If we do our best and they look their best, they'll get the best possible care.

"They love to be kissed, rocked, and loved. This one? When I touch her, she knows it. I know she knows it, that we are going to do our best."

Says Carol Gray, "Here, we believe that life is important, all life. So dressing the child well, getting the socks to match the ribbons, is making a statement about how we feel about that child. They are more than just a body; there's a spirit in there as well."

It is hard to look at a child like Lindsey, who is in her early teens now. She was born with severe cerebral palsy. She lies almost completely still, dreaming of who knows what—perhaps of a kindly touch, perhaps of nothing.

There is no way to know what may register, but the center's treatment of her has certainly registered with her mother, Brenda Fife. Brenda seems to enjoy life and knows that she can thank the center for that.

"I found it necessary to place Lindsey here. She was a handful—totally handicapped. She does not move independently and requires constant turning over, sitting up, feeding, and bathing. We had to place her here. It's one of the hardest things we ever did."

She reflects a moment: "But after we did, I could once again have a life. This place was a godsend."

After my visit, I have to agree—it is a godsend.

Rev. Ann Hayman of the Mary Magdalene Project

A Long Night's
Journey Into Day

Rev. Ann Hayman

WHEN IT COMES TO HUMANITARIANISM, it seems that
there are two kinds of people: Those whom everyone wants
to help, and those whom almost *no* one wants to help.

In the former category: Children. The hungry. The
elderly. The sick and, sometimes, even the poor.

In the latter: Prostitutes. Whores.

In particular, street hookers—the hard-looking women
in the short leather skirts, the hot pants, and the halter
tops you find flagging traffic on street corners in every
major city in America.

Nasty women. Dirty women. Bad women.

Who cares? Almost nobody.

"They wouldn't do that if they didn't like it" goes one
prevalent and wrongheaded notion, which usually goes
hand in hand with "they brought it on themselves."

And then there's the "victimless crime" scenario: Since
the men want sex and the women need money, no victim.
But there are at least two victims in ever case: Every last
one of us—society as a whole; and the woman herself,
the biggest victim of all.

Ann Hayman is fighting hard to restore these women
to lives of decent normality. And in many cases she is
winning.

Our journey to Los Angeles showed us three worlds—
one that is soft and phony, one that is hard and gritty,
and one that is probably real.

The first is that fabled and mythicized city by the
light of day. It's the world of health and sunshine and
money and glitz and glamour. Rodeo Drive. Beverly Hills.
Hollywood—a hip, smart "Julia Roberts, *Pretty Woman*"
kind of place.

By night, it's a different world. Our crews drove
through a world of shady ladies and twisted twenty-dollar
trystings—a world that is both cheap and cheapening

and a world filled with women for whom this society has no use and no sympathy, the people we see out of the corner of the eye, instantly disapproving and dismissing them.

We shake our heads and then go on our way. And "our way" is, of course, the easy road.

Said Ann Hayman, director of the Mary Magdalene Project:

"Here, we always remind ourselves that these women are someone's daughter, someone's sister; they're in some cases someone's mother."

The cycle of prostitution is almost impossible to break by conventional means.

Jail doesn't work. Jail time, in this world, amounts almost to vacation time. It's time "off the street," at public expense.

Welfare programs don't work—particularly in cases where the street prostitute must finance heavy drug or alcohol habits or the habits of her pimp.

The only thing that works is actually caring, actually providing the one thing that most of these women never had—a family that they could trust in a home that is secure.

That's what the Mary Magdalene Project does. More specifically, it's what the director, Ann Hayman, an ordained Presbyterian minister, does. She cares, hands-on.

Caring for these women requires *hearts*-on as well. Because what society has been almost pathologically unwilling to grasp is that, as little children, long before these women ever took to the streets, they were badly, badly damaged—and almost always, by men.

As Ann says, "Most of that is physical and emotional, but it includes things like abandonment. Incest is a big component. My guess is it probably runs 70- to 75-, maybe even 80 percent of them are incested. And those who weren't incested were sexually active with schoolteachers or ministers—you know, these guys they are supposed to be safe with. Right? Sure."

Some researchers suggest that fully 100 percent of

prostitutes were sexually abused early in life: Not all victims of sexual abuse become prostitutes—but almost all prostitutes are victims of sexual abuse.

From years of experience, Ann Hayman has known, "You don't get into prostitution if you've got any self-esteem at all. A lot of them go into prostitution as a way of taking control of their lives, probably for the first time ever. And it's usually the really young ones who are doing that, probably, oh, the thirteen-, fourteen-, fifteen-year-olds. A large number of these women got home from school one day to find that mom and dad had moved and left no forwarding address and made no arrangements for their care. And so, what are you going to do?

"You're not going to go to Social Services and say, 'Hey, take care of me, put me in a foster home,' you know, come on. And, of course, they usually seem to have girlfriends or live in a neighborhood or have access to prostitution, and it becomes a choice at that stage of the game. If you've been incested, and you see that as a kind of trap or situation over which you have no control, then to become a prostitute is very liberating because you can say no—not that they ever do, believe me—but you could," says Ann.

Another problem Ann encounters is that our culture is loaded with lingering myths about womanhood and about relationships, and these contribute further to the cycle of prostitution.

"I think a lot of them really bought the myth, hook, line, and sinker, that some man was going to take care of them. And prostitution lends itself really well to continued belief in that myth. You know, the reality is, especially if they've got a pimp, that they're taking care of him. But they can delude themselves into thinking that he is doing something for them."

Once they become prostitutes, they've added another problem to the already enormous pile they must live under: The *stigma* of being a prostitute.

All these problems further fuel the pain—and in this society, there seems to be but one preferred means of dealing with pain: We drug it.

"Fully 60 percent of them have abused alcohol and

drugs. They're usually substance abusers, and it's not just one or the other. You don't find one who just does alcohol or just does marijuana or just does cocaine."

Bottom line is, to get out of prostitution, most of these women still need what they never had—a home. A place that is safe, full of people they can trust. People who can accept them for what they are and who will help them to become what they want to be. And that's what the Mary Magdalene Project set out to provide.

It all started in the West Hollywood Presbyterian Church.

"Back in the late seventies," Ann recalls, "The pastor of the church, Ross Green, had prostitutes living in the fellowship hall, and he was trying to help them get out of this. He called a bunch of women together from the Presbytery, and they eventually wrote a grant to the National Church—United Presbyterian's Opportunity Giving Fund. In January 1980, they sent $30,000 to the Mary Magdalene Project, and that was the beginning."

As to the name, Ross Green came up with it.

Ann sort of objects.

"I'm sure Ross thought in his heart of hearts that Mary of Magdala was some kind of whore. My sense is that, having done a great deal of different kinds of Bible research and study, she was really tight with Jesus and probably one of the first apostles. And so I tend to lift that up. I mean, there's no Biblical evidence that she was a prostitute, none whatsoever. Not a word."

What's in a name? At the safe house in L.A., Ann dispenses the things these women need most: Love, plus discipline, plus education. Here, these women do what most women do. They cook. They eat. They clean up. They get ready to go to work somewhere besides on those murderous streets.

"We provide alternatives to women who have been involved in prostitution. And sometimes that includes their children as well. Not that the kids have been involved, but certainly they've paid the price for mom having participated in this.

"Everybody does pretty much the same thing here, but they all do it their own way. Everybody's in a job-training program, but not the same job-training program. Everybody is in some kind of an educational program. Some of them are finishing high school. Others are doing college-level work or quasi–college-level stuff. Others are doing parenting classes and self-esteem- and assertion-training classes. Some of them take sewing classes, some of them take cooking classes. It runs the gamut, but they are doing something that involves a classroom setting.

"And they're all doing therapy, at least individual and group. If they have eating disorders, if they have mental health issues, depression, those kinds of things, then they are involved in more specialized kinds of therapy. And then we also do group work with our graduates as well."

If these recovering street prostitutes have children, as many do, the kids get the same things. In cases where the state has taken the children away, if Ann and Mary Magdalene's board believe the woman has become fit to resume the role of a mother, they'll help to get the children back.

"For the first year here, it's strictly weekends and occasional school vacations, but they are short periods spent with mom. Then if the courts are willing, and if it seems to be a viable undertaking, and mom and the kids are doing well, then we do a sixty-day trial visit with the kids coming here. If that goes well, the state releases these kids and the moms take them back."

In a field that is filled with failures, Mary Magdalene's success ratio is nearly miraculous.

Out of the 135 women who have entered Mary Magdalene over the past fifteen years, only four have returned to prostitution—and these four were, sad to say, hopelessly addicted to heroin.

Ann does not judge her people by as strict or moralistic a code as other Christians might because she knows they've already been severely damaged by rejection and judgment.

"I don't fault them. I mean, they wanted to survive, they wanted to make it, and I think that in that kind of situation, it's important that they have something like prostitution to fall back on. That's sickening to say. You know, that all that our culture can offer them is a job as a street prostitute is just really, really disgusting.

"I think it should be decriminalized—especially when only the woman is going to be arrested. Come on, please. It does take two to do this... "

On our nighttime tour of L.A., we saw plenty of women getting into those cars on Santa Monica and Hollywood Boulevards, and we did notice that in every case, a man was driving.

Though there are far too few organizations like Mary Magdalene, other cities are beginning to follow the lead, and, like Mary Magdalene herself, are coming out of the darkness.

The last day we were there, we saw a perfectly normal scene at the Mary Magdalene Project House. It was a birthday party for one of the kids. She was there, her mother was there, and her friends were there.

No big deal. But for some reason, it will stay with us. It touched us.

Nasty women? Dirty women? Bad women?

Or people about whom we should care?

For that matter, about whom should we not care?

THE WAY BACK HOME

H.O.B.O.

IT'S ONE OF THE BIGGEST PROBLEMS facing America. And it's one we don't want to look at.

The raggedy man or woman on the street corner—dirty, beard matted, skin dried and cracked by the days of inescapable sunshine, winter, spring, summer, and fall—is an alien thing to behold, an ugliness we can shun.

We dismiss him as no longer a man, and we dismiss her as no longer a woman.

For us that is lucky. To see them is bad enough.

To actually have to talk to them would be unthinkable, a painful experience. But *not* because he or she is so much unlike us, or so horrible. But because we are all so very much the same.

As long as we can compartmentalize them as being other and apart, we don't have to see the truth, the thing they themselves know all too well:

Just like us, they never thought they'd be there, either.

This more than anything else was the most important lesson I learned from H.O.B.O.—which stands for Helping Our Brothers Out. It's an Austin organization that is making great strides in getting these "derelicts," these "losers," these "bums" back on their feet, not with handouts, but a helping hand.

I learned that one of the biggest obstacles to that resurrection of human life from those mean streets and back into "normal" life is the attitude of the society around them.

We were doing a segment on H.O.B.O. because we kept hearing about this program that offered something that few other social service agencies were focusing on: restoring dignity to these debased and destroyed lives.

And most of all, H.O.B.O. is giving the "bum's rush" to a lot of the myths that we've built up around these people—who, after all is said and done, are just that: people.

It began as an attempt to solve one of the biggest problems facing the out-on-the-street and down-on-their-luck: Time and space. Pure and simple.

Because the agencies that the homeless so desperately need in order to survive are often disparate, separate, and flung far about town, there soon develops for these people an almost hypnotic mind- and spirit-numbing order of march.

If they are lucky, they have slept in a shelter rather than beneath a bridge, but either way, first thing in the morning they have to find something to eat. That usually means seeking out a mission or the Salvation Army or a feeding program—most of which have set hours, and if you snooze, you lose.

Then, say you're one of the lucky ones, still at the stage at which all you need is a job and not psychiatric counseling or a substance-abuse program from those years of using alcohol or drugs to ease the pain of sleeping on a steamgrate, so it's double-time down to the Texas Employment Commission on the other side of town, working up a nice smelly sweat on the way over and an even better one as you jog off to the potential employer who tells you, no, you stink and your clothes aren't clean.

So now you jog back down to the bridge, get your clothes, and head for the laundry—but first you gotta have change for the washers and driers, and you're flat busted... so... you go downtown where the people are concentrated so you can borrow quarters for the laundry... and everybody assumes you want it for wine.

Hopelessness soon sets in on the heels of homelessness. It is the greatest enemy of these unlucky people. Everything they have to do in order to survive is fraught with obstacles, and living just another day is a Sisyphean undertaking.

The life and death of Diane Mulloy is an excellent case in point.

She became homeless on May 8, 1992, the day she was released from a San Antonio Hospital where she was being treated for tuberculosis. She had worked steadily for a telecommunications company for ten years, but the eight-month stay in the hospital had cost her her job and her apartment as well.

By May 20, she had showed up in Austin homeless

and looking for help. She was still very sick, and by June 5 was back in the hospital with pneumonia. And she was able to get back in touch with a long lost daughter, Sunday Metcalf. The two had lost touch, but while she was in the hospital, they began to correspond, rebuilding the relationship.

Sunday Metcalf invited her mother to come live with her, but Diane Mulloy declined, telling her daughter that she was "living with friends" in Austin. Like many homeless, she was too ashamed of her status to admit it, and yet too proud to reach out to family, fearing she would be a burden.

The basic stay at the Salvation Army is seven days, then, if you do not fit the criteria for entering an extended program, it's time to leave. She had a collapsed lung, but the acute pneumonia was gone. The Salvation Army referred her to the Legal Aid Society to file for possible disability benefits. But it's a process that can take as much as a year to complete.

She was living on the streets.

There, as most street women are sooner or later, she was raped. Reeling in physical and emotional pain, she began to self-medicate with drugs and alcohol.

Somewhere out there in the gritty and painful drunk and hungry whirl, she met a man named James Tyma, himself on the streets with nothing to offer except his friendship, which she hungrily accepted.

She still had to face the streets, but she didn't face them alone.

Except until the end.

It was a rainy month. And one night the water began to rise beneath the bridge on Sixth Street under which the poor, shabby couple were sleeping.

Tyma, who by then was Mulloy's fiancé, said he warned her about the rising water. She could not swim. He carried some belongings up to the top of the bridge to protect them from the floodwaters.

When he returned, she was gone. They found her body caught the next day, caught in debris where Waller Creek feeds into the town's downtown lake.

There were no witnesses to the actual event, so no

one can say for sure whether the waters came to claim her, or, more likely, that she stood there contemplating her life, saw that there was essentially nothing left of it, and jumped into those roiling, muddy waters.

And that end is by no means unexceptional. Once life lands you in the street, estimates are that you have, perhaps at best, five years to live.

Her death, highly publicized and well known to the street community, began to galvanize it into some constructive action. When these homeless people and the care providers who try to help them started comparing notes about the many "unimportant" deaths suffered by their number, it began to paint a picture of the true problem and its true deadliness, of which Mulloy was only a tiny part.

Quite a list, these "unimportant deaths," over the course of two years in just one medium-sized southwestern city.

A man known as Hammerhead had been beaten to death with a rock. Also murdered was Tommy "Cat Fish" Ferguson, forty-one, and Robert Horn. Jerry Dunlop, like Mulloy, had drowned. Chris SanMiguel fell from a fire escape. Michelle Pryor was run over by a car, as was Ramon S. Mays. Albert Valencia, forty-seven, and John Joseph Kirby, twenty-seven, died in the same fire at an abandoned house where they were staying. Jesse Hamminger died in a fire as well.

Then there were the "natural causes," the cirrhotic livers, the pneumonias, the general run-down health conditions leaving a host of inert, shabby bodies on the sidewalk; if the flood hadn't gotten Mulloy, the collapsed lung probably would have.

So?

A few dead bums.

Nobody knew 'em.

And that's the kind of thinking that reveals the other side of the attitude problem. Because the homeless are by no means "a few." By one survey, at least 13.5 million Americans have been homeless for at least a few days in their lives, and more than half a million are homeless on any given day. It is not only a problem of the big cities—

but it is true that in larger cities the problem is at its worst.

If they don't get off those streets, sooner more often than later, they will die there.

On just one cold, wintry night, there were 22,000 people bundled into New York's homeless shelters—and they were the lucky ones, because the number of beds in shelters fall vastly behind the number of people who need them.

These displaced people, these American refugees, include a truly depressing number of families—women with small children. A recent report by the U.S. Conference of Mayors says these comprise about 43 percent of all the homeless in the United States. There are children in the world today who have lived their entire lives in shelters; they enter the vicious cycle of homelessness at birth.

And then there's the "wino" thing. While it's true that in some cases, it was alcohol abuse that led them to their sad state, the reverse is more often true: The alcoholism is merely a symptom of their homeless status: Living on the street, baked by the sun in the summer and pierced to the bone by winter winds, universally reviled and held in low esteem, one is likely going to drink to kill the pain.

How else does one sleep in a cardboard box when the temperature is in the teens? How else does one bear the ants and the brown recluse spiders who also live beneath the bridge? The smell of garbage and human waste?

We were quite honestly just looking for stock shots to help us document the scope of the problem in America. While on the streets of Dallas, two hundred miles from Austin, our crews caught up with Anthony Wilson, American Homeless Man.

Our interview was the perfect snapshot of what these people go through.

They are like the pigeons with whom they share most downtown areas.

In the mornings, they have learned to fly to one place where they know at a certain hour there will be food; then to another location, where they hope they may find part-time jobs and money; in the afternoon, they must go flapping off frantically to a certain place for water, or wine, and in the evenings, to a certain place for shelter, or for still more cheap wine to kill the pain of not having found a place to stay the night.

Their lives are all movement; if they don't keep moving, they die.

Anthony Wilson is such a human pigeon. He lost his job first, after he was injured. Because he couldn't pay the rent, he lost his apartment. He and his family moved into a shelter. But his wife's parents thought that it was very embarrassing for her to have to do that and asked her to move in with them and bring the kids. And, naturally, she did.

The shelter was for families only, and since they were gone, Anthony had to leave.

Some nights, like the pigeons, he sleeps under the bridges, in an alleyway, wherever he can. Most nights he finds a shelter that will house him overnight—but even then, "they make you leave at 5:00 a.m., and there are not a lot of places to go at 5:00 a.m. So once I leave a shelter, I come over to the Stew Pot that opens at seven, and I sit here until some of the other places open up. I try to get bus tickets to go look for work.

"It's pretty hard. If you don't have any money, you can't even go find work, and at some of these places it's hard to even get bus tickets. I was going to donate some blood, just to have money so I could go look for work, and they said I couldn't do that because I didn't have a stable place of residence; they said that staying at a shelter is not considered a stable residence, but that is the only place I have to live right now."

Imagine that: You cannot even sell your own life's blood. But there are a million other barriers as well.

"How can you get a job if you don't have a phone number or an address? I went on an interview today, and I told this lady I was staying at shelters, and I told her I didn't have a number where she could reach me. She told me to come back by or give her a call.

"I was running around all day, and I still only got to go to one job interview because I was looking for bus tickets all day. I don't know what I am going to do. I don't have a car, and I can't just walk to some of these places.

"It's very difficult with things so spread out because it's like you never know where you are going to sleep, and if you don't get a job you don't know where your next meal is going to come from unless you go to another shelter to find a meal. Everything is so spread out that you live day to day. You are really just living on a prayer, you don't ever know what is coming up next, and you just hope that it will all fall into place.

"If you could've told me twenty years ago that this is where I was going to be, I probably would have rolled over and died. A lot of people think that it's your fault that you are in the position you're in. But we're all human and we all make mistakes. A lot of people think it could never happen to them.

"I realize that I should have appreciated a lot of the things I had; I took a lot of things for granted. But then, I never thought that I would be in a position like this, this type of a 'bottom,' and I feel like I am an outcast.

"I still feel as though I'm a human being, and I just wish I could gain their respect back, but it is hard when you're trying to start from the bottom again and you are having to do it by yourself, because people feel like since you are homeless, you are different and you don't count any more."

Too bad Anthony lives—if you call that living—in a city other than Austin.

Because H.O.B.O. is in Austin—and as far as we can tell, it's one organization that clearly, completely, and comprehensively understands these people and their needs. And the result of that understanding is that the organization is getting results.

H.O.B.O. takes out the speed bumps for these people—and the founder, Marion Morris, got that understanding the hard way, in a way that makes it soak in: He was homeless himself.

He, like hundreds of thousands of others, found himself out of a job. So he pulled up his roots and brought his family with him to a larger city—Austin—in hopes of finding one.

He immediately found himself with the same

difficulties facing anyone who doesn't have a place to stay. How are prospective employers going to find you if you don't have an address for them to write back to? How are you going to go to a job interview if you don't have gas for the car? How are you going to clean up for the interview if you don't have a shower? How are you going to get to where there is a shower if you don't have gas for the car... and if you sold the car would you have enough to feed the kids?

Once you are in it, it is a vicious cycle that takes on a life of its on. That which was once easy seems almost insurmountably difficult. Every aspect of every day is a giant question mark: How am I going to... ?

He and his family spent all of one afternoon in a Jim's Coffee Shop because they really didn't have anywhere else to go, and while they were there, Morris got lucky: In walked one of those rare human beings who does not have "the attitude" about the homeless. The man could tell by their hollow faces and long silent stares that Marion and his family were under some stress, and he approached them to ask what was the problem.

Marion told him.

And the fellow said, "Well, listen. I have an old rent house, and no one's living in it. It needs a lot of work, but if you're willing to fix it up you can live there until you can find yourself a job, save some money, and move on out on your own."

It worked. Morris, with a little help from a good Samaritan, was able to recover.

But once Morris was back on his feet, he didn't forget the tragic cases out there or that cycle that they were trapped in. He knew firsthand just how precarious are all of our situations.

So Morris dedicated every free moment over the next couple of years toward extending that good Samaritan, helping-hand concept to as many of the city's homeless as he could reach.

The idea was not merely to keep them alive by feeding them daily or clothing them when their clothes were falling off—those are only bandaids, really, and keep them living their bare-subsistent existence. Morris was determined to also give them back their dignity and self-respect and help them back into the mainstream.

He was determined to give them that which he himself had been given: a chance. He mobilized local interests and resources, put together a formal board of directors and chartered a formal organization to begin accepting contributions and grants, and, beginning with the essential basics, began helping people according to their individual needs so that they too had an opportunity to work their way out of homelessness.

The most important thing his organization brought to the table turned out to be what they only half-kiddingly call "one-stop shopping" to relieve that unending and grueling kind of unintentional "forced march," agency to agency, stewpot to shelter to day-labor recruiter.

Shower? Across town.

Medical care? Across town.

Alcohol or drug counseling? Across town.

And, sorry, no bus tickets today.

That is not the case with H.O.B.O. The premises are something of a mall for the homeless. The walks from one agency or service provider to another are a matter of crossing the hall. It's always open, the board being cognizant of the barriers of transportation and cleanliness.

Said H.O.B.O. counselor Bob Schwab: "It's kinda like you can give someone a fish dinner or teach them to fish. We feel that by providing people with haircuts, a place to receive their mail, phones to call potential employers, an answering service, showers, a laundry, and so on, we help people to get better prepared for job searching—and they are able to better hold on to it when they get one if they don't have to feel the shame of going into a place dirty or smelling bad. They can come here and not have that problem. They are more motivated. Being kind of scummy at the end of the day is not pleasant for anybody, and we provide a way out of that. It makes them feel better about themselves, and when people feel better about themselves, they are more likely to try and help themselves.

"And when they try to help themselves, they are more

likely to be successful. What we do is very important to taking people from discouragement and a complete loss of hope to helping them to begin to build themselves back up. We provide them with some of the dignity and self-respect they need to succeed."

Of course, H.O.B.O.'s assistance to the homeless goes far beyond laundries and showers. The Texas Employment Commission has a branch office there. So does the Travis County Health Department. There is job counseling and a free legal aid advisor and child care for mothers who are looking for jobs or settling into one.

Also under that one roof is an adult-education program to help with GED preparation and an office of Travis County Mental Health-Mental Retardation to help with the psychiatric problems that often lead to homelessness—or, at least as often, result from it.

There is an office of the Department of Veteran Affairs, because, sad to say, about a third of all homeless males, in their former lives, served their country.

There are job-skills programs, programs to help the homeless with transportation, treatment services for drug and alcohol abuse, and plans to bring in more such services.

H.O.B.O. is almost like a mom to some of these people: If you're going job-hunting, "she" will even pack you a sack lunch.

Perhaps the most important program of all is the transitional-housing program. Nationally, studies have indicated that the most important avenue of escape from homelessness is transitional housing, havens for people to stay and regularize their lives at reduced cost—in the way that that kind Jim's Coffee Shop patron did for Marion Morris back in 1987.

In this program, motivated and willing homeless persons are given apartments, duplexes, or houses—based on their family situations—while doing what Marion Morris did: get back on their feet.

To do that, though, they have to have a clean, safe place to lay their heads. To really rest. To regroup. It's a place that everybody has to have in order to live.

It's a place called home.

Obviously, that's what a person has to have, ipso facto, in order to stop being homeless.

So while the human resources center is the most visible aspect of H.O.B.O., that's just the entry point for the homeless. Where it really starts to come together is at the Monarch Apartments, which H.O.B.O. bought and then renovated, using the skills of their homeless work force.

"When we started," recalled Schwab, "there wasn't a single unit that was habitable. We began renovating each unit, moving in a family, and then moving on to the next unit. We furnish the units completely, as best we can, using donated furniture. And when a family moves in, that becomes their property; when they move out, they move all of that with them.

"We also provide all household supplies, linens, and that sort of thing. That's to help the family save money so that when they first earn some money, they don't have to go out and spend it on a dish drainer and a can opener."

This is more than just an unstaunched outpouring of a bleeding-heart philosophy—much more.

Says Schwab, "We help them to *save* money and make it a part of their monthly routine; the reason why many people become homeless in the first place is simply that they didn't have adequate reserves. Something unexpected came up and depleted all their money, and they could not pay rent."

They do not stay rent-free, but at a reduced rate; H.O.B.O. understands that to restore hope, you have to also restore a sense of responsibility and self-sufficiency. And there's a time limit of one year. Usually, most participants are back on their feet and ready to move out after ten months; at the end of that time, most clients have been able to save the $500 to $800 that's necessary to pay the deposit and first month's rent on a place of their own.

It is a misperception that these people "want" to be the way they are. Most of them are simply people who have lost, and seek to restore again, a home. Once they have one, they are no longer "homeless." They are people again.

H.O.B.O. is succeeding at giving that humanity back to the homeless at the rate of about three hundred a year. Contrasted with the huge numbers of homeless in America, that's not much.

But in the context of each human life it has touched, H.O.B.O. is lifesaving. There can be no doubt that the staff and volunteers at H.O.B.O. and other such programs are heroes. Every day they provide hands-on guidance and assistance to people most of us would rather not even look at or think about, much less touch.

All of us have a chance to be heroes as well. Sometimes a hero is just a person who makes a difference, maybe even someone who makes a small adjustment in attitude, hoping that others will follow.

As Schwab told us, "Sometimes, doing this work, I feel like I'm a civil rights worker in the early sixties—that people think it's okay to generalize about the homeless just as they did about minorities—an attitude of 'well, let's all agree that there is something wrong with them; otherwise, they wouldn't be homeless.' Probably one of our biggest battles is to make the public understand that people do not become homeless because of lack of character or integrity, but because of either bad luck or some very human mistakes they have made in life, experiences not so different from those of each and every one of us. Consider that everybody alive would change something he or she has done.

"And maybe some of us just have better options. Some of these people did not have the benefit of a middle or upper-class upbringing. Some didn't have the best role models in the world. There could be any number of problems associated with their ending up where they are. Nevertheless, these are human beings, these are Americans, they're members of our community, our culture, and our economy, and they have something to offer. It seems to me that everyone counts. And that includes the homeless."

They are, after all, also the children of God—who is reported to have said, "That which you do to the least of these... "

Lucy Narvaiz and family at her college graduation

Never Too Late

Lucy Narvaiz

AN UNSUNG HERO, TO ME, is not the person who gives millions to charity. For some, a million dollars is just a drop in the bucket, a pittance.

No, for me, the heroes of this world are people who give of the only thing that any of us has that is of any true value: ourselves.

In terms of status and stature, Lucy Narvaiz is tiny. But she's one of our biggest heroes.

She came up hardscrabble and dirt-poor in one of this nation's most impoverished states, New Mexico. She was raised in the rugged desert country outside Santa Fe, and now, at the other end of that long life, she is by no means rich. She lives in a little adobe house not far from where she was born.

But whatever is there that you need, you can have. Lucy feels rich. Many others agree. She's been changing lives there for decades.

Lucy was one of those people who actually did walk to school barefoot in the snow.

"I'd leave for school at 7:00 a.m. and usually wouldn't be able to get back home before dark. I went to a school where there was only one teacher. I went through the eighth grade, and then there was a problem: how to go to high school. I wanted and needed more education; I had seen that the people around me were very ignorant. They couldn't read or write. I didn't want that. I said, 'I'm going to learn.'"

But that's not the way life generally went for poor young girls of Latino extraction in New Mexico back during the Depression, and Lucy was no exception. Childhood for such people tends to end rather fast.

Almost before she knew it, Lucy was a wife and mother and had four kids of her own to raise. She spent most of her life caring for her husband and her family and others, as well. These Sangre de Cristo Mountains around Santa Fe are well known for attracting the great artists and craftsmen of the world. This is Georgia O'Keefe country, after all.

But what is not so well noted is that these mountains in northern New Mexico attract some of the poorest people in the world: thousands of desperate people from Mexico; people who are literally dying for work, for a second chance. For most of them, what they left behind can hardly be called a life, but ahead of them, for many, only uncertainty.

They are strangers in a strange land.

They cannot even speak the language, much less write it. They are undocumented in more than just the "citizenship" sense. No birth certificates. No drivers' licenses. No social security cards. Imagine being beamed down with only the clothes on your back into the middle of New Mexico, knowing only that you've got to make a go of it because there aren't any better alternatives and many that are worse.

If you were very, very fortunate, someone like Lucy Narvaiz would find you and take you under her wing. That is what she does, and what she has been doing for decades, free of charge, because that's all her students can afford.

On almost any given afternoon, you'll find that she has a houseful of "students" of all ages, scared but hungry to learn. She teaches them to speak English. She teaches them to read and write. She teaches them the ropes of employment, of dealing with the American bureaucracy, of learning to live here, and, for that matter, learning to learn. A mastery of English and the ability to read and write is what makes Lucy rich.

She's known it ever since she was a young girl who could read in a backward community—the only person for miles around, in fact, who could.

She was the one her neighbors came to if they wanted to decipher a land deed or a contract or a letter from home or the U.S. Government; they would not even know what it was they held in their hands, most times, until Lucy explained it to them.

"I hate to think where these people would be," she said, as her students practiced their lessons. "Learning the language is the most important thing; there's nowhere to go if you can't learn the language, and few people are willing to help them learn for free. I can't explain why I do it; it gives me a richness. My heart feels good, my soul feels good."

It's the knowledge that she is fortunate, by comparison, that makes her generous with her wealth.

But not too long ago, Lucy decided to do something for Lucy. Lucy finished high school. And then, in her seventies, she went to college. "I wonder myself how I went through with it. I was very scared that first day. I sat on the last seat in the room. The kids started getting smart, wanting to know who's the old lady at the back of the room; what's she doing here? Finally one of them asked the professor. He said, 'Who is she? I'll tell you who she is; she's a student.' They were all astonished, but after that I was just Lucy. They treated me like one of their own. Everybody helped me a lot."

After seven years of study, she graduated summa cum laude. "It was a great day for me. I got a standing ovation."

Armed with her sheepskin, she just went back to being Lucy to all those desperate immigrants, to whom, lost in the desert, she is an oasis, helping "them" to learn about "our" world.

"I figure that it's my destiny that I should help less fortunate people and to teach them by example. The example is that if I can go back to college and get a degree in my seventies, they can do anything they want to do. As long as I have life and health, I will help them—give them a beginning, get them started, and show them how."

She has one other project. While she was in college she discovered what she calls a "void in history" and the dearth of readily available information about the Latino contributions to the area.

So she's researching the rich history of her family and her neighbors, recording their tales and remembrances for a volume of voices from the past. "It's important to tell their stories," she says. Perhaps she's helping us to learn more about "them" as well.

And we'll all be richer for it.

Bobby Trimble of Christmas in April,
Midland, Texas

BUILDING BETTER LIVES

BOBBY TRIMBLE

UNLIKE MOST "HOMELESS," Minerva Ketter lost her little house the slow way: gently, over time.

In the poorest section of Hartsville, South Carolina, her little house slowly lost the battle with weather and grinding poverty. First it listed to one side. Then a part of it sank. Then the ceiling let in rain, and the front porch sagged until it was in the front yard.

Finally Minerva Ketter had to throw in the towel and leave the decaying and unsafe structure to move in with her father, who lived in only slightly better circumstances next door.

Minerva's story was unremarkable—except that one day Christmas came in April: a swarm of volunteers descended upon the little house that she'd given up on. Before she knew it, they were slapping on paint, hammering walls, shingling the roof, stabilizing the floor, and shoring up porches. By day's end, her house, like thirty-seven others in that town, had been delivered from ruin back into the owner's hands.

Before the last hammer blow sounded, the volunteers had used 400 gallons of paint, 7,000 feet of lumber, 800 pounds of nails, 5,000 squares of shingles, and 200 bags of cement.

But even more remarkable: The same scene was being repeated that day by 62,000 volunteers in 200 cities around the country, rehabilitating nearly 3,000 homes.

The program calls itself Christmas in April.

This volunteer project is not only homesaving, but lifesaving as well, because many of these impoverished homeowners and tenants would have been forced into a homeless life on the killing streets once their homes fell down around them.

From all across the country, these stories, because of the huge impact of the growing grassroots organization, come pouring in, along with letters revealing how deeply grateful are the beneficiaries. "I wish I could express my appreciation to all your volunteers personally for transforming my old home into a beautiful showplace," said a letter from Mrs. Rosa Row, a Seattle woman. "People who stop by have to do a double-take. This is the first time in my ninety-one years that anyone has done something so wonderful. I love you all."

You hear that a lot, especially from these older people, who need help with so much, but who are so surprised when someone helps them.

Then there was Julia Quintana, Española, New Mexico: "I've never had anything given to me. I've always had to work for everything. I can't believe all these people think I'm so important."

She had worked, indeed. A seventy-three-year-old great-grandmother, she'd raised twelve children, one of them with Down's syndrome, and helped to raise her thirty grandchildren.

She was worn out and so was the house; she spent most of her days depressed and alone sitting inside of it, even though it was getting ready to come down around her.

Fifty-plus volunteers blitzed the house, repairing the roof and stucco, installing a ramp to the outside, and repainting the house. Members of the Youth Ecology Corps landscaped her yard, gave her a new fence, picnic table and grill, and flowers and shrubs. When the tired volunteers trooped out, she was sitting amazed, looking out the window at her new yard. "This is the most important day of my life," she said.

It is every bit as meaningful to the volunteers, no matter who they are helping.

Jennifer Stowe: "I'll never forget the first time we met the Fonville family. Mr. Fonville, bedridden as a result of a stroke, slept under a gaping hole in his ceiling that leaked water on his bed when it rained and gazed out of a window broken by random stray bullets. Mrs. Fonville, a kindhearted woman who volunteers at the local prison, collects and donates damaged canned goods for the less fortunate. She is raising their four children."

There were leaks in the roof, broken window panes,

rusty and cracking gutters and downspouts, crumbling concrete on the front porch, unsafe stairs with no railings, and all eleven rooms needed a two-coat paint job.

Forty volunteers came and did the job... and many of them have never left, getting involved instead in helping the Fonvilles to better their situation. "Groups of us keep returning to spend time with people who have come to mean so much to us. One volunteer offered to sew curtains, and Rushell cried when she saw the new peach curtains against the freshly painted walls of her bedroom. We've spent a great deal of time with the four kids, teaching them how to paint, how to play softball... I've experienced the joy of giving something to a family that is struggling to carve out some normalcy in a difficult life."

There are many, many Fonvilles, people who give faces to the numbing national statistics. Five and a half million low-income homeowners in America are elderly, and the vast majority are women. Over one-third live alone, and 43 percent spend more than 40 percent of their income on housing expenditures. Twenty-two percent of all Americans are "shelter poor," meaning that they cannot afford basic minimum necessities after housing costs. It's a paradox: They have a home, but cannot afford to maintain it.

Like many of the organizations we encounter on "Unsung Heroes," Christmas in April had humble, grassroots beginnings—and that was the major thrust of this segment: that it's impossible to know how much good one kind, small act can do, once the ripple effect gets rolling.

It all started when Bobby Trimble, a sixty-six-year-old oil and gas scout who taught a young adults Sunday school class at Alamo Heights Baptist Church in Midland, Texas, looked around and saw that some of the elderly "widow-ladies" in the church were having some problems with minor home repairs. And he realized that some of the male members of the class could do these women a service by helping them with minor repairs.

At first, it was just a matter of repairing roofs and replacing a window pane or two—no big deal for able-bodied men. But it meant the world to these older women.

Then, in October 1973, Midland's Park Central YMCA began a cleanup campaign, and someone suggested that the campaign include the renovation of homes for people in dire need. Volunteers would have to furnish labor, equipment, materials, and payment for any expenses incurred while doing the job.

Bobby Trimble volunteered on behalf of his Alamo Heights Baptist Church Sunday school group to take on two houses.

After the October 1973 program, the YMCA board planned for another project the next April. In April 1974, the group renovated seventeen houses. One of the beneficiaries of this effort made the comment, "Wow, this is just like having Christmas in April." The organization had its name.

Christmas in April incorporated in 1980 with Bobby Trimble at the helm.

Said Bobby, looking at his work in some of the poorest of Midland's neighborhoods: "We can't roof every house in Midland, but we've done a pretty good job on this side of town."

And when it comes to the residents, where Bobby is concerned, it's like they're best friends.

I remember them all telling me the same thing—that Bobby Trimble was the best thing that ever happened to them. And it's true; he has given so much of himself that in turn, it makes others want to give.

Bobby told me, "If you'll just look around at one of our projects, you'll see that we're all a bunch of people of different colors, doing something for someone who needs help. Times like that make you realize that the U.S. is the most blessed country in the world. We're keeping people from being homeless. We're giving them dignity back, and more pride in their homes. Not just here, but in Washington and Baltimore, San Angelo and Harlingen. And with every nail that's driven, there's a story, and memories... "

Bobby Trimble stands looking at one of his first projects. "Sure enough, Miz Friday lived there in a tiny room with a half-bed, an apartment-sized stove, and a fridge. The whole thing was eight feet by ten. We decided we'd build her a house. And we did. It was only twenty by twenty, but when you go from eight by ten to a twenty by twenty, you've gone from a shack to a mansion."

"When she passed away..., " Bobby has to pause, suddenly choked up.

"When she passed, she gave me the property. That was where we got the money to buy our first warehouse. On account of that, we were able to do so many more things. That's what I like about Christmas in April. People do it out of love."

Today, Christmas in April is a nationwide effort whose mission is to improve the living conditions of low income, elderly, and needy folks.

This one day a year, thousands of volunteers sweep through neighborhoods and turn delapidated homes into places of pride.

Bobby told me, "You know, we're always talking about the homeless. Well, we're keeping people from being homeless, and we're giving them a little dignity back. They have a little more pride in their home and more to work with. So it's a bigger issue than just fixing up someone's house."

The first Texas city (outside of Midland) to implement the Christmas in April program was Cisco, a Dallas suburb, in 1982. In 1983, Washington, D.C., began a program. By 1989, the number of cities with programs at work had grown to an estimated twenty-seven, and the project had become a national organization, Christmas in April, USA, with headquarters in Washington, D.C. Today Christmas in April has branches throughout the United States and in other countries as well.

But this is no hidebound bureaucracy.

A good example of the enthusiasm people exhibit when they are offered not help, but a chance to be a helping hand, occurred in San Angelo, where in the first year the program was offered there, thirty-five homes were renovated during their first one-day blitz in April 1989. And the next year, more than 2,500 residents fixed up almost twice that number, sixty-seven.

And the numbers continue to grow: Once people get

an idea how much impact their day's work can have, the project just escalates in any town where it is initiated. It takes on a life of its own.

There is room for participation by almost everyone at every level and from every walk of life. For example, in San Angelo, the Junior League coordinated the fund-raising and raised $35,000 the first year for building supplies. The next year, they raised $50,000.

Now the program operates year-round. Christmas in April annually restores nearly 3,000 homes in 300 U.S. cities.

In excess of 11,000 homes have been renovated, free of charge, by this army of volunteers. It is contagious. And it could change the world. For example, 10 percent of the population of Hartsville, South Carolina, turned out for Christmas in April, carrying ladders, hammers, paintbrushes, and saws. That was eight hundred people, and in just one day, they did over $200,000 worth of work for people who could never have been able to afford it.

The event prompted the local paper to wonder aloud: "Imagine a goodwill project in New York City that turns out 10 percent of the population—1,000,000 people plus—to work a Saturday for free, helping those who can't help themselves... "

But think in numbers even larger if you want a picture of the real good that an organization like this can do: Picture 10 percent of 250,000,000 people.

Christmas in April recipient, Jimmie Rollins, praises Christmas in April: "Without Christmas in April, I don't know what I would do because we're on a fixed income. We wouldn't have any money to fix up our house. I just thank God for Mr. Timble and his volunteers. They work so hard and do so many things. And what they do, they do out of love!"

What is it that drives people like Bobby Trimble to fix up people's homes? In Bobby's case, it's not just one day a year. Bobby tends to the needs of his neighbors all year long. He has weathered the frustrations of organizing volunteers and squeezing favors and donations from others.

With every nail that is driven, every shingle that's laid, there are special memories for Bobby Trimble. Thanks to his efforts, Christmas in April is helping people all around the world.

Although the main workday for the volunteers is the last Saturday in April, Bobby Trimble is on the job year-round, securing materials needed for the work and remaining on call for emergency home repairs. And he does all of this while maintaining a full-time job and caring for a family.

Bobby is the heart of the Midland chapter of Christmas in April, and he is involved at the national level as well. Christmas in April is now in more than two hundred cities across more than twenty-eight states.

Bobby Trimble is a simple family man. He talks about having never finished high school and being a sharecropper's son, and yet look at what he has accomplished. An ordinary man who is making an extraordinary difference in this world.

Sister Mary at the St. Elizabeth Health Center

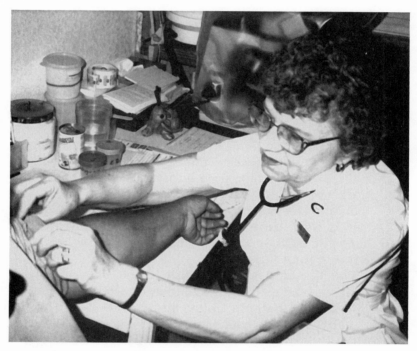

Eleanor Poe at her medical clinic in El Paso, Texas

With a Dream
and a Prayer

Sister Mary

and

Angel of Mercy

Eleanor Poe

As we do the research that leads to our programs, we often find that not only are some people angels, but also that these angels are kindred spirits—and that is the case with Sister Mary and Eleanor Poe.

We think of America's grinding rural poverty as being confined to small pockets. "Sure," we think, "there might be some—off on some deep Appalachian back road. Just a house or two."

But poverty has some mighty deep pockets, and broad ones as well. And some scenes from the "third world" that exist right in our own back yard are as stark as anything from Africa.

Take Gould, Arkansas. I wish I could say otherwise, but it's no different from hundreds of other little towns all across the southern United States.

A freight train roars along tracks that neatly divide this tiny Mississippi Delta town, where blacks live on one side and whites on the other. Situated in southeast Arkansas, this rural community is home to approximately 1,500 people. The land, good for growing crops, is not so good for its poorest residents, who seem destined to live out their lives without hope and without adequate health care. Chronic unemployment, illiteracy, teen pregnancy, and drug and alcohol abuse plagued this town. Its aging residents and sagging economy seemed all but forgotten.

There are homes here that still have no electricity or indoor plumbing. Sad, ragged laundry waves listlessly on the line. Here washing machines still have wringers on them if folks have them at all, and as often as not the washer is on the front porch.

The town has a dying, dilapidated feel, as though it is perennially at the point where Time and Nature have come to claim its tired old bones. Dreary, battered shanties dominate the landscape, along with run-down old, bare-shelved stores and little mom-and-pop outfits that cater to spending patterns of the poor.

The railroad tracks cut the town of Gould in half. But only 20 percent of the population lives on the right side of the tracks—the white side. On the other side struggles the rest of the population. Gould is 80 percent black.

And poor. Very poor. Unbelievably poor, but no more so than a lot of other southern towns.

In fact, Gould, Arkansas, is home to some of the richest land and the poorest people in the world, a place of bleak, grinding poverty and anonymous lives lived out miserably inside the darkened rooms of its tar-paper shacks.

Nearly half of the residents are past the age of sixty-five. For them, each day is just another battle with the infirmities of old age, exacerbated by malnutrition and disease. For the younger residents of Gould: chronic unemployment. Drugs. Teen pregnancy. Hopelessness.

And across the board, for almost every man, woman, and child (if they are black), a terrible lack of health care. The doctors all moved away to greener pastures as the white and more affluent population declined.

There once were two pharmacies. One closed, the other burned. And while there is health care in other towns fifty or one hundred miles away, few of these people have cars. And the ones who do can't afford health care anyway.

So for years, they simply did without, no matter how much sickness or suffering. Children might be born in these shacks and live their entire lives without ever seeing a doctor or dentist.

Gould, in other words, was a dying town where many people died young.

There was a mindset of hopelessness in Gould, Arkansas.

The people had accepted hardship as a way of life.

Then along came Sister Mary and the St. Elizabeth Health Care Center.

It started small—just outpatient care. But one seed of hope planted in such fertile soil has led to free transportation, adult education, a town cleanup committee, a thrift store, pregnancy-prevention programs, drug and alcohol counseling programs... and most important and absolutely necessary to the young people who will either need to leave Gould behind or stay and build it: self-esteem.

Beneath that nun's habit, Sister Mary is just a plain-jane, good old Iowa farm girl, and her sense of enthusiasm and optimism for the town has proven contagious. Such an attitude is even more remarkable, given that it flourishes in such an economically and emotionally depressed area.

As she makes her rounds about the town in her unassuming little car, she is constantly either smiling or waving—or if someone's riding with her, talking.

"If you love what you do, you never have to work a day in your life. I am close to that position. I get a lot of pleasure in the variety of people I get to work with; they are really delightful people. I couldn't have a better job," she says.

At first, residents told our crews they didn't know what to make of her. A white Catholic nun? Who wanted to help them solve all their problems? They thought it was probably too good to be true and figured that, like every good thing that had ever come to this town before, she, like the doctors and pharmacies, would one day simply be gone.

But she didn't leave. And the townspeople began to believe in the miracle.

In times past, when members of the Bynum family became ill, they couldn't afford to travel the eighty miles to the nearest hospital. Now they don't have to; they either go to St. Elizabeth's, or Sister Mary brings St. Elizabeth's to them.

As Wilma Bynum said when Sister Mary arrived at her door, "Oh, you never know when the angel's gonna come, but you know she will," and the hugging commenced.

Would it be a perfect world to expect adequate health care for people in need—a world in which people could rest knowing that somebody cares? That's what's happening in a place called Gould. Not much to look at, maybe, but a place where the quality of life is improving with every sickness that's cured and every pain that is conquered. Sister Mary and the staff and volunteers of the St. Elizabeth Health Care Clinic are working together to build a bridge of care and understanding in this little rural community.

It was a wonderful scene there in Gould, and I am glad to say that it was one that we had seen before, much farther south.

They have a great deal in common, Sister Mary in Arkansas and Eleanor Poe way out in west Texas. They both are angels of mercy, and neither of them particularly look the part.

If you saw Eleanor Poe on the street, you'd think she was just another grandmother—a pleasant-featured but unassuming fiftyish woman in a plain cotton dress. And for most of her life, she was decidedly average. She raised her family and kept house and went to church.

But one day, she says, God told her to do more.

Looking around her hometown of El Paso, she saw: There was plenty that *needed* to be done and plenty of problems to be solved—but the biggest of these was health care.

El Paso is separated from Juarez, Mexico, by only a chain-link fence and the Rio Grande, which is knee-deep at that point. And the two are hardly separated with the largest U.S. city abutting the border inextricably tied to her Mexican sister. It is estimated that more than 20,000 people live without running water in the area's colonias, and about 50,000 live without sewer systems. Many use contaminated water for their daily needs. And even better-off residents of Mexico pour into El Paso to get a better quality of health care.

Its health care system is short on primary-care doctors and overloaded by a population largely uninsured and unable to pay for care.

Twenty years ago Eleanor Poe opened a small clinic

with one doctor, one nurse, one patient, and one cotton ball. That first day is now only a blurred memory. Each Saturday hundreds of people crowd her little clinic's waiting room. For many of these folks, even the most basic medical care has forever been an unaffordable luxury, until now.

The barrios of El Paso are only three blocks from the border of Mexico. Thousands call this home. Poverty and squallor are a way of life here. This is where Eleanor Poe came to open her clinic, in the back of a small church. Eleanor has brought medical help to the suffering and the needy.

This is the clinic that turns none away. And they come. They come from the barrios of El Paso, from poverty-stricken towns across the border, from Juarez, from rural areas of southern New Mexico.

The doctors, nurses, pharmacist, even the receptionist, all are volunteers who give up their Saturdays each week to work at the clinic and offer hope to the sick and the suffering. Eleanor recruits her staff from all over the El Paso medical community. Every piece of equipment, every single pill is the result of her relentless dedication and efforts.

In this hard-pressed environment, Eleanor Poe and the Baptist Mission Clinic work everyday miracles—the kind that really work, guaranteed.

For instance, recently a man came to the clinic that Poe oversees. He'd been deaf for about three years. Almost instantly he was completely cured and able to hear again because the clinic doctor had discovered: impacted ear wax. And then there was the retarded boy a few years back who was in great pain. Though he was severely retarded, he was able to tell the staff how bad he was hurting and where. He could not urinate. A circumcision later, he was sent home.

And then there was the woman who came in five years ago fearing she had cancer but also refusing to believe it as well. The clinic did the tests—but the woman, in denial, didn't come back to learn that the results were indeed positive. She probably would have avoided knowing until it was too late.

Eleanor Poe tracked her down to a tiny house full of

children. "We sat in my car and talked and prayed and cried. She said all she wanted was ten dollars so she could get a Chihuahua to stay with her eldest daughter as she minded the children."

Eleanor Poe gave her the ten dollars—and took her to the hospital. Five years later the woman is alive and well.

Small miracles to middle America perhaps, but these are big miracles where they are happening in the woefully impoverished and underserved barrios of El Paso only three blocks from the border of Mexico where for thousands, poverty and squalor and illness are a way of life.

Most cannot afford even a minimally adequate diet, much less medical care. Adding to their list of woes is the fact that, since they are aliens, they cannot qualify for government assistance because of residency requirements.

Eleanor Poe and the Baptist Mission Clinic are, for many, the difference between life and death.

Eleanor, a nurse, just wanted to do something to help these people. She opened this small, privately funded free clinic. She was the nurse on duty. And the supply clerk, janitor, fund-raiser, recruiter, and administrator.

Now the fourteen doctors in the clinic see fifty or more patients every Saturday, offering primary care, immunizations, cancer screening, lab work, and physicals, and they are able to quickly refer an indigent patient to some of the best physicians El Paso has to offer.

More amazingly, everyone who works at the clinic is a volunteer. The clinic's first receptionist worked for free for more than fifteen years.

An El Paso laboratory provides all the lab work free of charge. Physicians volunteering at the clinic have brought colleagues into the pool of volunteers, and many accept every patient referred by the Baptist Clinic for further care, at no charge.

There is something like a miracle a minute here.

While our crews were there, for example, a twelve-year-old boy named Jesus and his mother swam across the Rio Grande from Juarez to come to the clinic. His chest pains got the staff's attention, as well as the fact that he was small for his age.

Diagnosis: enlarged heart. Before the day was out, clinic

physicians had lined up two heart specialists who volunteered to save the boy through surgery.

Said Jesus's mother, fighting back tears: "I couldn't have done anything without Eleanor's help. It is much too expensive and I do not have the money. They don't help people where I live. I prayed to God that someone would help me... "

And then she bursts into tears, because someone did.

The Reverend George Polk conducts services at the
Humble Chapel Baptist Church.

Taking Back our Neighborhood

Rev. George Polk

MIRACLE.

A good word for explaining some of the otherwise inexplicable good things that happen in our world.

There may in reality exist tangible explanations for them, but it makes us feel better to consider that, after all, Someone may be watching.

That is how the neighbors feel about the dove—the one that has nested in a sycamore tree in the yard of the unofficial mayor of Shropshire Street.

Neighbors believe that God sent the gentle, softly cooing bird and her downy brood as a symbol, a blessing, a confirmation of what they all know.

The neighborhood is a peaceful, restful one. It is like a black version of Mayberry RFD—and in the context of its surrounding environment, that is something of a miracle.

Because Shropshire Street in Fort Worth, Texas, is surrounded by some of the darkest, deadliest, drug-torn, and most dangerous of the city's many decaying neighborhoods. These are in an area that in fact are really not neighborhoods at all any more, but the dreariest backwaters of the human soul.

Crack is sold all day in broad daylight, and the prostitutes sell their bodies to obtain it. And that is followed by pop-pop of gunfire all of the long, long nights.

In these places, prostitution, addiction, murder, mayhem, and misery are a way of life—in fact a sort of living death.

Where there is life, there's hope, but sometimes it feels more as though the reverse is true: Is a life without hope worth living?

Yet here on Shropshire Street, an oasis. The weedy, unkempt, littered yards of the rotten and dilapidated housing (actually, human warehousing, each a shabby fortress, residents locked inside) all around the area

297

suddenly give way to tidy frame homes with neat yards, all newly painted and constantly maintained by the poor but hardworking and proud people of Shropshire Street.

That beautiful dove could have chosen, one block away, a vacant field of small trees and brush—much more habitable a nesting site for what is, after all, a bird of the woodlands.

She fascinated me as much as she did the neighbors. The crew and I couldn't get enough of gazing through our telephoto lenses, watching that beautiful bird presiding peacefully on her nest of twigs, allowing our lens to so clearly resolve her gentle, bright-eyed face. It was like being a foot away from her.

It will sound silly, I know, but she had an expression on her face that seemed to surpass the mere peacefulness of which her species is a symbol. The look said something even more wondrous: I am home. I am safe. This place, above all others I have seen where I have flown, is truly good.

The bird is in a sycamore tree, and the tree is in the yard of Reverend George Polk. It is not much of a tree, really, nor even much of a nest. As with any nest, it is whipped by wind and pelted by rain, as is the bird who sits on the new life growing within it.

But she gets one thing here that she would get nowhere else, however, and she seems to know it.

She seems to know that in the tiny but neat little house below, when her going gets tough, there's a man who always prays for her.

Mr. Polk prays in the night that the Lord will protect that bird and her babies—and when he hears her wistful yet contented coo once more in the morning, he prays again, a joyful prayer of thanks.

And as he prays to God to watch over the bird, the neighbors say the same prayer for him.

Because the neighbors all know that George Polk is the reason that Shropshire Street is different; that there is peace in this urban valley; that it has remained apart from the huge vale of tears and terror, sorrow and sorriness that surrounds them.

Because these good people know that these days individual goodness is not enough, that a glue is needed to bond them together, and on Shropshire Street, they know that George Polk is the source of their bonding and the synergy that provides their strength.

He and his wife, Zadie, have held this neighborhood together for more than thirty years, and the neighborhood, thus held together, has been able to keep the gunfire and drugs and prostitutes and trouble away for all of that time.

Other good people who live only a block away will tell you: They pray sometimes, too. They pray that they can someday live on Shropshire Street, where people take care of each other, and George Polk watches over them all.

When someone dies on Shropshire Street, it is always of natural causes. George and Zadie Polk are the ones who rally the neighbors to the survivors' sides with not mere sympathy but solid assistance, support, and succor.

When Vera Rollins's husband died and she was working at three jobs to feed herself and her son, she knew that young Derrell was safe, that the Polks were feeding him, raising him, and if necessary, disciplining him when she couldn't be there.

She knows that Derrell will likely not have to live in those hells that surround Shropshire Street because when she was not there, the Polks were there to love him.

This is true of all of Shropshire's young. They have been raised and guided by a man of peace, who shows them love and proves to them that it is always better than hatred.

That is what lies at the heart of the success of Shropshire Street: love.

There are a lot of things that Mr. Polk, like a lot of these people, has to do without. He earns not much more than minimum wage, driving a truck for Goodwill Industries plus whatever little the congregants can contribute to the support of his tiny but proud little ramshackle church, which is full of well-worn Bibles and equally hard-worn people who have remained nevertheless believers, thanks to their humble shepherd.

These are people who not only thump their Bibles, but live them, not out of blind allegiance, but because they have learned that applying its precepts results in a better life. These are people who not only call each other brother and sister in church, but take that attitude home with them the other six days of the week.

Whatever blessings are bestowed on his flock on Sundays seem to spread through Shropshire Street the rest of the time.

The kids here all say yes, sir and no, sir and please and thank you rather than yo, and yo mama, because George Polk has been a father to them all—and particularly the ones without fathers.

It takes a while for the irony of it to hit you, the sense of all we have lost, before you find yourself noticing that these kids are playing outside. In the street. Together and in complete safety.

It is sad that we live in a world where such things have become remarkable.

And if such things call to mind a lost and lamented bygone era, well, George Polk laments the passing of it, but only elsewhere, among the people who do not live on Shropshire Street. For love and neighborliness have tenaciously remained here.

"There are," he says, looking off at the surrounding urban grime and crime outside the borders of his gentle jurisdiction, "lots of things you could do back then that you can't do now."

In every direction off of Shropshire Street exists a dark and murderous anarchy. Those who do not live in an almost constant rage live in fear of the ones who do.

Terror and mankind's inhumanity have become not the exception but the rule, and it is the rule of the worst of human nature, red in tooth and claw.

Meanwhile, as the horrors rage all about, on Shropshire Street people all sit of an evening in the shade of their porches, talking to each other and greeting passersby. Because there are no drive-by shootings on Shropshire Street and there are no gang members. George Polk has been too good a father to allow that.

We found George Polk to be a remarkable man, and we found his humility, simplicity, and directness reassuring and refreshing.

Because of that unrelenting humility, we had a hard

time getting him to accept credit for this vast difference in the quality of life here. He was far more interested in talking about that dove.

"It makes me feel humble and thankful, and makes me know that I am blessed to live in a neighborhood where you can still hear the coo-coo of a bird. She has shown that there is hope for this area and for the children who grow up here.

"The neighborhood has been coming along real good. The kids are going to college, and the Lord has blessed us. We have taught the children to love one another. Without love and respect you have nothing at all. Things that I can be thankful for are health and friends, a wonderful wife, a nice home to live in, and all my children and grandchildren."

But we were still having a hard time getting him to tell us his secret for providing peace for his people in a violent world. He hemmed and dissembled and tried to place credit on any head but his own.

"I guess helping folks just runs in the family. My daddy and my mother, ever since I was big enough to remember, they was always helping people. Everybody loved one another in the community, and everyone shared the good things of the community; you just have to do the best you can."

But toward the end of our visit, he finally gave us a glimpse of that secret—its practicalities, rather than the pretty platitudes. Just a glimpse, but it may be all that any of us need to know to get along in the world, and help others get along in it as well.

"Oh," he finally said, standing in the yard beneath the sycamore tree, listening to his dove, "Oh, I just advise everybody to get acquainted with their neighbor and let them know that they care. If they find out that you care, then they'll care for you."

If each of us does that, follows that simple yet beautiful recipe, why, I believe that doves would come live in all of our yards.

While shooting this story, our photographer had a knife pulled on him in a drug-infested area just a few streets away from Shropshire Street. I can tell you firsthand that what happens on that street is nothing short of a miracle.

At the end of our shoot, George Polk invited me to attend his church service. The following Sunday I took him up on his invitation. My daughter and I attended his inspirational and heartwarming service in a tiny, rundown church building not too far from Shropshire Street. It was a hot Texas summer, and the only air conditioning was provided by a portable box fan that was sitting in a corner of the church. The church was filled to capacity with faithful worshipers who had come to expect miracles in most unlikely places. It was a day of worship that we will never forget.

DJ Kidd Kraddick of Kidd's Kids

KIDD'S KIDS

KIDD KRADDICK

I HAD HEARD of Kidd Kraddick. I had even listened to his morning radio show in the car because Bethany, my nine-year-old daughter, listened to it. While driving Bethany to school one morning, I heard Kidd Kraddick talking about a trip to Disney World for chronically and terminally ill children. It sounded like a good story.

Kidd Kraddick is a wild and crazy guy, and I think that's why the kids love him. He's just a big kid himself. But once he became a father, I think he changed a lot. He's still got a childlike quality, but children and "making a difference" have become very important to him.

Most young children we know are just that—kids, blissfully unaware of the harsher side of the world and its miseries. But not all of them are so lucky. There is misery in the world that sadly finds its way into the lives of the children. But if they are lucky, Kidd Kraddick finds them, too.

Kidd Kraddick is a Dallas DJ who spins tunes on KISS-106.1. His broadcasts are hip, irreverant, lively—everything you would expect from a top-forty DJ with an audience of teenagers and young adults. Kidd Kraddick is not a serious man except when it comes to the kids, the disadvantaged, the seriously, or even terminally, ill, the severly burned, or injured.

Kidd Kraddick tells the story best: "It started as an idea when my wife, Carolyn, was pregnant. In one sonogram, the baby looked like she had something very seriously wrong with her. And it turned out to be a mistake. But for four or five weeks we were so anxious about this. And I remember when I went back, the sonogram was clear and there wasn't the problem—a problem that probably would have prevented her ever walking. I promised God, when I thanked him profusely, that I would do something to help those parents who weren't so lucky."

At thirty-five, married, and with a child of his own,

he realized it was time to give something back. And he gave his huge audience of young adults a chance to do the same.

Kidd's Kids is an organization devoted to bringing light into some young lives.

"The mission: We try to be around for kids who haven't had it so great, whose parents weren't able to make it great for whatever reason, and quietly help them out."

The biggest fun of all came when Kidd Kraddick was able to pursuade Express One Airlines to fly the chldren on a special trip. Where did they go? Where does every kid want to go? To Disney World.

"I thought we would have to pay for every activity, for every plane ticket full fare, and the thing that surprised me most is how the corporations have a heart, that Disney World has made it free for everybody, that the Dolphin Hotel has made it as close to free as they possibly can, that an entire airline came forward and not only said we'll give you the plane, but the flight attendants will donate their time, the pilots will donate their time on their days off to fly these kids down and back. Everybody's made sacrifices for this.

"In the faces of the children I see the normal things you expect to see. I see normalcy in their faces. I see what I see in every face of a child at Disney World, and that is a look that these parents haven't seen forever, the look of awe in their children's faces is worth ten times what it costs to send them there. I think it is at least as valuable for the parents as it is for the kids. Not only are you suffering the trauma of your child being different than everybody else, having all these special needs, but also you know that you'll never be able to provide the things for that child because of that position. Because even those families who are insured, the deductibles that they are paying are wiping them out.

"For the kids this is better than any psychotherapy. They get to see children who have exactly what they have in some cases or similar in other cases, who've been through chemotherapy, who've had liver transplants, and they're able to exchange those stories, and it's amazing.

"You see these kids as they walk onto the airplane and look at their faces, then watch them come off. The difference is incredible; it's like the world has been lifted off their shoulders. And it's not just because they've been to Disney World and had a great time and been on some rides. It's because they've been hanging out with kids who've gone through the same thing they've gone through. Finally, for once, they can bond with somebody.

"I have a special opportunity to give back in a way that others can't, who don't have the power of the broadcast media like I do, and in this story there are thousands of unsung heroes. And I'm not worthy to hang with them; I'm not one of them. This is the easiest thing in the world for me to do, and I should get zero credit for it. Plus, it's so fun for me to hang out with these kids.

"I've been so lucky here, you know. With nominal talent I've been able to sustain some kind of career for a long time, and the listeners have just been incredibly nice to me. And so I wanted to—I hate the cliché "give something back," but I really felt like if you're going to have this forum on the radio every day, why not try to do something good with it.

"I'm really, really blessed and lucky in so many ways. God has just given me everything that I ever wanted, and for me to see this kind of thing happen, for me to be able to help other people realize some sort of satisfaction, some sort of dream—for the parents it's a dream for the kids.

"I can't help it—it's selfish, I know—I do it because I'm selfish, because of the way it makes me feel. It would feel so shallow for me to go on the air and entertain myself every day for four hours without doing something that I could go home at night and say, Maybe we've made some sort of difference here."

I paid the airfare for Bethany and me to fly with Kidd's Kids to Disney World to do this story. I didn't want to leave Bethany. Although I knew we would be working much of the time and she's been to Disney World before, I thought it would certainly be a different Disney World than she had seen in the past. She would be seeing it with some very special children. Bethany and I didn't have much time to ride rides, I must admit, but we definitely had one of the best trips of our lives. Kidd Kraddick and the great staff at KISS-106.1 put the trip together, and by the time it was over, Kraddick was almost as popular as Mickey Mouse to the kids and their families. I now listen to Kidd Kraddick with my daughter on a regular basis. We laugh, sing, and dance along to the program. And we remember what a difference people in the media can make.

Joy Bianchi and the residents of Helpers Homes.

JOY TO THE WORLD

JOY BIANCHI

IF EVER THERE WAS A GROUP of people entitled to be called Santa's helpers, it's Joy Bianchi and the residents of Helpers Homes. Joy is about as close to being a saint as anyone I've ever run across. She wants mentally retarded people to be treated with respect, and she has been ingenious in finding ways for them to support themselves. Through her efforts she provides them with beautiful homes and gives purpose to their lives.

Miracles are an everyday occurrence at 2626 Fulton Street. The shepherd of these sheep is Joy Bianchi, an energetic whirlwind of a woman who has been working with Helpers Homes for forty years. Joy's title is director. But the truth is that these people are her surrogate children. Like any mother, she wants her children to live in pleasant, happy surroundings. She wants them to have a sense of accomplishment. With Helpers Homes and the toys they produce for their Ghiarardelli Square store, they have both.

Joy started out working with the retarded as a young girl. She worked with a group of nuns in San Francisco who saw to the needs of families whose severely retarded children had no place to go.

"After the residents had lived with us a few months, we tried to get them into other programs. But at that time, there weren't many programs, and the few that we asked said no. It was the kind of thing that I really hated—people handicapped by retardation looking out a window doing nothing.

"So we started making Christmas balls and Christmas tags. I found that holding scissors or drawing something with a ruler is difficult for the retarded, and that these were not natural skills. And so when the work got better and better we realized that selling the handiwork was the next step toward helping the workers to self-sufficiency."

The adorable stuffed animals and figurines that are

311

created day in and day out are for sale at the Helpers Homes store in San Francisco's Ghiarardelli Square. Part of that was by design. These are, after all, based on the designs of PeeWee's Playhouse designer Max Robert. The rest of it comes from the heart. (Where minds may fail, hearts prevail.)

Joy speaks fondly of the cherished designer. "The inspiration behind the animals that we see today was Max Robert, my closest friend and my soulmate, who died of AIDS and worked at Helpers Homes for ten years.

"Anything special in life begins with a dream. As a young girl, when I used to go to state institutions and other places—even on the streets of San Francisco—I saw how people who were retarded were disheveled, and that just rocked my stomach. And when we began Helpers Homes, I remember someone saying, Why do they have to live in such beautiful homes? And I replied, Why not? I felt it was important for them to live in the same manner as I live.

"But the animals, these little creatures... there's something about them, to me, that tells the world that someone important made these. They're creatures of quality. And why are they quality? Because they mirror and reflect the beauty of our people, who are quality."

From Fulton Street we headed to Tiffany's on Post Street—two extremes in life. And yet, it has been said that a civilization is measured by how its people take care of "the least of these." Tiffany lets the residents of Helpers Homes know that their creations are the rarest jewels in their store. Tiffany proudly displays the Helpers Homes animals alongside their beautiful jewelry in the store windows during the Christmas holidays.

"I love the things of this world. I love jewelry, I love clothes. But people are certainly more important than things.

"My association with Helpers Homes is a fix for me. I love people. I meet little children—little children who are now parents of children—who come back year after year because they want the touch, they want the connection, they want the feel in their house.

"As I watch the residents of Helpers homes, I can

imagine that if they were to count the negatives rather than the blessings, they could choose to be unhappy. They *are* mentally retarded—some of them profoundly. People on the outside wonder what to call them. Disabled? Handicapped? Specially challenged? But they know what to call themselves. They call themselves family. They have not only learned to pull together, to cooperate, they have learned to create together, things of beauty.

"In homes throughout the United States, a tradition is being carried on as faithful followers and families add another treasure to their collection, a treasure with a red tag with the words 'handmade by the residents of Helpers Homes.'

"I hope when I meet God, that God says to me, Joy, you've made a difference in one person's life."

When I left that day I knew that, like Joy, I'd discovered that the spirit of Christmas exists 365 days a year. The act of unwrapping the beautiful Helpers Homes ornaments each Christmas brings special meaning to Bethany and me. And as we hang each one on our tree, we think of our wonderful friends at Helpers Homes.

"Ms. Richland Hills Nursing and
Rehabilitation Center," Lila "Cookie" Bailey

AGELESS BEAUTY

RICHLAND HILLS NURSING HOME

IT IS REMARKABLE TO ME how little effort it takes to become a hero. Sometimes it's simply a matter of doing something to make someone else happy.

You don't have to spend a million dollars, or raise the flag on Iwo Jima, or devote your entire life to a crusade. You don't have to be good, kind, loyal, brave, trustworthy... and all the rest of the Boy Scout oath every moment of every day to achieve hero status.

All you have to do is make someone smile, someone feel better about themselves—make other people feel valuable, special, loved, unique. You can even do it and get paid for it as part of your job.

As did the employees of a nursing home in the small Texas town of Richland Hills.

The origins of this little program call to mind those old episodes of "The Little Rascals," where Spanky or Alfalfa or Darla suddenly gets that inspirational look in the eyes and says, "I know! We'll put on a show!" As if that would solve all their problems and perhaps mankind's as well in one fell, decisive swoop.

But you would be surprised how many human problems such an idea *can* solve: the feelings of loneliness, uselessness, friendlessness that are attendant upon advanced old age.

So often nursing homes, even the cleanest and best of them, seem—to their occupants, saddest of all—to be nothing more than human warehouses, waiting areas for that final trip to parts unknown. It's hard not to think about death, that sentence without appeal, particularly when you notice as the days go by that some of the people who were there yesterday are not around any longer.

Nursing home staffs try to arrange for entertainment for their guests, but much of it is passive; wheel the old folks into the break area and let them listen to some kind, but usually nominally talented, local person sing them some hymns.

Cheerful stuff.

But somebody at the Richland Hills home looked around and said, "I know—we'll put on a show." A beauty pageant to be precise.

Starring, as contestants, the residents themselves. Sound stupid? Not if you live there. In fact, this is the one thing that many of these ladies look forward to all year long.

And if you think about it, you will see there is much value in giving these people something to look forward to, because so much of the time, all they have to occupy their minds is looking back, at what is over and gone. Spouses, houses, lives, and youth. Get them into the present and point them toward a future and you've more than halfway won the ever-present morale problem. The process of planning wardrobes, makeup, talent competitions gets them talking and thinking, and the competitive aspects make them, well, downright competitive.

The contest is timed to coincide with what can be the saddest of times in a nursing home, particularly for those whose loved ones are all gone to another city or have already passed on: the holidays. Hard on almost everyone, but murder on the residents, when loneliness competes with happiness and oftentimes wins.

Says Let's-put-on-a-show Wanda Boetel, the activities director:

"There is so much going on it's sometimes kind of hard to adjust to the holidays. Holidays are family oriented, so we wanted to put the residents in the spotlight and make it a bright time for them."

It is also a pretty good lure to draw in those family members who, well, don't visit as often as they should.

See Grandma all dolled up!

See Grandma on the stage!

See Grandma sing a song!

See Grandma wearing a crown while someone sings, Therrrre she is, Miss Richland Hi-ills Nurrr-sing Home!

See if that really is Grandma, just to be sure.

Before the show begins, the excitement is almost palpable—a rare state of affairs in a nursing home. Frantic last minute hair revisions. Agitated applications of makeup all too seldom applied. And the joy of, for once, being at the complete center of attention of families, staff, and friends.

Excitement! In a nursing home!

The emcee gets fired up. The staff gets fired up. And the ladies, well, the ladies get *real* fired up.

The judges get fired up too—but they will tell you: It's tough duty. Said Wanda: "I wouldn't be able to pick a winner. That's why I got all these judges. Each resident has her own glow, they all have that inner beauty."

The tension begins to mount. The question on everyone's mind: Who will wear the crown? But the only contest seems to be about who's having the most fun— the beauty school volunteers, the staff, the judges, or the contestants.

Onward they come, promenading past the judges. Never mind that some of the promenaders rely on walkers, wheelchairs, or canes. There truly is another kind of beauty than the one the media holds forth before us as the standard, before which most of us are doomed to fail.

It is a record of happiness and of sadness, of victories and defeats; these faces are the book covers of lifetimes, books written by the hand of God, and he who fails to see it is missing the most deeply beautiful part of life's story.

But none fail to see it here.

That is why, before the winner is announced, the judges report why all ten of them are winners; the judges tell all ten of them about their poise and grace and beauty—and it isn't idle flattery or just "jollying the old gal along."

Because the judges are talking about that beauty carved by time and burnished by thirty thousand sunsets over the course of eighty winters, eighty summers, eighty springs and falls.

This is a day that memories are made of, the kind of day to be remembered always.

Beauty and goodness know no age nor season and are natural in the world, and if they are allowed to blossom, bloom into human kindness. If there's anything I've learned over the course of the past three years, it is this:

That heroes are simply the people who are kind. And kindness is something we can take along wherever we go.

I love all my heroes. I have learned from them, in fact, what is at the core of every true hero, whether sung or otherwise:

Love.

May all of us receive it, and may all of us give it.

I think it's why we're here.

In Search
of Unsung
Heroes

EACH TIME A [PERSON] stands up for an
ideal, or acts to improve the lot of others... he
sends forth a tiny ripple of hope, and crossing
each other from a million different centers of
energy and daring, those ripples build a
current that can sweep down the mightiest
walls of oppression and resistance.
—Robert F. Kennedy

TWO THINGS STAND OUT foremost in our minds as a
result of our tours of the country over the past three years.

First is that there are many people out there who,
unselfishly and often at sacrifice to themselves, are still
willing to do good things, willing to help their fellow
human beings.

The other thing is: Our fellow human beings are
extremely grateful for what they receive—even if it's nothing
more miraculous than a decent place to lie down and die.

It has been a privilege to travel the highways and
byways of this country to meet the people you have read
about in this book. Some of their stories are very dramatic,
but there are others that we have met who are making
their daily contributions in a much simpler way: people
such as Thelma Kirkpatrick, who at age ninety-two
continues to compete in the Senior Olympics, proving
that life has purpose at any age; the staff at Camp John
Marc Myers, a wonderful, special camp for chronically
and terminally ill children; Don Kimbrell, a farmer who
not only marched on our nation's capitol to speak out
on behalf of America's farmers in need, but who has
helped save many of these farms and even the lives of
many desperate farmers; Kristen Kuykendall, a little girl

319

who was born with no arms and many other handicaps. Kristen is a top student in her class. She uses her feet as hands. She writes, cuts, even plays the piano with her feet. This brave little girl lets nothing stand in her way; the staff and volunteers of Texas Scottish Rite Hospital, an incredible medical facility for children that provides healthcare for children in need at no charge; Habitat for Humanity, the organization that former President Jimmy Carter and his wife, Rosalyn, support. They work with thousands of volunteers to build houses all around the world for those in need. While we visited with them, they were building fourteen houses and a daycare center in Liberty City, Florida, in just one week!

Betsy Weaver is one of education's best and brightest. As a first-grade teacher, she goes the distance to educate and communicate with children; Southwest Airlines is a company that has not only become a hero to its employees, but also the many charities, organizations, and individuals they have helped. They truly practice "LUV" Southwest-Airlines style.

The volunteers of "A Visit With St. Nick" are providing needy children with a special Christmas, while teaching them what the spirit of Christmas is all about. These people and the many, many others we met along the way all proved to me that each of us has the power to make a difference!

Our cameras sometimes capture some little image that will stay with us for years—not of fires and floods, or murder and mayhem or moon-shots, but the still, small shots of everyday people in everyday life who make us aware just how high the human spirit can soar.

It's for these moments that we travel the country, in fact. These moments are addictive. And they are quietly inspiring.

These unsung heroes have given us such moments. We are grateful for the privilege of meeting hundreds of unsung heroes who so inspire us for the further privilege of being allowed to use our time here to sing their songs.

In fact, it's what keeps us going.

J.C.

Duane Conder, Janet, and Jon Cermin
on location in Los Angeles